Advance Praise for *9/11 and American Empire: Intellectuals Speak Out*

"Read this. Read this now. And then tell someone else what it told you. If you wondered where morality, intellectual rigor, common sense and historical perspective went when they disappeared from public discourse, be reassured—the authors of these essays were keeping them safe for you, along with a surprisingly functional sense of humor. This is a massively important book about events which are still changing our world—forget the internet wingnuts, forget the blurry thinking and the blurry photographs, forget the government gibberish—if you want to know about 9/11 read this book. Read it. Read it now. And then tell someone else what it told you."

—A. L. Kennedy, *Paradise* and *Indelible Acts*

"For far too long, the very reasonable questions raised by 9/11 have been ignored and even ridiculed by America's press and politicians, who treat the subject with the sort of willful blindness that suggests a wish not to find out unpleasant truths. We, the people, therefore owe the editors of this important new collection our warm thanks for their intelligent and unrelenting work."

—Mark Crispin Miller, professor of culture and communications, New York University, and author of *Cruel and Unusual: Bush/Cheney's New World Order* and *Fooled Again: How the Right Stole the 2004 Election & Why They'll Steal the Next One, Too (Unless We Stop Them)*.

"Official versions of historical events should always be questioned. This book, dealing with 9/11 and much more, does just that, and from various points of view. It will provoke argument and that's a good thing."

—Howard Zinn, *A People's History of the United States*

"In *9/11 and American Empire: Intellectuals Speak Out*, David Ray Griffin and Peter Dale Scott point out that the book's publication 'signals the beginning of a new phase of the 9/11 Truth Movement, one in which scholars will play an increasingly larger role.' Griffin and Scott have assembled academics, scientists, engineers, and intellectuals with fine minds and courageous hearts to deliver the bitter pill—the official explanation of the events of 9/11 is false and the evidence indicating an inside job is significant. In doing so, they have returned scholarship to its rightful place of leading us back to excellence."

—Catherine Austin Fitts, assistant secretary for housing, first Bush administration

"It has long been clear that the Bush-Cheney administration cynically exploited the attacks of 9/11 to promote its imperial designs. But the present volume confronts us with compelling evidence for an even more disturbing conclusion: that the 9/11 attacks were themselves orchestrated by this administration precisely so they could be thus exploited. If this is true, it is not merely the case, as the Downing Street memos show, that the stated reason for attacking Iraq was a lie. It is also the case that the whole 'war on terror' was based on a prior deception. This book hence confronts the American people—indeed the people of the world as a whole—with an issue second to none in importance and urgency. I give this book, which in no way can be dismissed as the ravings of 'paranoid conspiracy theorists,' my highest possible recommendation."

—Ray McGovern, former CIA analyst and founder of VIPS (Veteran Intelligence Professionals for Sanity)

"All Americans who love their country enough to dig into the facts of these critical times will be well rewarded by examining David Griffin's books. 9/11 truth is a very important issue—with the power to bring lasting change to our country."

—The Rev. William Sloane Coffin Jr., former pastor of Riverside Church, New York

9/11 and American Empire
Intellectuals Speak Out

Edited by David Ray Griffin
and Peter Dale Scott

OLIVE
BRANCH
PRESS

An imprint of Interlink Publishing Group, Inc.
www.interlinkbooks.com

First published in 2007 by

OLIVE BRANCH PRESS
An imprint of Interlink Publishing Group, Inc.
46 Crosby Street, Northampton, Massachusetts 01060
www.interlinkbooks.com

Library of Congress Cataloging-in-Publication Data
9/11 and American empire : intellectuals speak out / edited by David Ray Griffin and Peter Dale Scott.
p. cm.
ISBN-13: 978-1-56656-659-9 (pbk.)
ISBN-10: 1-56656-659-2 (pbk.)
1. September 11 Terrorist Attacks, 2001. 2. War on Terrorism, 2001—Political aspects. 3. United States—Foreign relations—2001- 4. United States—Politics and government—2001- I. Griffin, David Ray, 1939- II. Scott, Peter Dale. III. Title: Nine-eleven and American empire.
HV6432.7.A128 2006
973.931—dc22

2006014385

Printed and bound in the United States of America

Cover image © AP Wide World Photos

Contents

Preface

David Ray Griffin and Peter Dale Scott

In the period since September 11, 2001, some researchers outside the mainstream of public discourse have increasingly been discovering and presenting evidence that contradicts the official account of what happened that day, including the official account of who was ultimately responsible for the attacks. Given the role that 9/11 has played in subsequent history—serving as the rationale both for a global "war on terror," which has thus far targeted Afghanistan and Iraq, and for extreme reductions in the civil liberties of Americans—the discovery that the official narrative about 9/11 was a lie would be a discovery of first importance. And yet thus far the mainstream media and most members of the academy have refused to explore the evidence that has been presented for this alternative narrative.

The main rationale for ignoring this evidence, insofar as a rationale is given, is that the so-called evidence need not be taken seriously because it has been presented by "conspiracy theorists." If analyzed, however, this charge provides no basis for discounting the proffered evidence.

For one thing, we are all conspiracy theorists. A conspiracy occurs whenever two or more people conspire in secret to do something illegal, such as robbing a bank, defrauding investors, or having a spouse killed. Our newspapers and television news shows are filled with stories about conspiracies. Insofar as we believe any of these stories, we are conspiracy theorists.

A second problem is that the official narrative about 9/11 is itself a conspiracy theory, alleging that the attacks were orchestrated entirely by Arab-Muslim members of al-Qaeda under the inspiration of Osama bin Laden in Afghanistan.

In light of these two considerations, an alternative theory about

9/11 cannot rationally be dismissed out of hand on the grounds that it is a conspiracy theory. Instead, the question becomes: Which of the two conspiracy theories is the more probable? And the only way to answer this question is to examine the relevant evidence, asking which of the competing hypotheses can better accommodate all the relevant evidence in a consistent and otherwise plausible way.

Confronted with this argument, journalists, editors, and educators may reply that the above argument is correct in principle but that when they use the term "conspiracy theorists" in a pejorative way, they have a more particular meaning in mind. They mean people who tend to see conspiracies, especially involving the US government, everywhere; who do not construct their theories on the basis of evidence but select and construe evidence in terms of their preconceived theories; and who, insofar as they appeal to evidence, use it to make wild inferences based on leaps of logic.

Conspiracy theorists in this sense of the term certainly exist within what has been called the 9/11 Truth Movement. But there are bad and even crazy theorists in every field, from quantum and relativity physics to evolutionary theory to the history of religion. Crazy theorists in these fields do not discredit the sensible ones. The same should be true in relation to 9/11 studies—assuming, of course, that this field of study has some sensible theorists.

This book, by demonstrating that it does, makes clear that alternative accounts of 9/11 cannot be dismissed on the grounds that they are offered only by people who fit the label of "conspiracy theorists" in the pejorative sense. All of the eleven contributors to this volume were well-respected members of establishment organizations before they got involved in the question of 9/11. Ten of them had earned the Ph.D. Nine of them were professors at well-regarded universities; one was employed at Underwriters Laboratories; one was a military officer in the Pentagon. The combined weight of their testimony cannot be dismissed lightly.

This combined testimony points to a twofold conclusion: the official account of 9/11 is false and this false account has been used to support an agenda that had been worked out in advance—the further extension of the American empire, most immediately into Afghanistan and Iraq.

Some of the chapters in this volume focus primarily on reasons to doubt the official account of 9/11. Some of them focus primarily on the way 9/11 has been exploited to further the American empire. And others deal somewhat equally with both issues.

The chapter by David Ray Griffin, which is based on a lecture that inspired this volume, presents an overview of the most important evidence suggestive of complicity by the US government in the attacks of 9/11. Then, pointing to evidence that the motive would have been to advance the American empire, he argues that this connection reinforces the contention, already apparent on other grounds, that the project to create an all-inclusive American empire must be considered, on the basis of moral norms that are common to all traditions, an immoral project.

The next three chapters focus primarily on evidence against the official account of 9/11.

Karen Kwiatkowski assesses this account from her perspective as a former military officer, a scientist, an academic, and a person who was present at the Pentagon on 9/11. Pointing out that the 9/11 Commission contained no people capable of assessing the evidence from a scientific perspective, she says that it did not answer or even address any of her questions about the official story. Especially valuable is her eyewitness testimony about the west wing of the Pentagon shortly after it was struck, in which she reports that she saw neither the debris nor the damage that would be expected from an attack by an airliner.

The chapter by physicist Steven Jones zeroes in on the collapses of the Twin Towers and Building 7 of the World Trade Center. He points to many features of these collapses that cannot be explained by the official theory, according to which the collapses were caused by fire (and, in the case of the Twin Towers, by airplane damage). He then shows that it is more probable that the buildings were destroyed in controlled demolitions, triggered by pre-set explosives.

Kevin Ryan, whose whistle-blowing action while he worked for Underwriters Laboratories is mentioned by Jones, argues that the question of the true cause of the collapse of the three World Trade Center buildings is of utmost importance, because it was what psychologically prepared Americans for the so-called War on Terror. Agreeing with Jones on the unscientific nature of the official report on the WTC collapses, which was put out by NIST (the National Institute of Standards and Technology), Ryan describes some of the behind-the-scene details in the failure by Underwriters Laboratories to protest NIST's distortion of evidence that it had supplied.

The next two chapters discuss background information that may be important to unraveling the truth about 9/11.

Peter Dale Scott focuses on the role of drugs and oil in American covert operations, especially the operation in Afghanistan in the 1980s involving so-called "Arab Afghans." Saying that the American people have been misled about the origins of al-Qaeda, he describes its origin in the use of drug-trafficking Muslims by the United States and American petroleum companies in their quest to control oil. He suggests that secrecy in foreign policy formation has led to short-sighted and disastrous strategies and that Congress should not give still more money to the very agencies that helped create the al-Qaeda network in the first place.

Swiss historian Daniele Ganser's contribution is relevant to one of the main a priori reasons Americans have had for rejecting the idea that 9/11 could have been orchestrated by our own government: the assumption that American political and military leaders simply would not do such a heinous thing. He presents evidence, widely discussed in Europe during the 1990s but hardly at all in the United States, that during the Cold War, the CIA and NATO (and hence the Pentagon) supported various right-wing movements in a "strategy of tension" to prevent left-wing electoral victories. The methods included staging "false-flag" terrorist attacks that would be blamed on the left to discredit them and justify their suppression.

The next three chapters discuss problems in the ability of the American public to engage in a rational discussion about the truth of 9/11.

Morgan Reynolds, as the first former member of the Bush-Cheney administration to declare 9/11 a false-flag operation, discusses the response by the academy: silence by most of it and ridicule and intimidation by his former university, Texas A&M, whose president, Robert Gates, was previously director of the CIA. Reynolds suggests that the kind of intimidation exercised by Gates may reflect a widespread problem within the academy, which would help explain the failure of most of its members to discuss the big lie of 9/11 and its connection to the government's global domination project.

Richard Falk, from whom Reynolds derived the phrase "global domination project," suggests that the Bush administration probably either allowed the 9/11 attacks, or conspired to cause them, in order to facilitate this project. Discussing the official management of suspicion in relation to 9/11 as itself suspicious, he suggests that the inability to discuss the truth about 9/11 reflects a fear that dark secrets will be exposed. But until the truth about 9/11 is publicly discussed, Falk suggests, its paralyzing effect will prevent us from facing the structural deficiencies in the present global order.

John McMurtry observes that the official story about 9/11 is transparently false; that the wars declared after 9/11 were in fact its strategic reasons; and that the so-called "liberation of Iraq" is an instance of what international law has determined to be "the supreme crime." To explain why most Americans cannot see these obvious truths, McMurtry proposes the concept of a ruling group-mind, which screens out everything that does not fit its preconceptions. One of the many novel elements in McMurtry's analysis is his explanation of why orchestrating 9/11 would have been entirely rational for the Bush administration and the class it serves, given their goals and their ability to control any subsequent investigation.

The final two chapters discuss the likely forces behind 9/11 in terms of the goal of global domination.

Ola Tunander observes that the major effect of 9/11 has been to allow policies that were developed by influential US thinkers during the 1990s to establish a "Pax Americana" to be put into practice under the guise of a global war on terror. Given the way in which state terrorism has been used in prior years, we can probably best understand 9/11 as an example of the kind of false-flag terrorism described in Ganser's chapter, used this time, however, to apply the "strategy of tension" to the world as a whole.

The idea of a group with a global domination agenda is explored in the chapter by sociologist Peter Phillips and two of his students. The global domination group, understood as the current version of what President Eisenhower called the "military-industrial complex," is seen as a segment of the higher circle policy elites—the segment with the most to gain from a US policy of global domination. Phillips suggests that investigations to determine ultimate responsibility for 9/11 and its cover-up might well begin with this group, the central members of which he seeks to identify.

The various chapters contain, of course, much more than can be indicated in these thumbnail sketches. Each chapter presents a multitude of facts that have seldom appeared on mainstream radio and television or in mainstream newspapers and magazines. These facts, and the connections between them, have also thus far been largely absent in college and university classrooms, even in departments most germane to discussing the various kinds of evidence, such as departments of physics, chemistry, architecture, engineering, aeronautics, history, political science, economics, sociology, philosophy, and religion.

The publication of the present volume—along with the

establishment of a new organization, Scholars for 9/11 Truth (for which one of our contributors, Steven Jones, serves as co-chair)—signals the beginning of a new phase of the 9/11 Truth Movement, one in which scholars will play an increasingly larger role. (See also Paul Zarembka, ed., *The Hidden History of 9-11-2001* [Amsterdam: El sevier, 2006].) We hope that this book, besides convincing members of the public and the mainstream media of the seriousness and importance of the issues raised by this movement, will also encourage specialists in the fields not represented in this volume to examine the relevant evidence that their educations have prepared them to evaluate.

We have put out this volume in the conviction that 9/11 was not only the largest and least-investigated homicide in American history but perhaps also the largest hoax, with extremely fateful consequences for human civilization as a whole. If our educational community cannot address this issue, then it risks remaining merely "academic" in the worst sense of that term.

ONE

9/11, the American Empire, and Common Moral Norms

David Ray Griffin

The thesis of this chapter is that the project to create an all-inclusive American empire, far from being a moral project, as its neoconservative supporters claim, violates universal moral norms, and this truth is dramatically illustrated by the connection between this project and 9/11. I will begin my argument in support of this thesis by unpacking the key terms in the title of this chapter: "9/11," "American empire," and "common moral norms," beginning with the final phrase.

Common Moral Norms

In speaking of "common moral norms," I am using the term "common" in both its senses. The moral norms in question are common to all humanity, rather than being unique to some particular religious or cultural tradition.[1] Also these norms are common in the sense of being very elementary, ordinary norms, rather than being deductions from some sophisticated moral theory. I have in mind moral principles such as:

Thou shalt not covet thy neighbors' oil.

Thou shalt not murder thy neighbors in order to steal their oil.

Thou shalt not bear false witness against thy neighbors, accusing them of illicitly harboring weapons of mass destruction, in order to justify killing them in order to steal their oil.

This language is, of course, language that we associate with the Abrahamic religions—Judaism, Christianity, and Islam. But the same basic ideas can be found in the other religious and ethical traditions.

It has been pointed out, for example, that the "golden rule," at least in its negative form— "Do not do to others that which you would not want done to yourself"—is common to the various religious and moral traditions.[2]

I turn now to "American empire," which has been a highly contentious expression.

American Empire: Divergent Views

In his 2002 book *American Empire*, Andrew Bacevich points out that it was long a "cherished American tradition [that] the United States is not and cannot be an empire." The words "American empire," he adds, were "fighting words," so that uttering them was an almost sure sign that one was a left-wing critic of America's foreign policy.[3] But as Bacevich also points out, this has all recently changed, so that now even right-wing commentators freely acknowledge the existence of the American empire. As columnist Charles Krauthammer said in 2002: "People are coming out of the closet on the word 'empire.'"[4] This new frankness often includes an element of pride, as exemplified by Krauthammer's statement that America is "no mere international citizen" but "the dominant power in the world, more dominant than any since Rome."[5]

Given this consensus about the reality of the American empire, the only remaining matter of debate concerns its nature. The new frankness about the empire by conservatives is generally accompanied by portrayals of it as benign. Robert Kagan has written of "The Benevolent Empire."[6] Dinesh D'Souza, after writing in 2002 that "American has become an empire," added that happily it is "the most magnanimous imperial power ever."[7] According to Krauthammer, the fact that America's claim to being a benign power "is not mere self-congratuation" is shown by its "track record."[8]

Commentators from the left, however, have a radically different view. A recent book by Noam Chomsky is subtitled "America's Quest for Global Dominance."[9] Richard Falk has written of the Bush administration's "global domination project," which poses the threat of "global fascism."[10] Chalmers Johnson was once a conservative who believed that American foreign policy aimed at promoting freedom and democracy. But he now describes the United States as "a military juggernaut intent on world domination."[11]

Andrew Bacevich is another conservative who has recently changed his mind. Unlike Johnson, he has not come to identify with the left, but he has come to agree with its assessment of the American empire.[12] He now ridicules the claim "that the promotion of peace, democracy, and human rights and the punishment of evil-doers—not the pursuit of self-interest—[has] defined the essence of American diplomacy." Pointing out that the aim of the US military has been "to achieve something approaching omnipotence," Bacevich mocks the idea that such power in America's hands "is by definition benign."[13]

9/11: Four Interpretations

If "American empire" is understood in various ways, the same is all the more true of "9/11."

For those Americans who accept the official interpretation of the event, 9/11 was a surprise attack on the US government and its people by Islamic terrorists.

For some Americans, "9/11" has a more complex meaning. This second group, while accepting the official interpretation of the attacks, thinks of 9/11 primarily as an event that was used opportunistically by the Bush administration to extend the American empire. This interpretation is effectively presented by writers such as Noam Chomsky, Rahul Mahajan, and Chalmers Johnson.[14]

For a third group of Americans, the term "9/11" connotes an event with a more sinister dimension. These citizens believe that the Bush administration knew the attacks were coming and intentionally let them happen. A Zogby poll indicated that 49 percent of the residents of New York City held this view in 2004.[15]

According to a fourth view of 9/11, the attacks were not merely foreknown by the Bush administration; they were *orchestrated* by it. Polls in Germany and Canada in 2003 and 2004, respectively, indicated that this view was held by 15 to 20 percent of their people. (A Zogby poll in 2006 showed that 42 percent of the US public believes that there has been a cover-up, but this poll did not distinguish between the third and fourth views.)[16]

9/11 and the American Empire

People who take humankind's common moral principles seriously will probably have very different attitudes toward the American empire, depending upon which of these four views of 9/11 they hold.

If they accept the official view, according to which America was the innocent victim of evil terrorists, then it is easy for them to think of America's so-called war on terror as a just war. This is the position taken by Jean Bethke Elshtain, a professor of ethics at the University of Chicago's Divinity School, in a book entitled *Just War Against Terror*.[17] From this perspective, the "war on terror" has nothing to do with imperial designs. It is simply a war to save the world from evil terrorists.[18]

The second interpretation of 9/11, according to which the Bush administration cynically exploited the 9/11 attacks to further its imperial plans, has quite different implications. Although it thinks of the attacks as surprise attacks, planned entirely by external enemies of America, it usually regards these attacks as "blowback" for injustices perpetrated (and sometimes terrorists trained) by US imperialists. This second view also typically regards the American response to the attacks of 9/11, which has already led to hundreds of thousands of deaths, as far worse than the attacks themselves. This interpretation of 9/11 would lead people who take universal moral principles seriously to support a movement to change US foreign policy.

An even stronger reaction would normally be evoked by the third interpretation, for it entails that the Bush administration allowed thousands of its own citizens to be killed on 9/11, deliberately and cold-bloodedly, for the sake of advancing its imperial designs, and then used this event as an excuse to kill hundreds of thousands of people in other countries, all the while hypocritically portraying itself as promoting a "culture of life." Of course, those who accept the previous interpretation know that hypocrisy with regard to the "sanctity of life" has long been a feature of official rhetoric. And yet most Americans, if they learned that their government had deliberately let thousands of their own citizens be killed, would surely consider this betrayal qualitatively different. For this would be a betrayal of the oath taken by American political leaders to protect their citizens.

If this third view implies that the Bush administration is guilty of a heinous and even criminal act, this is all the more the case with the fourth view. For many Americans, the idea that we are living in a country whose own leaders planned and carried out the attacks of 9/11 is simply too horrible to entertain. Unfortunately, however, there is strong evidence in support of this view. And if we find this evidence convincing, the implications for resistance to US empire-building are radical.

As Bacevich has emphasized, the only remaining debate about the American empire is whether it is benign. The interpretation of

9/11 is relevant to this debate, because it would be difficult to accept either the third or the fourth interpretation and still consider American imperialism benign.

I turn now to some of the evidence that supports these views. I will look first at evidence that supports (at least) the third view, according to which US officials had foreknowledge of the attacks.

Evidence for Foreknowledge by US Officials

A central aspect of the official story about 9/11 is that the attacks were planned entirely by al-Qaeda, with no one else knowing the plans. A year after the attacks, FBI Director Robert Mueller said: "To this day we have found no one in the United States except the actual hijackers who knew of the plot."[19] But there is much evidence that this claim was false.

For one thing, although the administration and the US military claimed that the threat that terrorists might use hijacked airlines as guided missiles was not recognized prior to 9/11, there is abundant evidence to the contrary. There had been many official reports about this threat, with some of them discussing al-Qaeda in particular and mentioning the World Trade Center and the Pentagon as likely targets. There had even been military exercises in 2000 and 2001 involving simulated attacks on these two structures. Also, there had been many warnings during the summer of 2001, several from foreign intelligence agencies, that there was going to be a spectacular attack on the United States in the near future. One of these was a CIA memo entitled "Bin Ladin Determined to Strike in US," which spoke of "preparations for hijackings and other types of attacks." The warnings were so many, in fact, that CIA Director George Tenet said that "the system was blinking red."[20]

These facts by themselves, to be sure, do not show that federal officials had specific foreknowledge. One could still, as did the 9/11 Commission, accept the conclusion published at the end of 2002 by the Congressional Joint Inquiry, according to which "none of [the intelligence gathered by the US intelligence community] identified the time, place, and specific nature of the attacks that were planned for September 11, 2001."[21]

A different conclusion must be reached, however, when we combine these warnings with the evidence supplied by an extraordinarily high volume of "put options" that were purchased in the three days before 9/11.

To buy put options for a particular company is to bet that its stock price will go down. These purchases were for two, and only two, airlines—United and American—the two airlines used in the attacks, and for Morgan Stanley Dean Witter, which occupied 22 stories of the World Trade Center. The price of these shares did, of course, plummet after 9/11. As the *San Francisco Chronicle* said, these unusual purchases, which resulted in profits of tens of millions of dollars, raise "suspicions that the investors... had advance knowledge of the strikes."[22]

The 9/11 Commission tried to scotch these suspicions. Its most important claim is that it found that 95 percent of the put options for United Airlines were purchased by "[a] single US-based institutional investor with no conceivable ties to al-Qaeda."[23] But this argument is viciously circular. What is at issue is precisely whether people other than al-Qaeda knew about the attacks in advance, perhaps because they had helped plan them. But the Commission simply assumes that al-Qaeda and only al-Qaeda planned and knew about the attacks. Accordingly, runs the Commission's logic, if the investors who purchased the put options in question had no ties with al-Qaeda, they could not possibly have had insider knowledge. They were simply lucky. The 9/11 Commission has, accordingly, done nothing to undermine the belief that the purchase of these put options indicated very specific prior knowledge of the attacks.

For our purposes, the most important implication of this story follows from the fact that US intelligence agencies monitor the market, looking for signs of imminent untoward events.[24] These extraordinary purchases, therefore, would have suggested to intelligence agencies that in the near future, United and American airliners were going to be used in attacks on the World Trade Center. This is fairly specific information, which implies the falsity of the Joint Inquiry's statement that "none of [the intelligence gathered by the US intelligence community] identified the time, place, and specific nature of the attacks." Indeed, one FBI agent reportedly said: "Obviously, people had to know.... It's terrible to think this, but this must have been allowed to happen as part of some other agenda."[25]

He was right. This would be terrible. There is considerable evidence, however, that the full truth is even more terrible—that the reason some US officials had foreknowledge of the attacks is because they had planned them.

Evidence that US Officials Planned and Executed the Attacks

The evidence for this fourth view consists largely of features of the attacks, in conjunction with behavior by US officials, that cannot be explained on the assumption that the attacks were planned and executed entirely by foreign agents. I will give four examples.

The Military's Failure to Prevent the Attacks and Its Changing Explanations: One feature of the attacks that suggests complicity by US officials is the twofold fact that the US military failed to prevent the attacks on 9/11 and then, since that time, has given us three mutually contradictory explanations for this failure. These changing stories suggest that the military has been trying to cover up the fact that a "stand-down" order was given on 9/11, canceling the military's own standard operating procedures for dealing with possibly hijacked airplanes.

It is clear that some agency—either the military, the FAA, or both—failed to follow standard procedures on 9/11. When these procedures are followed, the FAA, as soon as it sees signs that a plane may have been hijacked, calls military officials, who then call the nearest air force base with fighters on alert, telling it to send up a couple fighters to intercept the plane. Such interceptions usually occur within 10 to 15 minutes after the first signs of trouble. This is a routine procedure, happening about 100 times a year.[26] On 9/11, however, no interceptions occurred.

Why not? The military's first story was that no planes were sent up until after the Pentagon was hit. This would mean that the military leaders had left their fighters on the ground for almost 90 minutes after the FAA had first noticed signs of a possible hijacking. That story suggested to many people that a stand-down order had been given.

Within a few days, the military had put out a second story, saying that it *had* sent up fighters to intercept the airliners but that, because the FAA had been very late in notifying the military about the hijackings, the fighters arrived too late in each case. One problem with this story is that, if FAA personnel had responded so slowly, heads should have rolled; none did. An even more serious problem is that, even assuming the truth of the late notification times, the military's fighters still had time to intercept the hijacked airliners before they were to hit their targets. This second story implied, therefore, that standard procedures had been violated by the military as well as the FAA.[27]

To try to defend the military against this accusation, *The 9/11*

Commission Report gave us, amazingly, a third version, according to which the FAA, after giving the military insufficient warning about the first hijacked airliner, gave it absolutely no notification about the other three airliners until after they had crashed. But this account is wholly implausible. One problem is that it portrays FAA personnel, from top to bottom, as incompetent dolts. A second problem is that the 9/11 Commission's account rests on claims that contradict many credible and mutually supporting testimonies. In some of these cases, the fact that the Commission is simply lying is abundantly obvious. I will give two examples.

One obvious lie involves the time at which Vice President Cheney went down to the Presidential Emergency Operations Center (PEOC) under the White House. There is strong evidence that he went to the PEOC at about 9:15, perhaps the strongest being the testimony of Secretary of Transportation Norman Mineta, given in an open hearing to the Commission itself,[28] that when he entered the PEOC at about 9:20, Cheney was already there and fully in charge. But the Commission, simply omitting Mineta's testimony from its final report, claims that Cheney did not enter the PEOC until "shortly before 10:00, perhaps at 9:58."[29] According to this claim, therefore, Cheney did not take charge until about 20 minutes after the Pentagon had been hit (at 9:38). In accord with this timeline, there could be no truth to the idea—which is one possible interpretation of the content of Mineta's testimony—that Cheney had given a stand-down order: an order for the aircraft approaching the Pentagon not to be shot down.

Another obvious lie involves the time at which Cheney gave the authorization to shoot down any airliners that were still airborne. There is strong evidence that Cheney gave this authorization well before 10:00; Richard Clarke, for example, says that he received the authorization from Cheney shortly after 9:45, when the evacuation of the White House began,[30] but the Commission insists that Cheney did not give it until after 10:10. With this claim, the Commission is able simply to ignore the strong evidence that Flight 93, which crashed in Pennsylvania, was shot down by the US military. The Commission's implicit argument is that the military would not have done this without authorization from the White House; the vice president did not issue the authorization until at least seven minutes after Flight 93 had crashed; therefore, the US military could not have shot it down. This argument is made possible by the Commission's lies of omission; I have discussed its lies of distortion elsewhere.[31]

This third story implies that the military's earlier story, which it had been telling for almost three years, was almost entirely false. If our military leaders were lying to us all that time, why should we believe them now? And if our military is lying to us, must we not suspect that it is doing so to cover up its own guilt?

In sum, the behavior of the military both on 9/11 and afterward, combined with the fact that the 9/11 Commission had to resort to lies to make the US military appear blameless, suggests that military leaders were complicit in the attacks. A similar conclusion follows from an examination of the attack on the Pentagon.

The Strike on the Pentagon: One of the debates about this attack is whether the Pentagon was hit by American Airlines Flight 77, as the official account says, or by a military aircraft. Either story, however, implies that the attack was, at least partly, an inside job.

If we assume that the Pentagon was struck by Flight 77, we must ask how this could have occurred. The Pentagon is surely the best defended building on the planet, for three reasons. First, it is only a few miles from Andrews Air Force Base, which has at least three squadrons that keep fighter jets on alert at all times to protect the nation's capital. To be sure, part of the official story is that Andrews was not keeping any fighters on alert at that time. But as I argued in my critique of *The 9/11 Commission Report*, that claim is wholly implausible.[32]

Second, the US military has the best radar systems in the world. One of its systems, it has bragged, "does not miss anything occurring in North American airspace." This system is also said to be capable of monitoring a great number of targets simultaneously, as would be necessary in the case of a massive missile attack.[33] Given that capability, the official story, according to which Flight 77 flew toward the Pentagon undetected for 40 minutes, is absurd, especially at a time when the Pentagon knew the country was under attack. Any unauthorized airplane coming toward the Pentagon would normally have been detected and intercepted long before it got close.

Third, the Pentagon, according to people who should know, is ringed by anti-missile batteries, which are programmed to destroy any aircraft entering the Pentagon's airspace, except for any aircraft with a US military transponder.[34] If, by some fluke, Flight 77 had entered the Pentagon's airspace, it could have escaped being shot down only if officials in the Pentagon had deactivated its anti-aircraft defenses.

So, even if we accept the official story, according to which the

Pentagon was hit by Flight 77 under the control of al-Qaeda hijackers, we must conclude that the attack succeeded only because the Pentagon allowed it.

There are, furthermore, many reasons to reject the official story. First, the alleged pilot, Hani Hanjour, was a terrible pilot who could not possibly have flown the extremely complex and demanding trajectory allegedly taken by Flight 77.[35] Second, this aircraft hit the Pentagon's west wing, which for many reasons would have been the least likely spot for alien terrorists to target: Hitting the west wing required a very difficult maneuver; this wing was being renovated, so it contained very few people, and many of them were civilians working on the renovation; the renovation involved reinforcement, so that a strike on the west wing caused much less damage than would have a strike on any other part of the Pentagon; and Rumsfeld and all the top brass, whom terrorists would have wanted to kill, were in the east wing, as far removed from the west wing as possible. Third, whatever hit the Pentagon neither caused the kind of damage nor left the kind of debris that would be expected from the crash of a giant airliner—a fact testified to by both photographs[36] and eyewitnesses—including former Lt. Colonel Karen Kwiatkowski, whose testimony is provided in her chapter in the present volume.[37] Fourth, unlike the strikes on the Twin Towers, the strike on the Pentagon did not create a detectable seismic signal.[38] Fifth, the fact that the aircraft was not shot down by the Pentagon's anti-aircraft defense system suggests that it was a military aircraft, perhaps a missile, with a US military transponder.[39] Sixth, there are videos from nearby buildings that would show whether what struck the Pentagon was really a Boeing 757, but the FBI confiscated these videos right after the strike and, since then, the Department of Justice has refused to release them. In May of 2006, to be sure, two videos were released, but they did not show an airliner.[40]

Either way, therefore, the evidence indicates that the attack was, at least partly, an inside job.

The Collapse of the WTC Buildings: We can conclude the same thing about the attacks on the World Trade Center. Why? Because the collapses of the Twin Towers and Building 7 had to have been examples of controlled demolition, brought about by explosives placed throughout each of the buildings. Because this volume contains an entire chapter on this subject by physicist Steven Jones, I will simply summarize the main reasons for reaching this conclusion.

One reason for concluding that these three buildings were brought down by explosives is the very fact that they did collapse. High-rise steel-frame buildings have never—before or after 9/11—been caused to collapse by fire, even when, as in the Philadelphia fire of 1991 and the Caracas fire of 2004, the fires were much larger, much hotter, and much longer-lasting than the fires in the Twin Towers and Building 7 (the fires in the north and south towers lasted only 102 and 56 minutes, respectively).[41]

The second reason is the specific nature of the collapses, each feature of which points to explosives. For example, the buildings collapsed straight down, and at virtually free-fall speed. With regard to the Twin Towers in particular, many people in or near the buildings said that they heard or felt explosions.[42] Virtually all the concrete of these enormous structures was pulverized into very fine dust (try dropping a piece of concrete from a great height; it will merely break into small pieces, not turn into very fine dust particles). Much of this dust was blown out horizontally several hundred feet, as were pieces of steel and aluminum. Most of the steel beams and columns came down in sections short enough to be loaded on trucks. And many witnesses reported the existence of molten steel beneath the rubble, with some of them reporting that when steel beams were lifted from the depths of the rubble, one end would be dripping molten steel.[43] The existence of this molten steel cannot be explained by the fires, because open hydrocarbon fires under the most ideal conditions cannot exceed 1700° F and steel does not even begin to melt until it reaches 2,800° F. The molten steel is easily explained, however, by the use of explosives such as thermite or RDX, which are commonly used to slice steel. These and still other effects point to the existence of very powerful, precisely placed explosives.[44]

The third fact supporting the theory of controlled demolition is evidence of a deliberate cover-up. If the buildings' steel beams and columns had indeed been sliced by explosives, an examination of the steel would have revealed this fact. In this case, however, most of the steel was quickly hauled away, before it could be examined,[45] then put on ships to Asia, where it would be melted down.[46] Although it is normally a federal offense to remove evidence from a crime scene, the removal of the steel, which was carefully overseen, was facilitated by federal officials.[47]

When we look at all these features of the collapses, we can see that the official theory about the collapses of the Twin Towers—that they were caused by the impact of the airplanes plus the resulting fires—is ridiculous. The absurdity of the official theory is even clearer with regard to Building 7, which was not hit by a plane. Its collapse remains so impossible to explain, except as controlled demolition, that *The 9/11 Commission Report* did not even mention it—as if there were nothing remarkable about the fact that for the first time in history, fire, perhaps along with a little structural damage (which was alleged by some officials),[48] was said to have caused the sudden collapse of a steel-frame high-rise building—an event that would have been even more remarkable given the fact that the building was far from being engulfed in flames, according to some witnesses[49] and all of the available photographs.[50]

The evidence suggests, therefore, that the destruction of the World Trade Center was an inside job, with at least some of the insiders being at the federal level. No foreign terrorists could have obtained the kind of access to the buildings that would have been required, whereas the access of people hired by the Bush administration could be explained: Marvin Bush, one of the president's brothers, had served as a director of Securacom, the company in charge of security for the WTC, from 1993 until 2000, during which a new security system was installed, and the Bush brothers' cousin, Wirt Walker III, was the CEO from 1999 until January of 2002.[51] Also, al-Qaeda terrorists would probably not have had the courtesy to make sure that the buildings came straight down, rather than falling over onto other buildings. Foreign terrorists also could not have arranged for the removal of the steel or the failure of all the official investigations—as discussed in the chapter by Steven Jones—even to consider the possibility that the buildings were brought down by explosives. In sum, the destruction of the World Trade Center—like the strike on the Pentagon, the military's failure to prevent the attacks, and its changing stories— lead to the conclusion that the attacks must have been planned and executed by our own political and military leaders. The same conclusion can be inferred from the behavior of the Secret Service agents with the president that morning.

The Behavior of the Secret Service: As everyone who saw Michael Moore's *Fahrenheit 9/11* knows, President Bush was in a second-grade classroom in Florida when he was informed about the second strike on the World Trade Center. This report left no doubt that the country was suffering a terrorist attack. And yet the president simply sat there. Many people have asked why he did not spring into action, assuming his role as commander-in-chief.

But the real question, which Michael Moore mentions in passing, is why the Secret Service did not immediately rush him away from the school to a safe place. Bush's location had been highly publicized. And if the attacks were a complete surprise, executed solely by foreign terrorists, the Secret Service agents would have had no idea how many planes had been hijacked. They would have had to assume that the president himself might be one of the targets. For all they would have known, a hijacked airliner might have been headed toward the school at that very minute, ready to crash into it. And yet these agents, who are highly trained to respond instantly in such situations, allowed the president to remain in the classroom another 10 minutes. They then allowed him to deliver his regularly scheduled TV address, thereby announcing to any suicide hijackers that he was still there, giving them an even wider window of opportunity. This behavior makes sense only if the Secret Service knew that the planned attacks did not include an attack on the president. And how could this be known for certain unless the attacks were being carried out by people within our own government?

Although many more examples could be given, these four are sufficient to suggest that there is no escape from the frightening conclusion that 9/11 was engineered by members of the Bush administration, including the secretary of defense. As to why they would do this, at least part of the answer is clear from the way in which they have used 9/11: to advance the American empire. Immediately after 9/11, in fact, members of the Bush administration repeatedly referred to the attacks as an opportunity. Donald Rumsfeld, for example, said that the attacks created "the kind of opportunities that World War II offered, to refashion the world."[52] The *National Security Strategy of the United States of America*, published in the Bush administration in September 2002, frankly said: "The events of September 11, 2001 opened vast, new opportunities."[53] Seeing this connection between 9/11 and US imperial ambitions can be a stimulus to face up fully to the awful truth about the American empire.

Fully Facing the Truth about the American Empire

To be sure, as Chomsky, Falk, and Chalmers Johnson have illustrated, strong portrayals of American imperialism as far from benign can be drawn without any suggestion that the Bush administration arranged 9/11. These portrayals can be drawn from publicly available documents.

One such document is the "National Security Strategy of the United States of America," published by the Bush administration in September of 2002. David North says, not unfairly, that this document "asserts as the guiding policy of the United States the right to use military force... against any country it believes to be, or it believes may at some point become, a threat to American interests." "No other country in modern history," adds North, "has asserted such a sweeping claim to... world domination."[54]

Another such document, called "Vision for 2020," was published in February of 1997 by the US Space Command. The mission statement at the head of this document reads: "US Space Command—dominating the space dimension of military operations to protect US interests and investment."[55] There is no mention of democracy and human rights. In the body of the document, in fact, we find this amazingly candid statement: "The globalization of the world economy... will continue with a widening between 'haves' and 'have-nots.'" The point of this statement is that as the domination of the world economy by the United States and its allies increases, the world's poor will get still poorer, making the "have-nots" hate America all the more. We will need, therefore, the power to keep them in line.

The United States can do this—and this is the document's main message—through "full spectrum dominance," which will involve merging "space superiority with land, sea, and air superiority." Dominance in space will include, the document frankly says, the power "to deny others the use of space."

By speaking only of the Space Command's effort to develop a "missile defense system," the Pentagon and the White House like to suggest that its purpose is purely defensive. But the goal includes weaponizing space so as to give US forces, in the words of a more recent document, a "prompt global strike capability, whether nuclear or non-nuclear, [that] will allow the US to rapidly and accurately strike distant... targets."[56] The fact that the US Space Command's program is an aggressive one is announced in the logo of one of its divisions: "In Your Face from Outer Space."[57]

Simply from these and other documents, taken in conjunction with the actions of the Bush administration and the US military, we can see through the claim that the US project of creating the first truly global empire is a benevolent or at least benign enterprise. But we can *fully* grasp the extent to which this project is propelled by fanaticism based on a deeply perverted value system only when we realize that the terrorist attacks of 9/11 were orchestrated by our own leaders—and that they did this to provide the justification, the fear, and the funding for the so-called war on terror, which would be used as a pretext for enlarging the empire.

Whereas the fact that 9/11 has been used to provide the fear and the justification is obvious, there is also a clear connection between 9/11 and funding for these imperial efforts.

Shortly before the Bush administration took office in 2001, a document entitled *Rebuilding America's Defenses* was published by an organization called the Project for the New American Century,[58] founding members of which included Dick Cheney, Paul Wolfowitz, and Donald Rumsfeld. This document focused primarily on getting more tax money allocated for the technological transformation of the US military, with the centerpiece of this technological transformation being the US Space Command's project to weaponize and thereby control space. Because this transformation of the US military will be very expensive, the document said, it will probably proceed very slowly—unless America suffers "some catastrophic and catalyzing event—like a new Pearl Harbor."[59] It is interesting that on the night of 9/11, President Bush reportedly wrote in his diary, "The Pearl Harbor of the 21st century took place today."[60]

The Pearl Harbor precedent was also used in a document published in January 2001 by the Commission to Assess US National Security Space Management and Organization, which was chaired by Donald Rumsfeld. Speaking of the need for massive funding for the US Space Command, this Rumsfeld Commission, as it was generally called, asked whether such funding would occur only after a "Space Pearl Harbor."[61]

Then, on the evening of 9/11 itself, the attacks of that morning were cited as a basis for providing such funding. The occasion was a news briefing on the Pentagon attack held by Rumsfeld. Senator Carl Levin, the chair of the Senate Armed Services Committee, was present. He was asked: "Senator Levin, you and other Democrats in Congress have voiced fear that you simply don't have enough money for the large increase in defense that the Pentagon is seeking, especially for missile defense.... Does this sort of thing convince you that an emergency exists in this country to increase defense spending?"[62] Congress immediately appropriated an additional $40 billion for the Pentagon and much more later, with few questions asked.

Besides being a rousing success in obtaining increased spending for military purposes, 9/11 also provided the pretext for putting many military bases in Central Asia. Zbigniew Brzezinski, in his 1997 book, *The Grand Chessboard*, had said that doing so would be crucial for maintaining "American primacy," partly because of the huge oil reserves around the Caspian Sea. Indeed, it may have been from this book that the Project for the New American Century got its idea that a new Pearl Harbor would be helpful. Brzezinski, explaining that the American public had "supported America's engagement in World War II largely because of the shock effect of the Japanese attack on Pearl Harbor,"[63] suggested that Americans today would support the needed military operations in Central Asia only "in the circumstance of a truly massive and widely perceived direct external threat."[64] And indeed, thanks to the attacks of 9/11, the Bush administration was able to carry out its plan to attack Afghanistan—a plan that, we now know, had been formulated several months before 9/11.[65] The White House helped install a friendly government in Afghanistan and the Pentagon now has military bases there and in several other countries of Central Asia.

We also know that the intention to invade Iraq existed long before 9/11 and that this intention was based on imperial designs, not disgust with Saddam's wickedness.[66] In the Project for the New American Century's 2000 document, we read: "While the unresolved conflict with Iraq provides the immediate justification, the need for a substantial American force presence in the Gulf transcends the issue of the regime of Saddam Hussein."[67] Not long after the invasion, the US military started building several bases in Iraq, intended to be permanent.[68] The attacks of 9/11 again provided the pretext, as the Bush administration deceived a majority of the American people into believing that Saddam was connected with Osama bin Laden and even directly responsible for the attacks of 9/11.

I suggested earlier that seeing the true connections between 9/11 and the global domination project helps us understand how fully this project reflects "fanaticism based on a deeply perverted value system." This is a value system that is diametrically opposed to the value systems on which all the great religious and moral traditions of the world have been based. These traditional value systems say that we should not covet, steal, and murder, and that we should make sure that everyone has the necessary means for a decent life. But our government's project for global domination is carried out in the name of the greed of the "haves" of the world to have still more, even if it means killing hundreds of thousands of people and letting millions more die every year of starvation and poverty-related diseases. We can now see, furthermore, that some political and military leaders are so fanatically infected with these perverted values that they are willing to kill thousands of their own citizens, then endlessly use a deceptive account of these terrorist attacks to justify "a war on terror," in the name of which they claim the right to do virtually anything they wish, ignoring all principles of morality and international law.

How Should Morally Serious People Respond?

I now turn, finally, to the question of how people who take our common moral norms seriously should respond to 9/11 and the American empire. My discussion of this question must be very brief, consisting merely of four suggestions.

First, discover and then speak the truth: I would suggest that such people should—if they have not done so already—study about both 9/11 and the American empire to see if they find the claims made here about them true. If they do, then they should do everything in their power to make others aware of these facts.

Second, emphasize the total opposition between the values implicit in the global domination project and the common moral norms of humankind. This opposition must be emphasized over and over, because those who are behind the global domination project promote their policies in the name of moral values, especially freedom, democracy, and human rights. They have also convinced large numbers of Jews and especially Christians that they are promoting "biblical values." The fact that these claims are complete lies must be made so clear that it can be denied only by those who are completely impervious to evidence. For most people, a demonstration that 9/11 was orchestrated in order to facilitate US foreign policy would be the clearest possible demonstration of the fact that this policy is based on values diametrically opposed to the values that are shared by our various moral and religious traditions.

Third, use this appeal to common moral values to build a widespread movement opposing the global domination project. When elites finally turned against the war in Vietnam, they evidently did so primarily because they became convinced that it was a lost cause and was becoming counter-productive. But what generated the widespread anti-war movement was the growing conviction that the war was simply wrong—which meant, for one thing, that it was not a cause for which any more of our young people should die or for which any more of our tax dollars should be spent. Likewise, if a widespread movement in America against our government's global domination project emerges, the various members of this movement will probably not all share the same primary motives. But the basic conviction creating and sustaining the movement will surely be the conviction that the project to dominate the world is simply wrong—which will mean, for one thing, that it is not a cause for which any more of our young people should die or for which any more of our tax dollars should be spent.

Fourth, formulate proposals for a worldwide movement to subvert the global domination project. It seems clear that, given the global nature of the project, any movement opposing it, to have any chance of success, must be a worldwide movement. We need, therefore, concrete proposals that could, in principle, serve as the program for such a movement. I have published a brief statement of my own proposal, which is centered around the idea of global democracy.[69] Other people will favor different proposals. Whatever the nature of these proposals, however, it is important that they be based on moral principles that are common to all peoples and that this moral basis be made fully explicit. It is probably only such proposals, drawing explicitly on our common moral norms, that could serve as the basis for a worldwide movement.

I close with the observation that, insofar as Americans participate in this anti-imperialist movement, their activities will be deeply patriotic, because they will be seeking to call our nation back to its moral ideals, which stand diametrically opposed to the values implicit in the global domination project.[70]

TWO

Assessing the Official 9/11 Conspiracy Theory

Karen Kwiatkowski

M y co-workers and I stood watching CNN record the image of an airplane impacting the south tower, in view of an already smoking north tower. Prior to the second impact, some of us commented on how the north tower impact could have been an accident, entailing faulty coordinates or computer data, equipment malfunction, FAA controllers asleep at the wheel, or some other problem. But after the south tower was hit, a certain coolness seemed to enter the room. Some of us began to wonder if we were under attack, literally. Shortly thereafter, we heard a "boom," and all eyes flew from the television in the corner to the center-facing window of our fifth-floor, seventh-corridor, B-ring office in the Pentagon. In our direct view, an unforgettable fireball, 20 to 30 feet in diameter, appeared to be resting quietly on the flat fifth-story roof, about a third of the way around from where we were standing. To me, it looked like an explosive had fallen from above, rather than like a mass of energy forcing its way up through four stories to bloom in flames on the Pentagon roof (according to the official account, the fire came from the explosion of American Airlines Flight 77 after it crashed into the first floor of the Pentagon's west wing).

Some people remember a shake of the building, but I did not feel it. Also, no noticeable fire alarms went off. But we locked safes, vaults, and doors, then gathered our things and exited the building on the Mall side, which looks out toward Rosslyn, Virginia. Directly opposite the impact, near the Mall side, is the River exit, which services the offices of the secretary of defense and most of his undersecretaries and service chiefs. I remember hearing, as I was walking out, a short announcement repeated over and over on the hallway intercom—not an alarm but some kind of instruction. It was scratchy, unintelligible, and irrelevant, because the hallways were already mostly empty. Blessedly for me and my coworkers, there was no smoke or fire, no screams or horrific smells in the 7th corridor or the E-ring on the Mall and River sides.

Outside the Mall entrance, we stood for a while, listening to loud jets overhead, and wincing. Would they hit, as rumor had it, via another airplane inbound for the Pentagon? The idea that it was an airplane made sense, as we had been watching airplanes hit buildings only minutes before. Before long, we were ushered south some distance from the building to a spot between the Naval Annex and the south lawn of the Pentagon. From this elevated vantage point, a few thousand people all stared in disbelief at a smoking gash in the Pentagon, directly between the just completed and mostly unoccupied "wedge" on the right and its older, unrefurbished, sister wedge to the left. The older part of the building looked more damaged. Surreal is the word that kept coming to mind as we stared, transfixed.

People were responding in different ways. Some had come through smoke, others were noticeably stressed and emotional, still others curious and quiet. Most of us were just staring at the green lawn and the damaged building on that vividly bright morning.

At some point, authoritative folks came by, calling for all those in uniform to report to the flat lawn near the helicopter port for stretcher duty. Those of us in uniform, along with a few reservists with day jobs as civilian Pentagon employees or contractors, quickly reported and formed lines of four, ready for our forecasted stretcher duty. But no person or thing emerged from that side of the Pentagon. We heard that survivors and injured folks were being rescued from the inside, from the center area known affectionately as Ground Zero, and out the River exit into ambulances. Not long after we had been called, we were dismissed and disbanded back up to the highway above the lawn, in safety further away from the building.

In the days that followed, we all watched a lot of television, seeing the Twin Towers collapse on their moorings over and over again. We saw the Pentagon fires largely put out and watched that big American flag flap near the damaged wall, in a defiant and proud and patriotic gesture. We heard a lot of news, rumors, and tall tales regarding what had happened and who did what. And we waited to hear about the dead.

This was September 11, 2001, and the days that followed. Although from a general American perspective, things began slowly, from a Pentagon perspective, they did not. Shortly after 9/11, the anthrax letter events occurred, causing varied kinds of anxiety in the Pentagon, both before and after we knew that the anthrax was the Ames strain, manufactured just up the road in Maryland. The invasion plan for Afghanistan was moving rapidly. At the time, I wondered how we could do the planning and the work as quickly as we did. But I found out later that the plans to topple the Taliban had been in place months before 9/11 and that Iraq was discussed openly as a target within days of 9/11.

I remember thinking how strange it was that although the hijackers, according to the published lists, were mostly Saudis and Egyptians, the enemies to be attacked were Afghans and, it was hoped, Iraqis. Of course, Osama bin Laden seemed a perfect villain. He was a public enemy of both the Saudi government and Washington, a man with a past record of attacks against both entities, a wealthy Wahhabist with a British education and excellent English, and a person with whom we had once worked well in a previous incarnation of the American-led global war for freedom and democracy.

When I think about 9/11, I do so as a retired military officer, as an academic and a teacher, as a scientist (both political and zoological), as a storyteller, as a taxpayer, and as a person who was physically present for a small portion of the events that day. Like many people in Washington and in the military, I spent the months and years after 9/11 reading and watching and questioning, trying to learn more, understand more, and get up to speed on what was happening. Like most Americans, this effort at self-education was marred by the insistent drumbeat of the "one true path" as broadcast by the administration, most of Congress, and the mainstream media.

Until I embarked on a personal quest to understand what we were doing with our security and foreign policies, I thought of the mainstream media as simply "the media." I didn't fully comprehend its important political role. I would not begin to comprehend that role until months later in 2002. Then, in my position as a staff officer assigned to the Under Secretary for Policy, Near East and South Asia, I was able personally to observe a coordinated and effective move by the White House and a host of neoconservative and evangelical politicos to publicly rationalize an all-out invasion of Iraq, with 9/11 as a recurring, if blatantly false, pillar of justification.

Iraq and 9/11 are related, of course. We did not care to occupy Afghanistan, and it seems we were never concerned about finding Osama bin Laden. That task, to the extent that it was and is pursued, has been the job of our friendly Unocal hand, Hamid Karzai, along with our friends in Pakistan. In March 2002, only months after 9/11 and the invasion of Afghanistan, President George W. Bush himself stated: "I don't know where [Bin Laden] is. You know, I just don't spend that much time on him."[1] By May 2002, Arabic, Pushtun, and Dari speakers from the Fifth Special Forces Group in Afghanistan were abruptly replaced five months into their work by members of Third Special Forces Group, which focuses on West Africa and Central America and is trained in French and Spanish. Sadly, perhaps catastrophically, for the work accomplished up to that time in Afghanistan and the work that would follow, Third Group replacements in Afghanistan spoke no Arabic, no Pushtun, no Dari. The operational military must have realized that, at least in this case, the president was being absolutely forthright regarding his views toward the ostensible perpetrator of 9/11.

The 9/11 Commission Report

Honesty is a strange and debatable thing. What is truth, and what is reality? How can we know? In the case of 9/11, this most human of challenges is made even more complicated. Average people, interested citizens, or even trained researchers of the journalistic or scientific variety are not encouraged to inquire about what happened on that day, what had happened in the months and years preceding it, or about what came afterward. This work was to be done, of course, by the president's appointed commission. After I read the report, it seemed to me to be a complete waste of time and effort. None of my own personal questions about that day had been answered. Most of them were not even addressed. Why would the difficult questions, and also some very easy ones, be avoided by the 9/11 Commission?

After reading the 9/11 Commission's report, I wrote in August 2004:

The 9/11 Commission "discovered" the main problem is not technology or information or even leadership—it was the government rule-set. The rules they used didn't allow our Jabba the Hutt commanders in Washington to properly predict and then respond to the millions of possibilities that constitute daily reality. If only the government could have more rules and regulations, more mandates and controls, if only we could centralize control, things would be much better, so says the 9/11 Commission. One wonders if the entire commission wasn't secretly replaced by pod people from the old Soviet Central Committee.

I naïvely expected more constructive and useful information in the report. A detailed discussion of FBI whistleblower Coleen Rowley and how her observations and actions led to change would be nice. She merited a brief mention in footnote 94. That is all.

I expected to hear how WTC 7 collapsed. The lease-holder of the building told the media it was "pulled."[2] I expected to see more discussion of the mechanics of that presumably unplanned demolition in the evening of 9/11 as well as the collapse of both 110-story towers, both impacted differently, both falling almost identically. Do we have an engineering design flaw no one knew about? It didn't come up in the report.

The Commission concluded that the FAA was not really capable of giving the military what it needed to know. Things have certainly gone downhill since 1999, when Payne Stewart's twin engine Learjet quietly drifted off its flight plan, and was escorted by military jets from Eglin AFB and Tyndall AFB in Florida, ANG out of Tulsa, and out of Fargo, for several hours across several states before it ran out of gas and crashed in South Dakota. The difference was that Stewart was just a guy in a single private plane off course with no explanation, while on 9/11, it was one, no two, wait—three, I mean four, jumbo passenger jets. Unlike Stewart's plane, which simply left its flight plan and was unresponsive, the FAA actually had hijack warning on AA 11 at 8:19 AM and UA 175 at 8:52 AM. After two hijack warnings, AA 77 made an unauthorized turn at 8:54 AM. The Herndon Control Center knew UA 93 was hijacked at 9:34 AM.

The commission reports the first fighter jets from Otis ANG Base were scrambled for AA 11 thirty-four minutes after the first hijack alert and again, from Langley AFB, a half hour or so later. At 10:38, fighter jets from Andrews AFB were airborne. None had a visual on any of the four planes plane until it was too late. In 1999, more military jets were on the job watching a lone Learjet over the Midwest than in the 2001 response to multiple hijacks on the densely populated East Coast. Rumsfeld and Wolfowitz should have both been fired at the time, saving us the trouble and expense of criminal trials for their roles in fomenting the unjustified and gratuitous Iraq war.

The report refers to the many cell phone calls that were made from the speeding airplanes, yet most people who have tried to do this find that reception, cell switching software, and other factors often prevent even a connection, much less a conversation.[3] The 9/11 commission should have taken the opportunity to clear up that technological debate. It did not.

Why were the only gas stations mentioned those where terrorists were spotted before 9/11—and not the Citgo directly in line with the Flight path of AA 77 as it aimed for the Pentagon? The security video from Citgo was confiscated by law enforcement—no hints as to what it recorded were provided in the Commission report. In fact, as the Citgo gas station employee noted, "The FBI was here within minutes and took the film."[4] Sounds like the FBI had its eye on the ball—at least after the attacks!

Having walked from the Pentagon into the vivid sunlight the morning of 9/11, to stare in disbelief with thousands of my coworkers at the burning gash in the structure, I'd like to understand more about the events of the day itself. Why the Towers and the Pentagon or other governmental buildings would be targeted by al-Qaeda or any other adversary is self-evident; why American policies and practices create enemies around the world is also no mystery. The slow and highly debatable rate of improvement in our ability to defend the country—while the cost of doing business for Americans everywhere has skyrocketed—is also predictable. George W. Bush himself admitted the truth as he almost happily noted, "We are a nation in danger."[5]

[You better believe it, Mr. Bush. We have an incompetent, bankrupt, obese federal government bureaucracy led by ignoramuses who dream of empire, with continued zero accountability to either the facts on the ground or to the people who pay for it all]

That was my initial reaction to the government's assessment of 9/11, an assessment weakly offered by the administration almost three years after the fact. But in retrospect, my frustration was clearly the result of my expectation that a set of both questions and answers would be provided, and that a scientific, policy, and, yes, political assessment would be delivered. But this product did not appear even to be an assessment! And if it was, what was being assessed? What criteria were used to produce the final document?

Could an assessment of the actual facts be accomplished by the commission, given the myriad of information that was available—and the myriad that was not available due to the lack of retention of crime-scene evidence? Were any scientists or technicians or academics on the commission?

The Commission had ten members plus an executive director. Thomas Kean, the chair, is a teacher and politician, with a Master's degree from Columbia University's Teacher's College; Lee Hamilton, the vice chair, is a lawyer, as are Richard Ben-Veniste, Fred Fielding, Jamie Gorelick, Slade Gorton, Timothy Roemer, and James Thompson. Bob Kerrey was trained as a pharmacist; after military service, he started a chain of restaurants and health clubs; he later served as a Nebraska governor, representative, and senator. John Lehman, an investment banker and Reagan's secretary of the navy, completed the Ph.D. with a dissertation entitled "Functional Analysis of Congress and the Executive in Foreign Policy." The executive director, Philip Zelikow, is an academic student of the presidency.

It would appear that only Lehman and Zelikow had the kind of academic training needed to examine what really happened and why, and their training equipped them only to deal with the political dimension of 9/11. In terms of science, engineering, technology, psychology, economics, intelligence, and practical law enforcement, no one on the Commission seems to have been remotely qualified to examine the evidence and assess what happened, and what it signified. The government assigned no thinkers, no scientists, no engineers, and no intelligence analysts to the official task of assessing what happened on 9/11. Instead, Washington and the Bush administration apparently believed itself best served by legal tacticians, politicians, political theorists, and political supporters.

The Commission's product is thus necessarily a non-scientific document. It is an ad hoc document, absent any critical or complete examination of facts on the ground. As in the old Soviet Union where TASS and *Pravda* pretended to report the news and citizens pretended to believe it, this massive tome was put forth as the first and final answer for Americans interested in understanding how and why 9/11 occurred. Perhaps the real message Americans should take away from the report is how tremendously important this report—in all its nonsensical glory—is held to be by the Bush administration. And nothing more.

I believe that the Commission failed to deeply examine the topic at hand, failed to apply scientific rigor to its assessment of events leading up to and including 9/11, failed to produce a believable and unbiased summary of what happened, failed to fully examine why it happened, and even failed to include a set of unanswered questions for future research.

Sadly, I also understand that pointing out any of these failures brings on self-righteous government wrath and mainstream media condemnation. Thou shalt not be a curious observer, or else thou shalt be labeled a "conspiracy theorist" or worse. This seems to be the message and, years later, the Bush administration and the mainstream media are still preaching it.

Thinking about 9/11 from a Variety of Perspectives

How then might we think of 9/11—the event itself and its significance in American political history? I have been told by reporters that they will not report their own insights or contrary evaluations of the official 9/11 story, because to question the government story about 9/11 is to question the very foundations of our entire modern belief system regarding our government, our country, and our way of life. To be charged with questioning these foundations is far more serious than being labeled a disgruntled conspiracy nut or an anti-government traitor, or even being sidelined or marginalized within an academic, government-service, or literary career. To question the official 9/11 story is simply and fundamentally revolutionary. In this way, of course, questioning the official story is also simply and fundamentally American.

Even in this environment of official discouragement, Americans are able to discuss 9/11 from a variety of perspectives. There are so many unanswered questions, so many flaws and inconsistencies in the government's official conspiracy theory. I do not have the complete set of answers, or knowledge, but after some study it appears that I, as a regular citizen, may know more than the 9/11 Commission—or at least more than they put in their Report. This observation is meant to be forthright, not frightening. Sadly, it is both.

From a Military Perspective: As a retired member of the military, I would expect that a paramilitary-style attack on mainland United States territory as witnessed on 9/11 would be more rigorously examined by both law enforcement and military agencies, and more openly discussed as a prior possibility. Understandably, both law enforcement and the military had failed to protect the nation, but even a desire to avoid self-incrimination does not explain the calculatedly incompetent response to the event, and the superficial analysis of what happened afterward. According to the official account, nineteen hijackers on four passenger planes conducted the kind of attack I had read about four years earlier in a Tom Clancy book, one of the Jack Ryan series, *Executive Orders*. Here, Jack is made president when a passenger airplane is purposely crashed into the US Capitol, killing the president, vice president, and speaker of the house. I thought most people in the military read Tom Clancy novels in the 1990s. And yet, military leaders and spokespersons consistently expressed shock and surprise at such a possibility. Donald Rumsfeld, General Richard Myers, and other Pentagon leaders simply had no idea such a thing was possible, they claimed. Was Tom Clancy really more savvy than the entire Pentagon?

From an Academic Perspective: As an academic and a teacher, I often have to check facts, review for faulty footnoting and plagiarism, and assess a written document's effectiveness and attention to detail. In *The 9/11 Commission Report*, the names of the hijackers are listed, with detailed descriptions of what they did, despite the fact that no witnesses survived. Yet in late September 2001, several of the purported hijackers were found to be alive and well, some of them protesting their innocence and their amazement.[6] I checked to see if this real-world information had found its way into the 9/11 report—certainly there had been time—and was shocked to find reportedly living men listed as dead hijackers. The Commission did not indicate any uncertainty as to hijacker identities, even though the FBI itself admitted publicly that several identities were uncertain, with Saudi Arabian pilot Waleed al-Shehri, two different Saudis named Abdulaziz Al Omari (one a pilot and one an engineer), Saeed Alghamdi, and possibly Khalid al-Midhar, all giving post 9/11 interviews, in person and on television.[7] When I evaluate a paper, if I see stupid mistakes that indicate gross negligence in the research and note failures to address serious well-published challenges to the writer's assumptions or argument, the writer's credibility is devastated. In the present case, I wonder what else the 9/11 Commission failed to examine, and what other less obvious or more subtle mistakes are present in the report.

From a Scientific Perspective: It is as a scientist that I have the most trouble with the official government conspiracy theory, mainly because it does not satisfy the rules of probability or physics.

The collapses of the World Trade Center buildings clearly violate the laws of physics and probability (as the essay in this volume by

Steven Jones demonstrates). The government explains the collapses as the natural result of the forces admitted into the equation—primarily the heat from the fires and the force of gravity—but none of the story works, assuming we are using known principles of physics, algebra, or calculus. It may work using some new kind of math, or perhaps new rules of physics, known to the Bush administration, but these alternatives are not proposed. Given the curiosities of three steel skyscrapers collapsing at virtually freefall speed (something that had never happened before) and doing so identically in spite of varying degrees of fire and different types of structural damage), I, as a scientist, would have expected extremely careful and detailed crime-scene analysis and investigation. I would have expected to observe subsequent widespread global alarm about the apparently flawed and highly vulnerable design of steel skyscrapers everywhere. These logical extensions of such a major event not only failed to occur; they were actively discouraged by the US government. Physical evidence was taken away under lock and key and destroyed almost in its entirety. If I were an insurance investigator examining the situation in the weeks and month of cleanup, I would certainly have been able to tally up some salvage profit, as the steel beams bypassed any after-accident laboratory delay and were sold post-haste to overseas scrap metal processors. But to me as a scientist, the crime-scene investigation was mystifying in its absence.

This goes double for the attack on the Pentagon. There was a dearth of visible debris on the relatively unmarked lawn, where I stood only minutes after the impact. Beyond this strange absence of airliner debris, there was no sign of the kind of damage to the Pentagon structure one would expect from the impact of a large airliner. This visible evidence or lack thereof may have also been apparent to the secretary of defense, who in an unfortunate slip of the tongue, referred to the aircraft that slammed into the Pentagon as a "missile." These aspects of the morning of September 11 combine to make me quite wary of the subsequent statements and actions taken by federal officials. This wariness might be easily eliminated with more detailed and forthcoming evidence—perhaps even a reconstruction of the aircraft that was reported to have hit the Pentagon. Unlike the painstaking reconstruction of civilian aircraft that we have witnessed in past decades, most recently in Flight 800—which exploded midair and crashed into the ocean—any physical remains of the aircraft that hit the Pentagon were quickly carted away to some unknown location, so we have no physical evidence that the aircraft really was Flight 77 or even a Boeing 757.

Like many people who watch a lot of television news and the Discovery Channel, I have seen post-passenger airline crash videos and post-accident computerized reconstructions of such events. Typically in these cases, a great deal of debris in all shapes and sizes is present, and an amazing amount of this debris is recoverable and useful in post-accident reconstruction. Yet in the case of the Pentagon attack, I saw nothing of any significance at the point of impact—no airplane metal or cargo debris was blowing on the lawn in front of the damaged building as smoke billowed from within the Pentagon. Strangely, none seemed to be produced afterward in any attempted accident analysis or reconstruction. This is even stranger in light of public reports afterward estimating that the large airplane was in fact flying low and turning, suggesting that one wing would have hit the ground before the aircraft nose hit the Pentagon, leaving a terrific amount of debris. Having only minutes before observed the televised crashes against buildings in New York, all of us staring at the Pentagon that morning were indeed looking for such debris, but what we expected to see was, in fact, not evident.

The same is true with regard to the kind of damage we expected. I would think that if a 100-plus-ton aircraft constructed of relatively lightweight materials and designed for lift, loaded with passenger seating, luggage, odds and ends and passengers, going several hundred miles an hour were to hit the Pentagon, it would cause a great deal of possibly superficial but visible damage to the wide swath of the side of the building and the entire area of impact. But I did not see this kind of damage. Rather, the façade had a rather small hole, no larger than 20 feet in diameter. Although this façade later collapsed, it remained standing for 30 or 40 minutes, with the roof line remaining relatively straight.

The scene, in short, was not what I would have expected from a strike by a large airliner. It was, however, exactly what one would expect if a missile had struck the Pentagon. I was not thinking at the time that it was a missile. My mindset was completely oriented toward the idea that a hijacked airliner had crashed into our building. I do remember thinking at the time how fortunate it was that the impact was diametrically opposite the offices of the secretary of defense and the service secretaries.

From a Storyteller's Perspective: As a storyteller, I find the government's account, according to which the planes were taken over by 19 hijackers who were motivated by hate for American "freedom" and a desire for 70 virgins, simply unbelievable. The entire story—from the president's reading a book about a goat with schoolchildren for many minutes after he is informed of the situation, to the authoritative dominance of the vice president barking commands in the aftermath, to the strange statements made by the Pentagon leadership,[8] to the out-of-place collapse of the undamaged WTC 7 (see Steven Jones's chapter), and the complete and simultaneous failure of both NORAD and the FAA systems of hijack response—this entire story is so unrealistic that even the most talented and creative novelist would never attempt to advance such a plot.

After the incidents, the lack of detailed agency investigations into the events and the complete and conscious government refusal to hold anyone responsible likewise defies literary common sense. In the marketplace of theories and explanations, no one would buy the official story. Consider the surprise attack on Pearl Harbor, an event repeatedly called to mind in 2001—and an event for which we did have some prior sense of possibility, given widespread concern in Washington over Japanese aggression in Asia. On December 17, 1941, only ten days after the attack on Pearl Harbor, President Roosevelt, through his Navy and Army secretaries, relieved Admiral Kimmel and General Short of their commands. After 9/11, this type of executive response would have been logical, and indeed many Americans expected the dismissal of the respective heads of NORAD and the FAA, and possibly even the USAF chief of staff and the FBI director. But here again, the government story defies historical precedent as well as logic.

From a Taxpayer's Perspective: As a taxpayer, I am concerned that the largest military and intelligence and law-enforcement investment on the planet was rendered completely ineffective by 19 people of average criminal capability operating on a low budget. "Concerned" is not the right word. As a taxpayer, I am enraged, appalled, and infuriated. Not that it matters, of course. But it is indeed galling that the 9/11 Commission's solution is to assign no blame to any government agency, then ask for even more money and a larger bureaucracy. This seems, in retrospect, self-serving beyond anything even Franklin Roosevelt himself could have conceived.

From the Perspective of a Person Who Was Present: Finally, as a person who was physically present for a small portion of the events that day at the Pentagon, I am disappointed that so many of my questions remain unanswered by the US government, my employer at the time. I want to understand what happened, and I would like honest information that can be reconciled with my own observations, particularly at the scene of the Pentagon crime. While some may believe that the morning of 9/11 was confusing and crazy, I witnessed a great degree of calm and intelligence among my co-workers and compatriots who work in the Pentagon. They were not afraid of the truth then, and it seems that the only people who fear this truth are those ostensibly charged to keep us all protected and safe. The truth needs no protection, and the Department of Defense and other affected agencies have no reason—assuming the basic truth of the official account—not to be both forthcoming and enthusiastic in publicly determining exactly how the events of 9/11 occurred, as well as exploring motivation and coordination possibilities beyond the simplistic explanation that young unhappy Middle Eastern men hate us because we are free. As someone who was personally affected by the events of 9/11, I do not accept the casual disregard and callous abandon with which the federal government, Congress, and the executive branch and its agencies have all approached the crime-scene analysis and systemic autopsy of 9/11.

Conclusion

More information is certainly needed regarding the events of 9/11 and the events leading up to that terrible day. Interestingly, several opportunities for the investigation to be pursued and for new light to be shed emanate from FBI whistleblowers like Sibel Edmonds and military whistleblowers who have attempted to bring forward Pentagon, CIA, and law enforcement advance knowledge and past surveillance of suspected participants in the attack.[9] Questions remain about relationships between key Bush administration policymakers and the Pakistani intelligence service, as well as about information that other US allies and beneficiaries knew and had observed regarding the suspected 9/11 hijackers. None of these questions have been officially answered. In fact, in lieu of official inquiries or congressional and judicial fact-finding sessions, we see executive agency stonewalling and judicially enforced gag orders on whistleblowers, government-initiated process obstructions, claims of possible damage that the truth will do to national security, and government destruction of evidence. This is all very strange and, as with so much relating to 9/11, further undermines the credibility of the government's story.

It does, however, lend credence to all of the other more compelling and logical explanations for the events before, on, and after 9/11. These alternate "conspiracy" theories have a distinct disadvantage for Americans. They place the conspirators—conscientious and incompetent alike—in western suits and ties, rather than in turbans with prayer rugs. This is indeed unfortunate for all of us. But H. L. Mencken—a longtime observer of government excess, incompetence, war-making, and a concomitant loss of domestic freedoms of speech, thought, and action in a previous era—explained in his personal credo what we must all remember, and hold on to unreservedly, as though in the midst of a hurricane. He wrote:

> I believe that no discovery of fact, however trivial, can be wholly useless to the race, and that no trumpeting of falsehood, however virtuous in intent, can be anything but vicious.... I believe in complete freedom of thought and speech—alike for the humblest man and the mightiest, and in the utmost freedom of conduct that is consistent with living in organized society.... I believe in the capacity of man to conquer his world, and to find out what it is made of, and how it is run. I believe in the reality of progress....
>
> But the whole thing, after all, may be put very simply. I believe that it is better to tell the truth than to lie. I believe that it is better to be free than to be a slave. And I believe that it is better to know than to be ignorant.

I imagine Mencken would not be in the least surprised today at the great dilemma in which the US finds itself, struggling to understand its own government, explain its (apparent) incompetence, divine its goals, and know the ground truth about 9/11.

THREE

Why Indeed Did the WTC Buildings Collapse?

Steven E. Jones

In this paper, I call for a serious investigation of the hypothesis that WTC 7 and the Twin Towers were brought down not by impact damage and fires but through the use of pre-positioned cutter-charges. I consider the official FEMA, NIST, and 9/11 Commission reports, according to which fires plus impact damage alone caused complete collapses of all three buildings. And I present evidence for the controlled-demolition hypothesis, which is suggested by the available data and scientifically testable but has not yet been analyzed in any of the reports funded by the US government. I should note from the start that although readers can follow the discussion of the evidence here, the visual data—the numbered photographs and video clips referred to in this paper—are necessary to appreciate the argument fully. All of the visual information I mention can be accessed from my website.[1]

I begin with the fact that large quantities of molten metal were observed in basement areas under rubble piles of all three buildings. Eyewitness evidence regarding this metal at ground zero has been caught on video.[2] A photograph by Frank Silecchia shows a chunk of hot metal being removed from the north tower rubble about eight weeks after 9/11. The bright yellow-orange color of the lower portion of the extracted metal tells us much about the temperature of the metal and provides important clues regarding its composition, as we shall see.

Consider next the collapse of the 47-story WTC 7, which was never hit by a jet. Three photographs of the building—before 9/11, on the afternoon of 9/11 after the collapse of the Twin Towers (looking the same, if through smoke, as in the first photograph), and the rubble pile after its own collapse a few hours later—show how unbelievable the official explanation for this event.

For the following discussion of laws of physics, especially laws of motion, it would be best if readers look at some video clips of the collapse of this building that are easily accessible on the Web.[3] Notice in particular the following features:

Symmetry: The building collapses straight down, nearly symmetrically, rather than toppling over.

Virtually Free-Fall Speed: The southwest roof corner, according to measurements made by my students and me, fell in 6.5 (+- 0.2) seconds. An apple dropped from that spot would fall in 6.0 seconds in a vacuum (through the air it would be a little slower).

Squibs: Note the puffs of smoke/debris coming out of the building, especially the sequence and fast timing of observed puffs, sometimes called "squibs."

On the basis of photographic and video evidence as well as related data and analyses, I provide thirteen reasons for rejecting the official hypothesis, according to which fire and impact damage caused the collapse of the Twin Towers and WTC 7, in favor of the controlled-demolition hypothesis. The goal is to promote further scrutiny of the official government-sponsored reports as well as serious investigation of the controlled-demolition hypothesis. No rebuttal of my argument can be complete, of course, unless it addresses all of these points.

1. Molten Metal, Flowing and in Pools

There are several published observations of molten metal in the basements of all three buildings—the Twin Towers (WTC 1 and 2) and WTC 7—following their collapses. For example, Dr. Keith Eaton, after touring Ground Zero, stated in the *Structural Engineer*: "They showed us many fascinating slides... ranging from molten metal which was still red hot weeks after the event, to 4-inch thick steel plates sheared and bent in the disaster."[4] The observation of molten metal at Ground Zero was emphasized publicly by Leslie Robertson, who was a member of the firm that designed the Twin Towers. According to his report: "As of 21 days after the attack, the fires were still burning and molten steel was still running."[5]

Sarah Atlas was part of the New Jersey Task Force One Urban Search and Rescue team and was one of the first on the scene at Ground Zero. Stating that "nobody's going to be alive," she said that fires burned and molten steel flowed in the pile of ruins still settling beneath her feet.[6]

Dr. Allison Geyh was one of a team of public health investigators from Johns Hopkins who visited the WTC site after 9/11. According to her report, "In some pockets now being uncovered they are finding molten steel."[7] The video available on the internet shows that some six weeks after 9/11, the observed surface of the metal was still reddish-orange. This suggests that there was a large quantity of a metal with fairly low heat conductivity and a relatively large heat capacity. It is, therefore, more likely to be iron or steel than aluminum. Like magma in a volcanic cone, such metal can remain hot and molten for a long time, if it remains in a fairly well insulated underground location. Moreover, as I will hypothesize, thermite reactions may have resulted in substantial quantities of molten iron (which was observed in pools), initially at very high temperatures, above 2,000°C (3,632°F). At these temperatures, aluminum materials from the buildings should continue to undergo exothermic oxidation reactions with materials also entrained in the molten metal pools, including metal oxides, which will then keep the pools molten and even growing for weeks, in spite of radiative and conductive losses. It is clear that molten metal was repeatedly observed in the rubble piles of the WTC Towers and WTC 7, metal that looked like molten steel or perhaps iron. Scientific analysis would be needed to ascertain the actual composition of the molten metal.

These observations are consistent with the use of high-temperature cutter-charges such as thermite, HDX, RDX, or some combination thereof. These are explosive materials that are routinely used to melt or cut steel. Thermite is a mixture of iron oxide and aluminum powder. The end products of the thermite reaction are aluminum oxide and molten iron. The thermite reaction, in other words, generates molten iron directly and is hot enough to melt and even evaporate steel that it contacts during the reaction. Thermite contains its own supply of oxygen (from iron oxide), so the reaction cannot be smothered, even with water. Use of sulfur in conjunction with the thermite—in "thermate," for example—will accelerate the destructive effect on steel. And, as the FEMA report stated, sulfidation of structural steel was indeed observed in some of the few recovered members from the WTC rubble.[8] Buildings that fall down without the aid of thermite or equivalent, by contrast, have insufficient directed energy to result in the melting of large quantities of metal. Indeed, demolition expert Brent Blanchard told me that he had never witnessed molten metal at the site of any building that had been brought down by demolition without thermite, and he had seen hundreds of these.[9]

Experts have pointed out that the fires in the WTC buildings would not have caused any of the steel to melt. For example, Thomas Eagar, a professor of materials engineering at MIT who supports the official view of the collapses, wrote in 2001:

> The fire is the most misunderstood part of the WTC collapse. Even today, the media report (and many scientists believe) that the steel melted. It is argued that the jet fuel burns very hot, especially with so much fuel present. This is not true.... *The temperature of the fire at the WTC was not unusual, and it was most definitely not capable of melting steel.*
>
> In combustion science, there are three basic types of flames, namely, a jet burner, a pre-mixed flame, and a diffuse flame.... A fireplace is a diffuse flame burning in air, as was the WTC fire. Diffuse flames generate the lowest heat intensities of the three flame types.... The maximum flame temperature increase for burning hydrocarbons (jet fuel) in air is, thus, about 1,000°C [1,832°F].... But it is very difficult to reach [even] this maximum temperature with a diffuse flame. There is nothing to ensure that the fuel and air in a diffuse flame are mixed in the best ratio.... This is why the temperatures in a residential fire are usually in the 500°C to 650°C [932–1,202°F] range.[10] It is known that the WTC fire was a fuel-rich, diffuse flame as evidenced by the copious black smoke.... It is known that structural steel begins to soften around 425°C [797°F] and loses about half of its strength at 650°C [1,202 °F].[11] This is why steel is stress relieved in this temperature range. But even a 50 percent loss of strength is still insufficient, by itself, to explain the WTC collapse.... The WTC, on this low-wind day, was likely not stressed more than a third of the design allowable.... *Even with its strength halved, the steel could still support two to three times the stresses imposed by a 650°C [1,202°F] fire.*[12] [Emphasis added.]

Likewise, Frank Gayle, a metals expert working with the National Institute for Standards and Technology (NIST), stated: "Your gut reaction would be the jet fuel is what made the fire so very intense, a lot of people figured that's what melted the steel. Indeed it did not, the steel did not melt."[13] What Gayle clearly meant is that the jet fuel could not have melted the steel, and that is correct. The evidence shows, nevertheless, a considerable amount of flowing molten metal just before the collapse of WTC 2 and molten-metal pools following the collapses of all three buildings.

The NIST Report, to which Gayle contributed, is the final official government report on the WTC collapses. This report admits that the fires were insufficient to melt steel beams. That admission raises the obvious question: Where, then, did the molten metal come from?

All of the official reports—the FEMA Report, *The 9/11 Commission Report*, the NIST Report—have failed to tackle this mystery. Yet the presence of molten metal is a significant clue to what caused the towers and WTC 7 to collapse. We need an analysis of the composition of the metal by a qualified scientific panel. This analysis could well become an *experimentum crucis*.

Even without a direct elemental analysis, we can, on the basis of available data, rule out some metals. The first photograph I mentioned shows a chunk of the hot metal being extracted at Ground Zero. The hottest portion is the lowest, which was deepest down in the slag, and the metal is seen to be yellow-hot, certainly above cherry-red hot. Data regarding the melting temperatures of lead, aluminum, structural steel, and iron, along with approximate metal temperatures by color, are well-established.[14] According to this information, the solid metal being extracted in the picture existed at salmon-to-yellow-hot temperature, or between 845–1,040°C (1,550 and 1,900°F). This temperature is well above the melting temperatures of lead and aluminum, so these metals can be ruled out since they would be runny liquids at much lower temperatures (cherry-red or below). The observed hot specimen could be structural steel (from the building), or iron (from a thermite reaction), or a combination of the two. Additional photographs of the hot metal could provide further information and advance the research.

The next photograph evidently shows solidified metal with entrained material stored—at least as of November 2005—in a warehouse in New York. The abundance of iron (specifically as opposed to aluminum) in this slag is indicated by the reddish rust observed. When a sample is obtained, a range of characterization techniques will quickly give us information we seek. X-ray energy-dispersive spectrometry (XEDS) will yield the elemental composition, and electron energy-loss spectroscopy will tell us the elements found in very small amounts undetectable with XEDS. Electron-backscattered diffraction in the scanning electron microscope will give us phase information; the formation of certain precipitates can tell us a minimum temperature the melt must have reached. I will endeavor to obtain and publish these data, whatever they reveal.

Additional photographic evidence of the use of thermite, or a sulfur-containing derivative such as thermate, is provided by the next photograph, taken by Rob Miller of the *New York Post*.[15] It shows debris and dust as WTC 1 (the north tower) collapses, with WTC 7, across the street, seen in the foreground. Another photograph on my website shows, for comparison, a small thermite reaction with a grayish-white aluminum-oxide dust plume extending upward from the white-hot molten iron "blob" from the reaction.[16] Two ladder-like structures, consistent with steel structures observed in the core of WTC 1, are captured in Miller's photograph. Observe the grayish-white plumes trailing upward from white "blobs" at the left-most extremities of the upper structure. (The lower structure is mostly obscured by dust.) It is possible that thermite cut through the structural steel and that what we now observe is white-hot iron from the reaction adhering to the severed ends of the steel, with grayish-white aluminum oxide still streaming away from the reaction sites. The observations are consistent with the use of thermite or one of its variants. Further analysis of this and additional photographs from the series are necessary, however, before any firm conclusions can be drawn about this line of evidence.

"Superthermites" use tiny particles of aluminum known as "nanoaluminum" (<120 nanometers) in order to increase their reactivity. Mixed with fine metal oxide particles such as micron-scale iron oxide dust, nanoaluminum in superthermite becomes explosive. This is another form of thermite that should be investigated in relation to 9/11.[17] In any case, if some variation of the thermite reaction was indeed used to sever steel beams, as suggested by the visual evidence, then particulate-size aluminum oxide should be found in unusual abundance in the toxic dust from the collapses of the Twin Towers and WTC 7. One should certainly look for the residual end-products—molten iron and aluminum oxide—to test this hypothesis. Other explanations for the observations are sought, of course.

Are there any examples of buildings toppled by fire, or any reason other than deliberate demolition, that show large pools of molten metal in the rubble? I have posed this question to numerous engineers and scientists, but so far no examples have emerged. It is strange, then, that three buildings in Manhattan, supposedly brought down solely by fire—or, in the case of the Twin Towers, fire and the impact of the airplanes—all show these large pools of molten metal in their basements after their collapses. It would be interesting if underground fires could somehow produce molten steel, but then there should be historical examples of this effect, since there have been many large fires in numerous buildings. But no such examples have been found. It is not enough to argue hypothetically that fires could possibly cause all three pools of molten metal. One needs at least one previous example.

Dramatic footage reveals salmon-to-yellow-hot molten metal dripping from the south tower shortly before its collapse. The yellow color implies a molten-metal temperature of approximately 1,000°C (1,832°F), far above that which the dark-smoke hydrocarbon fires in the towers could have produced. If aluminum—from the plane, for example—had melted, it would have flowed away from the heat source at its melting point of about 650°C and thus would not have reached the yellow color observed for this molten metal. Thus, molten aluminum is ruled out with high probability. But molten iron with the characteristics seen in this video is consistent with a thermite reaction attacking the steel columns, thus weakening the building just prior to its collapse. (The reader may wish to compare the dripping molten metal observed on the corner of the south tower just before its collapse with the dripping molten metal from known thermite reactions.[18])

We thus find substantial evidence supporting the current conjecture that thermite (solid aluminum powder plus Fe_2O_3, with possible addition of sulfur) was used on the steel columns of the south tower to weaken the huge steel supports, not long before explosives finished the demolition job. Roughly 3,000 pounds of RDX-grade linear-shaped charges (which could have been pre-positioned by just a few men) would then suffice in each tower and WTC 7 to cut the supports at key points so that gravity would bring the buildings straight down. The estimate is based on the amount of explosives used in controlled demolitions in the past and the size of the buildings. Radio-initiated firing of the charges is implicated here. Using computer-controlled radio signals, it would be an easy matter to begin the explosive demolition near the planes' points of entry.

The very high temperatures of the molten metal, determined by the color data, are difficult to explain in the context of the official theory, according to which the collapses were caused by dark-smoke hydrocarbon fires. The data clearly imply some highly exothermic reactions, such as the thermite reaction, which produces molten iron as an end product, and/or explosives such as HDX and RDX (or some combination).

The official reports by NIST, FEMA and the 9/11 Commission, rather than trying to explain the large quantities of molten metal observed in the basement areas of WTC 7 and the towers, simply omit any mention of these extraordinary facts. This failure provides compelling motivation for continued research on the WTC collapses.

2. Observed Temperatures around 1,000°C and Sulfidation in WTC 7 Steel

One of the relatively few peer-reviewed papers relating to the WTC collapses provides, as its title says, "An Initial Microstructural Analysis of A36 Steel from WTC Building 7." This brief but important paper by J. R. Barnett and two colleagues, which deals with one steel beam recovered from WTC 7, states:

> While the exact location of this beam could not be determined, the unexpected erosion of the steel found in this beam warranted a study of microstructural changes that occurred in this steel. Examination of other sections in this beam is underway.
>
> ANALYSIS: Rapid deterioration of the steel was a result of heating with oxidation in combination with intergranular melting due to the presence of sulfur. The formation of the eutectic mixture of iron oxide and iron sulfide lowers the temperature at which liquid can form in this steel. This strongly suggests that the temperatures in this region of the steel beam approached 1,000°C [1,832°F] by a process similar to making a "blacksmith's weld" in a hand forge.[19]

How were these 1,000°C (1,832°F) temperatures in the steel beam achieved? As noted in the quotation from Thomas Eagar, it is difficult to reach temperatures above 650°C (1,202°F) in the type of diffuse hydrocarbon fires evident in the WTC buildings. It would be even harder for this temperature to be reached in steel beams that were part of an enormous steel structure, as in the WTC buildings, because heat at any one location would be quickly dispersed throughout the structure. So the high steel temperatures deduced by Barnett and his colleagues are indeed remarkable.

Another mysterious phenomenon reported in this paper is sulfidation of the steel. What is the origin of this sulfur? No solid answer is given in any of the official reports. The NIST Report and the report by the 9/11 Commission do not, in fact, even mention it.

There is, of course, a straightforward way to achieve 1,000°C temperatures (and well above) in the presence of sulfur, and that is to use thermate (or some other variation of thermite). Thermate, a high-level cutting thermite-analog developed by the military,[20] combines aluminum powder and iron oxide (thermite) with barium nitrate (29 percent) and sulfur (typically 2 percent, although more sulfur could be added). The thermate reaction proceeds rapidly and is much faster than plain thermite in degrading steel and thereby leading to structural failure. Both the unusually high temperatures and the extraordinary observation of steel-sulfidation can thus be accounted for—if the use of thermate is admitted into the discussion.

Sulfidation could also have occurred if the steel member had been exposed to a molten metal pool (discussed above), since there were sulfur-bearing materials, such as gypsum, in the buildings. But the analyzed steel sample was evidently found near the top of the rubble pile, not near the deep-underground pool.

Finally, sulfidation was observed in structural steel samples recovered from both WTC 7 and one of the towers, as indicated in the FEMA report.[21] It is quite possible that more than one type of cutter-charge was involved on 9/11—for example, HDX, RDX, and thermate in some combination.

3. Near-Symmetrical Collapse of WTC 7

As shown in the videos mentioned earlier, WTC 7 collapsed not only very rapidly but also almost straight down and almost symmetrically, even though fires were randomly scattered in the building. WTC 7 fell about seven hours after the second of the Twin Towers collapsed, even though it was not hit by an airplane and no major persistent fires are visible in any of the available photographs. WTC 7 contained 24 huge steel support columns as well as huge trusses, arranged non-symmetrically, along with 57 perimeter columns.[22]

WTC 7 was not hit by a plane. Even if, as NIST claims, twelve of the columns were damaged by debris from the collapse of WTC 1 (some 350 feet away), this damage would have been non-symmetrical and would not have severed any of the core columns.

A near-symmetrical collapse, as observed, evidently requires the simultaneous "pulling" of many of the support columns (see below, particularly the discussion of the paper by Bazant and Zhou). The likelihood of complete and nearly symmetrical collapse due to random fires, or any other cause other than controlled demolition, is exceedingly small. Without the use of explosives, incomplete and non-symmetrical failure is much more likely, as shown in the photographs of collapses brought about by earthquakes. By contrast, when buildings are brought down with the use of cutter-charges or explosives to produce an implosion, a complete, straight-down, symmetrical collapse is what is expected. Examples of controlled demolitions, which can be seen on the Web, are instructive to watch.[23]

Support for these arguments is provided by a concluding remark in the FEMA report, which says:

> The specifics of the fires in WTC 7 and how they caused the building to collapse remain unknown at this time. Although the total diesel fuel on the premises contained massive potential energy, the best hypothesis [a collapse caused by diesel-fuel-fed fire plus damage from debris] has only a low probability of occurrence. Further research, investigation, and analyses are needed to resolve this issue.[24]

That is precisely the point: We do indeed need further investigation and analyses, including serious consideration of the controlled-demolition hypothesis, which is neglected in all of the government reports (those by FEMA, NIST, and the 9/11 Commission). Note that *The 9/11 Commission Report* does not even mention the collapse of WTC 7. This is a striking omission of data highly relevant to the question of what really happened on 9/11.

4. No Previous Skyscraper Collapse Due to Fires

A *New York Times* article in 2001 was entitled "Engineers Are Baffled Over the Collapse of 7 WTC; Steel Members Have Been Partly Evaporated." This article provides some highly relevant information, saying about WTC 7: "Experts said no building like it, a modern, steel-reinforced high-rise, had ever collapsed because of an uncontrolled fire."[25] Fire engineering expert Norman Glover agrees, saying:

> Almost all large buildings will be the location for a major fire in their useful life. No major high-rise building has ever collapsed

from fire.... The WTC [itself] was the location for such a fire in 1975; however, the building survived with minor damage and was repaired and returned to service.[26]

That is correct: Before 9/11, no steel-beam high-rise had ever completely collapsed due to fires, and none has done so since. What a surprise, then, for such an occurrence in downtown Manhattan: three skyscrapers completely collapsed on the same day, presumably without the use of explosives. The same *Times* article continued:

> Engineers have been trying to figure out exactly what happened and whether they should be worried about other buildings like it around the country.... Most of the other buildings in the [area] stood despite suffering damage of all kinds, including fire.... "Fire and the structural damage.... would not explain steel members in the debris pile that appear to have been partly evaporated," Dr. [Jonathan] Barnett said.

The "partly evaporated" steel members are particularly upsetting to the official theory, because fires involving paper, office materials, and even diesel fuel cannot generate temperatures anywhere near the 2,860°C (5,180°F) needed to evaporate steel. But RDX, thermite-variants, and other commonly-used incendiaries or explosives (cutter-charges) can readily slice through steel, thus cutting the support columns, and reach the required temperatures. This mystery needs to be explored, but it is not mentioned in the official reports.

5. Squib-Timing during the Collapse of WTC 7

As we saw in videos mentioned earlier, horizontal puffs of smoke and debris, sometimes called "squibs," emerge from the upper floors of WTC 7, in regular sequence, just as the building starts to collapse. The upper floors have evidently not moved relative to one another yet, from what one can observe on the videos. In addition, the timing between the puffs is less than 0.2 seconds, so air expulsion due to collapsing floors, as suggested by defenders of the official account,[27] is evidently excluded. Since this is near the initiation of the collapse, free-fall time for a floor to fall down to the next floor is significantly longer than 0.2 seconds: The equation for free fall yields a little over 0.6 seconds.[28] The official reports lack an explanation for these squibs.

On the other hand, the presence of squibs proceeding up the side of the building is common when pre-positioned explosives are used, as can be observed on several videos at the website www.implosionworld.com.

These videos also show that it is common for these explosive squibs to occur in rapid sequence. Accordingly, the squibs going up the side of WTC 7 in rapid sequence provide additional significant evidence for the use of pre-placed explosives.[29]

6. Early Drop of North Tower Antenna

The FEMA Report admits a striking anomaly regarding the collapse of the north tower (WTC 1):

> Review of videotape recordings of the collapse taken from various angles indicates that the transmission tower on top of the structure began to move downward and laterally slightly before movement was evident at the exterior wall. This suggests that collapse began with one or more failures in the central core area of the building.[30]

We can see for ourselves in photographs and videos of the north tower collapse that the antenna drops first.[31] A *New York Times* article also notes this behavior:

> The building stood for more than an hour and a half. Videos of the north tower's collapse appear to show that its television antenna began to drop a fraction of a second before the rest of the building. The observations suggest that the building's steel core somehow gave way first.[32]

But how? What could have caused the 47 enormous steel columns in the building's core (which supported the antenna) to give way nearly simultaneously? This mystery was not resolved in any of the official reports. The NIST report notes that photographic and videographic records taken from due north of the WTC 1 collapse appeared to indicate that the antenna was sinking into the roof. When records from east and west vantage points were viewed, it was apparent that the building section above the impact area tilted to the south as the building collapsed.

This report, however, provides no quantitative analysis showing that this tilting of the building section was sufficient to account for the large apparent drop of the antenna as seen from the north. Furthermore, FEMA investigators also reviewed "videotape recordings of the collapse taken from various angles" but asserted that "collapse began with one or more failures in the central core area of the building."[33]

The early antenna drop on the north tower provides one more indication that the core columns may have been cut by explosives or incendiaries prior to the tower's collapse; the matter needs to be investigated further.

7. Eyewitness Accounts of Flashes and Loud Explosions

Multiple loud explosions in rapid sequence were heard and reported by numerous observers in and near the WTC towers, consistent with explosive demolition. Firemen and others described flashes and explosions in upper floors near where the plane entered, and in lower floors of WTC 2, far below the region where the plane had struck the tower, just prior to its collapse.[34] For instance, at the beginning of the collapse of the south tower, a Fox News anchor gave this report: "There is an explosion at the base of the building... white smoke from the bottom.... [S]omething happened at the base of the building! Then another explosion."[35]

Firefighter Edward Cachia independently reported: "[We] thought there was like an internal detonation, explosives, because it went in succession, boom, boom, boom, boom, and then the tower came down.... It actually gave at a lower floor, not the floor where the plane hit."[36]

And Assistant Fire Commissioner Stephen Gregory provides additional information, saying during an interview:

> When I looked in the direction of the Trade Center before it came down, before No. 2 came down, ... I saw low-level flashes. In my conversation with Lieutenant Evangelista, never mentioning this to him, he questioned me and asked me if I saw low-level flashes in front of the building, and I agreed with him because I thought—at that time I didn't know what it was. I mean, it could have been as a result of the building collapsing, things exploding, but I saw a flash flash flash and then it looked like the building came down.
>
> Q. Was that on the lower level of the building or up where the fire was?
>
> A. No, the lower level of the building. You know like when they demolish a building, how when they blow up a building, when it falls down? That's what I thought I saw. And I didn't broach the topic to him, but he asked me. He said I don't know if I'm crazy, but I just wanted to ask you because you were standing right next to me.... He said did you see any flashes? I said, yes, well, I thought it was just me. He said no, I saw them, too.[37]

William Rodriguez, who worked in the north tower for many years, provided this eyewitness account privately, in November 2005:

> About my experience. My basis was, like I told the Commission, there was an explosion that came from under our feet, we were pushed upwards lightly by the effect, I was on basement level 1 and it sounded [like] it came from B2 and B3 level. Rapidly after that we heard the impact far away at the top. My assertions are [that] my 20 years experience there and witnessing prior to that many other noises [enable me] to conclude without any doubt where the sounds were coming from…. Some of the same people that I saved gave testimonies in interviews of the same experience prior to my actually being reunited with them after the event.[38]

It is highly unlikely that jet fuel was present to generate such explosions, especially on lower floors and so long after the planes hit the buildings. Shyam Sunder, lead investigator for NIST, stated: "The jet fuel probably burned out in less than 10 minutes."[39] Pre-positioned explosives, however, provide a plausible and simple explanation for the observed detonations.

8. Ejection of Steel Beams and Debris-Plumes from the Towers

The horizontal ejection of steel beams for hundreds of feet and the pulverization of concrete to flour-like powder, observed clearly in the collapses of the WTC towers, provide further evidence for the use of explosives.[40] Some debris-plumes (squibs) are observed far below the pulverization region and are therefore deserving of particular attention. A photograph on my website shows clearly a horizontal plume of smoke coming out of the north tower well below the point of the plane's impact.

Unlike WTC 7, the Twin Towers appear to have been exploded "top-down" rather than proceeding from the bottom—which is unusual for controlled demolition but clearly possible, depending on the order in which explosives are detonated. That is, explosives may have been placed on higher floors and exploded via radio signals so as to have early explosions near the regions where the planes entered. Certainly this hypothesis ought to be seriously considered in an independent investigation using all available data.

9. Rapid Collapses and the Conservation of Momentum

The NIST team admits that their report "does not actually include the structural behavior of the tower after the conditions for collapse initiation were reached."[41] Quite a confession, since much of the external evidence for explosive demolition typically comes after collapse initiation, as seen in cases of acknowledged controlled demolition.[42]

The rapid fall of the towers and WTC 7 has been analyzed by several engineers and scientists.[43] The roof of WTC 7 falls to earth in less than 6.6 seconds, while an object dropped from the roof in a vacuum would hit the ground in 6.0 seconds. (This follows from an equation for free fall.[44]) Likewise, the Twin Towers fall very rapidly to the ground, with the upper part falling nearly as rapidly as ejected debris, which demonstrate the free-fall speed through the air.[45] Where is the delay that must be expected due to the Law of the Conservation of Momentum, one of the foundational laws of physics? That is, as higher falling floors strike lower floors, including intact steel support columns, the fall must be significantly impeded by the impacted mass. If the central support columns remained standing, then the effective resistive mass would be less, but this is not the case: somehow the enormous support columns failed or disintegrated along with the falling floors. How do the upper floors fall so quickly, then, and still conserve momentum in the collapsing buildings? This contradiction is ignored by the FEMA, NIST, and 9/11 Commission reports, none of which analyzed conservation of momentum and the fall times. The contradiction is, however, easily resolved by the explosive demolition hypothesis, according to which explosives quickly removed lower-floor material, including steel support columns, and allowed near free-fall-speed collapses.[46]

The hypothesis that such explosives were used also readily accounts for the fact that the falling towers turned to fine dust as the collapse ensued. Given NIST's hypothesis of a non-explosive-caused progressive collapse, we would have expected a huge pile of shattered concrete. Instead we find that most of the material (concrete, carpet, computers, steel, and so on) was converted to flour-like powder while the buildings were falling. The collapses of the Twin Towers were not typical implosions, but quite possibly series of "shock-and-awe" explosions coupled with the use of thermate incendiaries. At least the evidence points strongly in this direction. The hypothesis ought to be explored further.

Those who wish to preserve fundamental physical laws as inviolate may wish to take a closer look at the collapse of the south tower.[47] We observe that approximately 30 upper floors began to rotate as a block, to the south and east. They began to topple over, as favored by the Law of Increasing Entropy. The torque due to gravity on this block was enormous, as was its angular momentum. But then—and this I am still puzzling over—this block turned mostly to powder in mid-air! How can we understand this strange behavior, without explosives? This is a remarkable, amazing phenomenon, and yet the US government-funded reports failed to analyze it. The NIST report's analysis, as we have seen, "does not actually include the structural behavior of the tower after the conditions for collapse initiation were reached." Nothing could better illustrate the fact that a serious official analysis of the collapses still remains to be carried out.

Indeed, if we seek the truth of the matter, we must not ignore the data to be observed during the actual collapses of the towers, as the NIST team admits it did. But why did they, in deliberately ignoring highly relevant data, follow such a nonscientific procedure? The business smacks of political constraints on what was supposed to be an "open and thorough" investigation.[48]

10. Controlled Demolition "Implosions" Require Skill

The occurrence of nearly symmetrical, straight-down, and complete collapses of WTC 7 and the towers is particularly upsetting to the official theory that random fires plus damage caused all these collapses. Even with high-level cutting charges, achieving such results requires a great deal of pre-planning and expertise. As Tom Harris, an authority in this field, has explained:

> The main challenge in bringing a building down is controlling which way it falls. Ideally, a blasting crew will be able to tumble the building over on one side, into a parking lot or other open area. This sort of blast is the easiest to execute [because it is favored by the Law of Increasing Entropy]. Tipping a building over is something like felling a tree. To topple the building to the north, the blasters detonate explosives on the north side of the building first....

> Sometimes, though, a building is surrounded by structures that must be preserved. In this case, the blasters proceed with a true implosion, demolishing the building so that it collapses straight down into its own footprint (the total area at the base of the building). This feat requires such skill that only a handful of demolition companies in the world will attempt it.

> Blasters approach each project a little differently.... [A good]

option is to detonate the columns at the center of the building before the other columns so that the building's sides fall inward.... Generally speaking, blasters will explode the major support columns on the lower floors first and then a few upper stories. [N.B.: The upper floors then fall as a tamper, resulting in "progressive collapse"—this is common in controlled demolition using explosives.][49]

Careful observation of the collapse of WTC 7 on the videos demonstrates a downward "kink" near the center of the building first, suggesting "pulling" of the support columns, then the building's sides pull inward such that the building "collapses straight down into its own footprint." The plumes of debris that are observed on upper floors of WTC 7 as the collapse begins appear to be consistent with explosive cutting of supports for "a few upper stories," as outlined above. FEMA admitted that WTC 7 collapsed onto a well-confined footprint: "The collapse of WTC 7 had a small debris field as the facade was pulled downward, suggesting an internal failure and implosion.... The average debris field radius was approximately 70 feet."[50]

Evidently FEMA and I agree that the collapse of WTC 7 involved a beautifully done implosion. If, as Tom Harris contends, this is a feat that "requires such skill that only a handful of demolition companies in the world will attempt it," a few questions emerge. Why would foreign terrorists undertake straight-down collapses of WTC 7 and the towers, when causing them to topple over would require much less work and would do much more damage in downtown Manhattan? And where would they obtain the necessary skills and access to the buildings for a symmetrical implosion anyway?

One of the people who should be questioned in a thorough investigation is demolition expert Mark Loizeaux, president of Controlled Demolition, Inc. Speaking of the way the WTC buildings came down, he said in an interview: "If I were to bring the towers down, I would put explosives in the basement to get the weight of the building to help collapse the structure."[51]

The idea of "explosives in the basement" agrees with eyewitness reports of pre-collapse explosions down low in the buildings. Also, this would be the best way to sever the support columns, and this way would be consistent with both the apparent initial drop of the north tower's communication antenna and the "kink" in the middle of WTC 7 as its collapse began.

Also, as president of Controlled Demolition, Inc., Loizeaux would know the "handful of demolition companies in the world" that could attempt such a controlled demolition.[52] His company, certainly one of these, was hired to do the rapid clean-up work following the building collapses.

If you still have not looked at the rapid symmetrical collapse of WTC 7 for yourself, why not do so now?[53] Watch for the initial "kink" or drop in the middle, and for the "squibs" blowing in sequence up the side of the building, and notice the symmetrical, straight-down collapse. All of these features are common in controlled demolitions.

11. Steel Column Temperatures of 800°C Needed: A Problem in the Argument of Bazant and Zhou

A mechanical engineering professor suggested that I review a paper by Zedenek P. Bazant and Yong Zhou, which I did. These authors write: "The 110-story towers of the World Trade Center were designed to withstand as a whole the forces caused by a horizontal impact of a large commercial aircraft. So why did a total collapse occur?"[54] They are correct: Jet collisions did not cause the collapses. MIT's Thomas Eagar concurs, "because the number of columns lost on the initial impact was not large and the loads were shifted to remaining columns in this highly redundant structure."[55] Bazant and Zhou continue, saying that the "conflagration, caused by the aircraft fuel spilled into the structure, causes the steel of the columns to be exposed to sustained temperatures apparently exceeding 800°C." But the NIST final report said that the "initial jet fuel fires themselves lasted at most a few minutes" (179). Certainly jet fuel burning was not enough to raise steel to sustained temperatures above 800°C. Even the burning of office materials is insufficient in this regard, as we will see.

Having made that problematic claim, Bazant and Zhou then make an even more problematic one: "Once more than half of the columns in the critical floor... suffer buckling (stage 3), the weight of the upper part of the structure above this floor can no longer be supported, and so the upper part starts falling down onto the lower part below." They do not explain how "more than half of the columns in the critical floor... suffer buckling" at the same time, so as to precipitate the complete and nearly symmetrical collapse observed. There were 47 huge steel core columns in each of the Twin Towers, and 24 such support columns in WTC 7.[56]

The basic problem here is that, even if we suppose that temperatures above 800°C were achieved, they have given no explanation as to how fires from burning office materials could have heated up more than half the columns in each building almost simultaneously. NIST notes that office materials in an area burn for about 15–20 minutes, then are consumed (117, 179). This is not long enough to raise steel column temperatures as high as the Bazant–Zhou model requires, given the enormous heat sinks of the structures. And to have three buildings completely collapse due to this unlikely mechanism on the same day strains credulity. Moreover, the final NIST report on the Twin Towers admits that:

> Of the more than 170 areas examined on 16 perimeter column panels, only three columns had evidence that the steel reached temperatures above 250°C.... Only two core column specimens had sufficient paint remaining to make such an analysis, and their temperatures did not reach 250°C.... Using metallographic analysis, NIST determined that there was no evidence that any of the samples had reached temperatures above 600 °C. (176–177)

As for WTC 7, Bazant and Zhou say little, but they do mention in a separate "addendum" that burning natural gas might have been a source of the needed heat (370). This issue is addressed in Chapter 5 of the FEMA report: "Early news reports had indicated that a high pressure, 24-inch gas main was located in the vicinity of the building [WTC 7]; however, this proved not to be true."

12. Problems in the NIST Report: Inadequate Steel Temperatures and Tweaked Models

I have read through the hundreds of pages of the final NIST report on the collapses of the WTC towers. It is interesting to note that NIST "decoupled" and delayed their final report on WTC 7, which is long overdue as of this writing. I agree with some of the NIST report, such as this statement:

> Both WTC 1 and WTC 2 were stable after the aircraft impact, standing for 102 min and 56 min, respectively. The global analyses with structural impact damage showed that both towers had considerable reserve capacity. This was confirmed by analysis of the post-impact vibration of WTC 2 . . . where the damaged tower oscillated at a period nearly equal to the first mode period calculated for the undamaged structure. (144)

At any given location, the duration of [air, not steel] temperatures near 1,000°C was about 15 min to 20 min. The rest of the time, the calculated temperatures were near 500°C or below. (127)

NIST contracted with Underwriters Laboratories, Inc. to conduct tests to obtain information on the fire endurance of trusses like those in the WTC towers.... All four test specimens sustained the maximum design load for approximately 2 hours without collapsing. (140)

While agreeing with all those statements, I (along with many others) challenge NIST's collapse theory. NIST maintains that all three building collapses were fire-initiated, despite the observations above, particularly the fact that fire endurance tests with actual models did not result in collapse. In a paper by fire-engineering experts in the UK, we find:

The basis of NIST's collapse theory is... column behaviour in fire.... However, we believe that a considerable difference in downward displace between the [47] core and [240] perimeter columns, much greater than the 300 mm proposed, is required for the collapse theory to hold true.... [Our] lower reliance on passive fire protection is in contrast to the NIST work where the amount of fire protection on the truss elements is believed to be a significant factor in defining the time to collapse.... The [proposed effect] is swamped by thermal expansion.... Thermal expansion and the response of the whole frame to this effect has not been described as yet [by NIST].[57]

I agree with these pointed objections, particularly that the "response of the whole frame" of each building should be considered, especially heat transport to the whole frame from localized fires, and that the "core columns cannot pull the exterior columns in via the floor."

The computerized models of the Twin Towers in the NIST study, which incorporate many features of the buildings and the fires on 9/11, are less than convincing. The final NIST Report states:

The Investigation Team then defined three cases for each building by combining the middle, less severe, and more severe values of the influential variables. Upon a preliminary examination of the middle cases, it became clear that the towers would likely remain standing. The less severe cases were discarded after the aircraft impact results were compared to observed events. The middle cases (which became Case A for WTC 1 and Case C for WTC 2) were discarded after the structural response analysis of major subsystems were compared to observed events. (142)

The NIST report makes for interesting reading. The less severe cases based on empirical data were discarded because they did not result in building collapse. But one must "save the hypothesis," so more severe cases were tried and the simulations tweaked, as the NIST report admits:

> The more severe case (which became Case B for WTC 1 and Case D for WTC 2) was used for the global analysis of each tower. Complete sets of simulations were then performed for Cases B and D. To the extent that the simulations deviated from the photographic evidence or eyewitness reports [that complete collapse occurred, for example], the investigators adjusted the input, but only within the range of physical reality. Thus, for instance,... the pulling forces on the perimeter columns by the sagging floors were adjusted (142).... The primary role of the floors in the collapse of the towers was to provide inward pull forces that induced inward bowing of perimeter columns. (180)

How fun to tweak the model like that, until one gets the desired result! But the end result of such tweaked computer hypotheticals is, of course, not compelling. Notice that the "the pulling forces on the perimeter columns by the sagging floors were adjusted" to get the perimeter columns to yield sufficiently—one suspects these were "adjusted" by hand quite a bit—even though the UK experts complained that "the core columns cannot pull the exterior [that is, perimeter] columns in via the floor."[58]

I also agree with Kevin Ryan's objections regarding the NIST study. Ryan, at the time a manager at Underwriters Laboratories (UL), makes a point of the non-collapse of actual WTC-based models in his letter to Frank Gayle of NIST:

> As I'm sure you know, the company I work for certified the steel components used in the construction of the WTC buildings. In requesting information from both our CEO and Fire Protection business manager last year... they suggested we all be patient and understand that UL [Underwriters Laboratory] was working with your team.... I'm aware of UL's attempts to help, including performing tests on models of the floor assemblies. But the results of these tests... indicate that the buildings should have easily withstood the thermal stress caused by... burning [jet fuel, paper, et cetera].[59]

The fact that models of WTC trusses at Underwriter Laboratories subjected to fires did not fail is also admitted in the final NIST Report, which says:

NIST contracted with Underwriters Laboratories, Inc. to conduct tests to obtain information on the fire endurance of trusses like those in the WTC towers.... All four test specimens sustained the maximum design load for approximately 2 hours without collapsing.... The Investigation Team was cautious about using these results directly in the formulation of collapse hypotheses. In addition to the scaling issues raised by the test results, the fires in the towers on September 11, and the resulting exposure of the floor systems, were substantially different from the conditions in the test furnaces. Nonetheless, the [empirical test] results established that this type of assembly was capable of sustaining a large gravity load, without collapsing, for a substantial period of time relative to the duration of the fires in any given location on September 11. (141)

So how does the NIST team justify the WTC collapses, when actual models fail to collapse and there are no examples of fire-caused high-rise collapses? Easy: NIST concocted computer-generated hypotheticals for very "severe" cases, called cases B and D (124–138). Of course, the details are rather hidden to us. And they omit consideration of the complete, rapid, and symmetrical nature of the collapses."

Indeed, NIST makes the following startling admission in a footnote on page 80 of their final report:

The focus of the Investigation was on the sequence of events from the instant of aircraft impact to the initiation of collapse for each tower. For brevity in this report, this sequence is referred to as the "probable collapse sequence," although it does not actually include the structural behavior of the tower after the conditions for collapse initiation were reached.

Again, on page 142, NIST admits that its computer simulation only proceeds until the building is (allegedly) "poised for collapse," thus ignoring any data from that time on: The results were a simulation of the structural deterioration of each tower from the time of aircraft impact to the time at which the building became unstable, that is, was poised for collapse."

What about the subsequent complete, rapid, and symmetrical collapse of the buildings? What about the observed squibs? What about the antenna dropping first in the north tower? What about the molten metal observed in the basement areas in large pools in both towers and WTC 7 as well? Never mind all that: NIST did not discuss at all any data after the buildings were "poised for collapse." Well, some of us want to look at *all* the data, without "black-box" computer simulations that are "adjusted," perhaps to make them fit the desired outcome. A hypothesis that is not refutable in principle is not scientific. Occam's razor, by contrast, suggests that the simplest explanation that addresses and satisfies all the evidence is most probably correct.

13. NIST's Failure to Show Visualizations

An article in the journal *New Civil Engineering* (NCE) lends support to concerns about the NIST analysis of the WTC collapses. It states:

> World Trade Center disaster investigators [at NIST] are refusing to show computer visualizations of the collapse of the Twin Towers despite calls from leading structural and fire engineers, NCE has learned. Visualizations of collapse mechanisms are routinely used to validate the type of finite element analysis model used by the [NIST] investigators. The collapse mechanism and the role played by the hat truss at the top of the tower has been the focus of debate since the US National Institute of Standards & Technology (NIST) published its findings....
>
> University of Manchester [England] professor of structural engineering Colin Bailey said there was a lot to be gained from visualizing the structural response. "NIST should really show the visualizations; otherwise the opportunity to correlate them back to the video evidence and identify any errors in the modeling will be lost," he said....
>
> A leading US structural engineer said NIST had obviously devoted enormous resources to the development of the impact and fire models. "By comparison the global structural model is not as sophisticated," he said. "The software used [by NIST] has been pushed to new limits, and there have been a lot of simplifications, extrapolations and judgment calls."[60]

Here we have serious concerns about NIST's WTC collapse report raised by structural and fire engineers, augmenting the arguments raised here by a physicist.

The thirteen points above provide scientific data and analyses that seriously challenge the official story and support my call for an immediate investigation of 9/11 events. A few other considerations provide further motivation for the proposed urgent investigation.

"Burning Questions that Need Answers"

I totally agree with the urgent yet reasoned assessment of expert fire-protection engineers, as boldly editorialized in the journal *Fire Engineering*:

> Respected members of the fire protection engineering community are beginning to raise red flags, and a resonating theory has emerged: The structural damage from the planes and the explosive ignition of jet fuel in themselves were not enough to bring down the towers....
>
> *Fire Engineering* has good reason to believe that the "official investigation" blessed by FEMA and run by the American Society of Civil Engineers is a half-baked farce that may already have been commandeered by political forces whose primary interests, to put it mildly, lie far afield of full disclosure. Except for the marginal benefit obtained from a three-day, visual walk-through of evidence sites conducted by ASCE investigation committee members— described by one close source as a "tourist trip"—no one's checking the evidence for anything.
>
> Some citizens are taking to the streets to protest the investigation sellout. Sally Regenhard, for one, wants to know why and how the building fell as it did upon her unfortunate son Christian, an FDNY probationary firefighter. And so do we.
>
> Clearly, there are burning questions that need answers. Based on the incident's magnitude alone, a full-throttle, fully resourced, forensic investigation is imperative. More important, from a moral standpoint, [are considerations] for the safety of present and future generations.[61]

Analysis by Whistleblower Ryan

Kevin Ryan, the whistleblower from Underwriters Laboratories mentioned earlier, did his own brief statistical analysis in the letter to Frank Gayle regarding the NIST report, arguing that probabilities of collapse-initiation needed to be calculated. NIST nowhere provides such a likelihood analysis for their non-explosive collapse model. Ryan estimates that the probability that fires and damage could cause the complete collapse of the Twin Towers is less than one in a trillion, and the probability is still less when the complete collapse of WTC 7 is included. Nor does NIST (or FEMA or the 9/11 Commission) even mention the molten metals found in the basements of all three buildings (WTC 1, 2, and 7).

So where does that leave us? I strongly agree with Kevin Ryan when he says:

This [official] story just does not add up.... That fact should be of great concern to all Americans.... There is no question that the events of 9/11 are the emotional driving force behind the War on Terror. And the issue of the WTC collapse is at the crux of the story of 9/11.[62]

Faculty Support Investigation

I presented my objections to the official theory at a seminar at Brigham Young University on September 22, 2005, to about 60 people. I also showed evidence and scientific arguments for the controlled-demolition theory. In attendance were faculty from physics, mechanical engineering, civil engineering, electrical engineering, psychology, geology, and mathematics (from both BYU and Utah Valley State College). The discussion was vigorous and lasted nearly two hours. After I had presented much of the material summarized here, including actually looking at and discussing the collapses of WTC 7 and the towers, I asked how many agreed that further investigation of the WTC collapses was called for. Only one professor disagreed. The next day, this professor said that after thinking about it further, he agreed that more investigation was needed. He joined the others in hoping that the 6,977 segments of video footage and 6,899 photographs, largely from private photographers, that are held by NIST,[63] plus others held by the FBI, would be released for independent scrutiny. Therefore, I along with others call for the release of these data to a cross-disciplinary, preferably international, team of scientists and engineers.

Inconsistencies in Official Models

Finally, and by way of review, we consider the variations and inconsistencies in the fire-damage-caused collapse models with time. The earliest model, promoted by various media sources, was that the fires in the Twin Towers were sufficiently hot to actually melt the steel in the buildings, thus causing their collapse. For example, Chris Wise in a BBC piece spouted out false notions with great gusto, saying:

> It was the fire that killed the buildings. There's nothing on earth that could survive those temperatures with that amount of fuel burning.... The columns would have melted, the floors would have melted and eventually they would have collapsed one on top of the other.[64]

But as we have seen from serious studies carried out later, most of the jet fuel burned out within minutes following impact. And let me repeat

Frank Gayle's refutation of the notion that fires in the WTC buildings were sufficiently hot to melt the steel supports: "Your gut reaction would be the jet fuel is what made the fire so very intense, a lot of people figured that's what melted the steel. Indeed it did not."[65]

Then we have the model of Bazant and Zhou, which requires the majority of the 47 huge steel columns on a floor of each of the Twin Towers to reach sustained temperatures of 800°C and buckle at the same time. But as we have seen, it would be very difficult for burning office materials to heat steel up to such temperatures, especially give the fact that in these interconnected steel structures, the heat would have been wicked away.[66] The theory becomes even more implausible when we realize that it entails that half of the core columns had to fail at the same time. This scenario is far too improbable to be taken seriously.

That approach was, understandably, abandoned in the next investigative effort, that by FEMA. The FEMA team largely adopted the theory of Thomas Eagar,[67] which had been presented in a *Nova* show called "Why the Towers Fell."[68] Instead of having the columns fail simultaneously, FEMA suggested that fires caused floor pans in each tower to warp, that the floor connections to the (vertical) columns broke, and that the warped floor pans then fell down onto the floor pans below, initiating the "pancaking" of one floor pan on another, all the way down. Very simple.

But not so fast. What happens to the enormous core columns to which the floors were firmly attached? Why do not these remain standing like spindles with the floor pans falling down around them, since the connections are presumed to have broken away? This interconnected steel core was founded on bedrock. FEMA does not totally ignore the core:

> As the floors collapsed, this left tall freestanding portions of the exterior wall and possibly central core columns. As the unsupported height of these freestanding exterior wall elements increased, they buckled at the bolted column splice connections and also collapsed.

Note that by the second sentence here, the "possibly central core columns" have been forgotten. This approach completely fails to account for the observed collapse of the 47 interconnected core columns, which were massive and designed to bear (along with the smaller perimeter columns) the weight of the buildings. It also has the striking weakness of evidently requiring the connections of the floor pans to the vertical columns to break, both at the core and at the perimeter columns, more or less simultaneously.

That was too implausible, so NIST went back to the drawing board. Its report does not require the connections of the floor pans to vertical columns to fail (contrary to FEMA's model). Rather, it requires that the floor pans "pull" with enormous force, sufficient to pull the perimeter columns inward, leading to final failure (contrary to objections of ARUP Fire experts, discussed above). Also, NIST constructs a computer model. Its realistic cases, however, did not actually lead to building collapse. So it "adjusts" inputs until the model, employing the most severe cases, finally shows collapse initiation. The details of these "adjustments" are hidden from us, in their computerized hypotheticals, but the hypothesis is saved. NIST also, as we saw above, had Underwriters Laboratories construct models of the WTC trusses, but the models withstood all fires in tests and did not collapse.

We are left without a compelling fire-plus-impact-damage model, unless one blindly accepts the NIST "black-box" computer simulation while ignoring the model fire-tests, which I am not willing to do. NIST did not even do the routinely-used visualizations to validate their finite-element analysis model. And none of the official models outlined above accounts for what happens to each building after it is "poised for collapse"[69]—namely the rapid, nearly-symmetrical, and complete collapses.

There are still other omissions. Reports of explosions, heard and seen, are not discussed. These official reports ignore the squibs seen ejected from floors in the Twin Towers far from where the jets hit. They also ignore those seen in WTC 7, where no jet hit at all. Finally, we are back to where we started: What about the molten metal under the rubble piles of all three WTC buildings and the yellow-white hot molten metal seen flowing from the south tower just prior to its collapse?

The controlled-demolition hypothesis, by contrast, accounts for all the available data rather easily. The core columns on lower floors are cut using explosives and/or incendiaries, near simultaneously, along with cutting charges detonated up higher so that gravity acting on now-unsupported floors helps bring down the buildings quickly. The collapses are thus near-symmetrical, rapid and complete, with accompanying squibs—what demolition experts would expect to see. The use of thermite, whose end product is molten iron, on some of the steel beams readily accounts for the molten metal, which then pooled beneath the rubble piles, as well as for the sulfidation observed in steel from the rubble piles of both WTC 7 and the towers.

This is a straightforward hypothesis, much more probable than the official one. It deserves scientific scrutiny, beyond that which I have been able to outline in this chapter.

Conclusions

I have called attention to glaring inadequacies in the reports funded by the US government. I have also presented multiple evidence for an alternative hypothesis. In particular, the official theory lacks repeatability in that no actual buildings, before or since 9/11, have been observed to suffer total collapse due to fire-based mechanisms. On the other hand, dozens of buildings have been completely and symmetrically demolished through the use of pre-positioned explosives. And high-temperature chemical reactions can account not only for the large pools of molten metal under buildings but also the sulfidation of structural steel. The controlled-demolition hypothesis cannot be dismissed as "junk science," because it better satisfies tests of repeatability and parsimony. It ought to be seriously (scientifically) investigated and debated.

A truly independent, cross-disciplinary, international panel should be formed. Such a panel would consider all viable hypotheses, including the pre-positioned-explosives theory, guided not by politicized notions and constraints, but rather by observations and calculations, to reach a scientific conclusion. If possible it would question, under oath, the officials who approved the rapid removal and destruction of the WTC steel beams and columns before they could be properly analyzed.

None of the government-funded studies have provided any analyses of the explosive demolition hypothesis. Until the above steps are taken, the case for accusing ill-trained Muslims of causing all the destruction on 9/11 is far from compelling. It just does not add up.

That fact should be of great concern to Americans. Clearly, we must find out what really caused these three WTC buildings to collapse as they did. The implications of what happened on 9/11 clearly supersede partisan politics. Physics sheds light on the issue that we ignore to our peril as we contemplate the wars that have been, and others that may yet be, justified on the basis of 9/11 and its official interpretation.

To this end, NIST must release the 6,899 photographs and over 300 hours of video recordings — acquired mostly by private parties —

which it admits to holding. In particular, photos and analyses of the molten metal observed in the basements of the Twin Towers and WTC 7 need to be brought forth to the international community of scientists and engineers immediately. Therefore, I with others call for the release of these and all relevant data for scrutiny in a truly open and thorough investigation by an independent, cross-disciplinary, international team of researchers.[70]

FOUR

Propping Up the War on Terror: Lies about the WTC by NIST and Underwriters Laboratories

Kevin Ryan

"Already there is near-consensus as to the sequence of events that led to the collapse of the World Trade Center."
—Shankar Nair, quoted in the *Chicago Tribune* on September 19, 2001

T urn on C-Span, or *Meet the Press*, or any other media program presenting federal officials. Whatever the issue, it always comes back to the same thing. Our government really has nothing else to offer us but protection from another 9/11. It uses this painful story to cut public services, eliminate our basic rights, and plunder the national coffers. But for many of us, it is not entirely clear from whom we most need protection.[1] As our debt explodes and our freedoms diminish, it would be wise to maintain focus on the origins of our war on terror. No matter where this war leads us, we will need to keep the beginning in mind if we ever hope to see an end.

The Point of Origin: The Collapse of the WTC

Many have found that the 9/11 Commission not only failed to help us understand what happened; it also omitted or distorted most of the facts.[2] But if we really want to zero in on the exact turning point around which we plunged into chaos, we need to focus in particular on the collapse of the World Trade Center buildings. This is where our hearts were wrenched and our minds were made ready for never-ending war, torture, and apparently the end of everything that was American. If we are ever to emerge from this insanity, we need to know how three tall buildings collapsed due to fire, all on the same day, when no such thing has ever happened before.

It would help to begin with an accurate description of the WTC towers in terms of quality of design and construction. In July of 1971, the American Society of Civil Engineers (ASCE) presented a national award judging the buildings to be "the engineering project that demonstrates the greatest engineering skills and represents the greatest contribution to engineering progress and mankind."[3] Others noted that "the World Trade Center towers would have an inherent capacity to resist unforeseen calamities." This capacity stemmed from the use of special high-strength steels. In particular, the perimeter columns were designed with tremendous reserve strength whereby "live loads on these columns can be increased more than 2,000 percent before failure occurs."[4]

One would expect that any explanation for the destruction of such buildings would need to be very solid as well. Four years after 9/11, the National Institute of Standards and Technology (NIST) finally did give us their version of "why and how" two of the buildings collapsed, but its explanation may be even less effective than the 9/11 Commission report.[5] Now that the official story has been given, however, we can see just how weak and ill-defined our basis for this war on terror has been all along. Additionally, we can track the evolution of official comments about collapse and see who was involved.

Selling the Official Story: Some Key Players

Shankar Nair, whose statement opens this chapter, was one of those "experts" on whom the government depended to support what turned out to be an ever-changing, but always flimsy, story. Many of the scientists involved in the investigation were asked to examine ancillary issues, like escape routes and other emergency response factors. But those few who attempted to explain what really needed explaining—the unique events of fire-induced collapse—appear to have engaged in what can only be called anti-science. That is, they started with their conclusions and worked backward to some "leading hypotheses."

Not surprisingly, many of the contractors who contributed to the NIST investigation, like the company for which Nair works, just happen to depend on good relationships with the government in order to earn their living. What may be a surprise is just how lucrative these relationships can be. For example, Nair's company, Teng & Associates, boasts of Indefinite Quantity Contracts, long-term relationships with federal government agencies and federal projects worth in excess of $40 million.[6]

Others who worked so hard to maintain the official story included Gene Corley, a concrete construction expert listed by the National Directory of Expert Witnesses as a source for litigation testimony.[7] Corley was more than just a witness, however. He had led the Oklahoma City bombing investigation and then was asked to lead the initial ASCE investigation into the WTC disaster. Perhaps someone else, with less experience in bombings and more experience in fires, would have been a better choice. But without authority to save samples or even obtain blueprints, the ASCE investigation was ineffective anyway. Corley himself ended up being a very versatile resource, however, providing testimony supporting the pre-determined conclusions many times, and even posing as a reporter during an NIST media session.[8]

There was really no need for phony media coverage. As with *The 9/11 Commission Report* and the lead-up to the Iraq War, the major media simply parroted any explanations, or non-explanations, given in support of the official story. One example is from a television program, *The Anatomy of September 11th*, which aired on the History Channel. Corley took the lead on this one as well, but James Glanz, a *New York Times* reporter, was also interviewed and helped to spread what is probably the worst excuse for collapse given. He told us that the fires heated the steel columns so much (the video suggested 2,500°F) that they were turned into "licorice." Other self-proclaimed experts have been heard promoting similar theories.[9] They will probably come to regret it.

This is because the results of physical tests performed by NIST's own Frank Gayle proved this theory to be a ridiculous exaggeration, as some people already knew. The temperatures seen by the few steel samples saved, only about 500°F, were far too low to soften, let alone melt, even un-fireproofed steel. Of course that result could have been calculated, knowing that 4,000 gallons of jet fuel[10]—not 24,000 gallons or 10,000 gallons, as some reports have claimed— were sprayed into an open-air environment over several floors, each comprised of more than 1,000 metric tons of concrete and steel.

Another expert who served on NIST's advisory committee was Charles Thornton, of the engineering firm Thornton and Tomasetti. Thornton's partner, Richard Tomasetti, was reported to be behind the unprecedented and widely criticized decision to destroy most of the steel evidence.[11] Early on Thornton said: "Karl, we all know what caused the collapse." He was talking to Karl Koch, whose company erected the WTC steel. Koch attempted to clarify as follows.

> I could see it in my mind's eye: The fire burned until the steel was weakened and the floors above collapsed, starting a chain reaction of gravity, floor falling upon floor upon floor, clunk— clunk—clunk, the load gaining weight and momentum by the nanosecond, unstoppable. Once enough floors collapsed, the exterior walls and the core columns were no longer laterally supported and folded in.[12]

This is a description of what was called the Pancake Theory, the most widely accepted version of what happened.

The Pancake Theory was promoted by an influential 2002 show on PBS's *Nova*, "Why the Towers Fell," in which Corley (yet again) and Thornton were the primary commentators. Both of them talked about the floors collapsing, and Thornton described how the perimeter columns buckled outward, not inward as Koch had described. The video made a number of false claims, including exaggeration of the temperatures (2,000°F), remarks about melting steel, and the incredible statement that two-thirds of the columns in the north tower were completely severed by the airplane's impact. NIST's report now indicates that only about 14 percent of the columns were severed, and in some pre-collapse photos we can count most of these for ourselves.[13]

NIST and Underwriters Laboratories
In August 2004, Underwriters Laboratories evaluated the Pancake Theory by testing models of the floor assemblies used in the WTC buildings. Despite all the previous expert testimony, the floor models did not collapse. NIST reported this in its October 2004 update, in a table of results that clearly showed that the floors did not fail and that, therefore, pancaking was not possible.[14] NIST more succinctly stated this again in its June 2005 draft report, saying: "The results established that this type of assembly was capable of sustaining a large gravity load, without collapsing, for a substantial period of time relative to the duration of the fires in any given location on September 11th."[15]

At the time of the floor tests, I worked for Underwriters Laboratories (UL). I was very interested in the progress of these tests, having already asked some sensitive questions. My interest began when UL's CEO, Loring Knoblauch, a very experienced executive with a law degree from Harvard, surprised us at the company's South Bend location, just a few weeks after 9/11, by saying that UL had certified the steel used in the WTC buildings. Knoblauch told us that we should all be proud that the buildings had stood for so long under such intense conditions. In retrospect it is clear that all of us, including Knoblauch, were ignorant of many important facts surrounding 9/11 and did not, therefore, see his statements as particularly important.

Over the next two years, however, I learned more about the issues, like the unprecedented destruction of the steel evidence and the fact that no tall steel-frame buildings have ever collapsed due to fire. And I saw video of the owner of the buildings stating publicly that he and the fire department made the decision to "pull"—that is, to demolish—WTC 7 that day,[16] though demolition usually requires many weeks of planning and preparation. Perhaps most compelling for me were the words of a genuine expert on the WTC. This was John Skilling, the structural engineer responsible for designing the towers.[17] (The PBS *Nova* show, incidentally, gave this credit to Leslie Robertson. But Robertson, who never claimed to have originated the design, was only a junior member of the firm of Worthington, Skilling, Helle and Jackson. Skilling was known at the time to be the engineer in charge.) In 1993, five years before his death, Skilling said that he had performed an analysis on jet plane crashes and the ensuing fires and that "the building structure would still be there."[18]

By 2003, all of this information was available to anyone who cared. The details were, without a doubt, difficult to reconcile with testimony from officials, reporters, and scientists who were supporting the official story. But in November of that year, I felt that answers from UL were needed. If, as our CEO had suggested, our company had tested samples of steel components and listed the results in the UL Fire Resistance Directory almost 40 years ago, Skilling would have depended on these results to ensure that the buildings were sufficiently fire resistant. So I sent a formal written message to our chief executive, outlining my thoughts and asking what he was doing to protect our reputation.

Knoblauch's written response contained several points. He wrote: "We test to the code requirements, and the steel clearly met those requirements and exceeded them." He pointed to the NYC code used at the time of the WTC construction, which required fire resistance times of 3 hours for building columns, and 2 hours for floors. From the start, his answers were not helping to explain fire-induced collapse in 56 minutes (the time it took WTC 2, the south tower, to come down). But he did give a better explanation of UL's involvement in testing the WTC steel, even talking about the quality of the sample and how well it did. "We tested the steel with all the required fireproofing on," he wrote, "and it did beautifully."[19]

This response was copied to several UL executives, including Tom Chapin, the manager of UL's Fire Protection division. Chapin reminded me that UL was the "leader in fire research testing," but he clearly did not want to make any commitments on the issue. He talked about the floor assemblies, how these had not been UL tested, and he made the misleading claim that UL does not certify structural steel. But even an introductory textbook lists UL as one of the few important organizations supporting codes and specifications because they "produce a Fire Resistance Index with hourly ratings for beams, columns, floors, roofs, walls and partitions tested in accordance with ASTM Standard E119."[20] He went on to clarify that UL tests assemblies of which steel is a component. This is a bit like saying "we don't crash test the car door, we crash test the whole car." In any case, Chapin suggested that we be patient and wait for the report from NIST, because the investigation into the "collapse of WTC buildings 1, 2, and 7" was an ongoing process and that "UL is right in the middle of these activities."[21]

For the most part, I did wait, although I shared my concerns with Chapin again at UL's Leadership Summit in January 2004. I encouraged him to ask for a company news release on our position, but this did not happen and I never heard from him again. By the time UL tested the floor assembly models in August of that year, I had been promoted to the top management job in my division, Environmental Health Laboratories, overseeing all company functions. Two months later, NIST released an official update that included the floor test results, as well as Frank Gayle's results, in which steel temperatures were predicted. These results clearly invalidated the major theories of collapse, because pancaking could not occur without floor collapse and steel does not turn to licorice at the temperatures discussed.

After reviewing this update, I sent a letter directly to Dr. Gayle at NIST. In this letter, I referred to my experiences at UL and asked for more information on the WTC investigation and NIST's soon-to-be-published conclusions. NIST had planned at the time to release its final report in December, with time allowed for public comment. After I allowed my letter to become public,[22] this date was moved to January 2005, and then nothing was heard from NIST for several months.

Other than UL's involvement in testing the steel components, the facts I stated had all been reported publicly, but when I put them together plainly, they were considered outrageous. Five days after I sent my letter, I was fired by UL for doing so. The company made a few brief statements in an attempt to discredit me, then quickly began to make it clear that its relationship with the government, perhaps due to its tax-exempt status, was more important than its commitment to public safety.

For example, in spite of Tom Chapin's previous statements, UL suggested that it had played only a "limited" role in the investigation. Despite what our CEO, Loring Knoblauch, had written and copied to several executives, UL said there was "no evidence" that any firm had tested the steel used in the WTC buildings.[23] In doing so, UL implied that its CEO not only had fabricated this story about testing the WTC steel but had also spoken and written about it for several years without anyone in the company correcting him. As I see it, the only other option was that the company claiming to be our "Public Safety Guardian" was lying to us about the most important safety issue of our lives.

My experiences give a taste for the delicate nature of our critical turning point. But to keep our focus, we should examine what NIST did with the results of its physical tests, which had failed to support its conclusions. Did NIST perform more tests, at least to prove its key argument that much of the fireproofing on the steel in the Twin Towers popped off due to the impact of the airliners? No, it did not. Instead, NIST put together a black box computer model that would spit out the right answers. This black box model was driven by initial parameters that could be tweaked. When the parameters that had initially been considered "realistic" did not generate results that "compared to observed events," NIST scientists performed their final analysis using another set of parameters they called "more severe."[24] When they were finished, their model produced video graphics that would enable anyone to see the buildings collapse without having to follow a train of logic to get there.

Tom Chapin of UL was one of those doomed to make public comments in support of NIST's final report. His comments were innocuous enough but he did hint at something of value. "The effect of scale on test assemblies," Chapin said, "requires more investigation."[25] This may be the closest thing to a straightforward statement that we will ever see from UL on the matter. But it seems clear enough that results showing zero floor collapse, when scaled-up from the floor panels to a few floors, would still result in zero floor collapse. Perhaps a more direct version of Chapin's comment would be that test results negating predetermined conclusions should not be used to prove them.

Other than the video, NIST left us with only some vague statements about a few sagging floors suddenly destroying two hundred super-strong perimeter columns and forty core columns. But since sagging floors do not weigh more than non-sagging floors, it is difficult to see how this might occur, especially so uniformly. NIST claimed the perimeter columns saw increased loads of between 0 and 25 percent due to the damage, but it never reconciled this with the original claim that these columns could resist 2,000 percent increases in live load. And the outward-buckling theory, suggested by Thornton, was changed again to inward buckling—apparently the forces involved were never well defined. Additionally, NIST suggested that the documents that would support testing of the steel components, along with documents containing Skilling's jet-fuel-fire analysis, could not be found.[26]

Ultimately, NIST failed to give any explanation for the dynamics of the towers as they fell, about how and why they dropped like rocks in free-fall. For both buildings, the NIST report simply stated that "once the upper building section began to move downwards…, global collapse ensued," as if just saying so was enough (197). As for WTC 7, NIST as of yet has not elaborated on its "working collapse hypothesis," which was vaguely presented in June 2004.[27]

The bottom line is that, after more than four years, it is still impossible for the government even to begin to explain the primary events that drive this war on terror. So much has been sacrificed, and so much has been invested in this story, that we all have a need for supportive answers. But when we look for those answers, all our "mind's eye" can see is this smoky black box, where scientific results are reversed to support politically correct, predetermined conclusions. That critical point of divergence, where our lives were turned upside down and all logic followed, has always been too painful to imagine. But now, without expert accounts of pancaking floors and licorice steel, it cannot be imagined at all.

Some of us remain hopeful that we can still achieve a critical mass awareness of the need for truth, and in doing so pull the support out from under what John McMurtry in this volume calls "the 9/11 wars." But if we cannot, even as the hopes for peace fade and the number of 9/11 families continues to grow, we should remember how we got this story and how it was propped up despite all the evidence against it. Because whatever happens next, after the smoke clears, our children may have a need to know.

FIVE

The Background of 9/11: Drugs, Oil, and US Covert Operations

Peter Dale Scott

Just as the American people have been seriously misled about the reasons for America's invasion of Iraq, they have been seriously misled about the origins of the al-Qaeda movement, which was blamed for the 9/11 attacks.

The truth is that for at least two decades, as the United States has engaged in energetic covert programs to secure US control over the Persian Gulf and also to open up Central Asia for development by US oil companies, the US has used so-called "Arab-Afghan" warriors as assets—the very jihadis whom we loosely link with the name and leadership of al-Qaeda.[1] American's were eager to gain access to the petroleum reserves of the Caspian Basin (in the 1980s estimated to be "the largest known reserves of unexploited fuel in the planet"[2]). To this end US covert operations, as late as the 1990s, worked with Arab Afghans, who, in country after country, were involved in trafficking Afghan heroin.

America's sponsorship of drug-trafficking Muslim warriors, including those now in al-Qaeda, dates back to the Afghan War of 1979–1989, sponsored in part by the CIA's links to the drug-laundering Bank of Credit and Commerce International (BCCI).[3] It was part of CIA Director William Casey's strategy for launching covert operations over and above those approved and financed by a Democratic-controlled Congress.

The most conspicuous example of this alliance with drug-traffickers in the 1980s was the Contra support operation. Here again, foreign money and drug profits filled the gap after Congress denied funds through the so-called Boland amendments. Government funds were used to lie about the Contras to the American people.[4] This was followed by a massive cover-up, in which a dubious role was played by then-Congressman Lee Hamilton, who was to become co-chair of the 9/11 Commission.[5]

The lying continues. The report of the 9/11 Commission assures Americans that "Bin Ladin and his comrades had their own sources of support and training, and they received little or no assistance from the United States" (56). This misleading statement ignores several facts:

1) Al-Qaeda elements received considerable indirect US government assistance, first in Afghanistan until 1992, and thereafter in other countries such as Azerbaijan (1992–1995). Before 1992, for example, the Afghan leader Jallaladin Haqqani organized and hosted the Arab-Afghan volunteers known later as al-Qaeda, and Haqqani "received bags of money each month from the [CIA] station in Islamabad."[6] The Arab Afghans were also trained in urban terrorism (including car bombings) by Pakistani ISI operatives, who were themselves trained by the CIA.[7]

2) Key members of the network that became al-Qaeda, such as Sheikh Omar Abdel Rahman, Ali Mohamed, Mohamed Jamal Khalifa, and lead hijacker Mohamed Atta, were granted visas to enter the United States, despite being suspected of terrorism.[8] Al-Qaeda foot soldiers were also admitted to the United States for training under a special visa program.[9]

3) At Fort Belvoir, Virginia, an al-Qaeda operative was given a list of Muslim candidates for al-Qaeda's jihad.[10]

4) When Sergeant Ali Mohamed of the US Army Special Forces, a key al-Qaeda operative, trained al-Qaeda personnel in the United States, he was still on the US Army payroll.[11]

5) Repeatedly al-Qaeda terrorists were protected by FBI officials from investigation and prosecution.[12]

In part, America's limited covert assistance to al-Qaeda after 1989 was in order not to offend al-Qaeda's two primary supporters, which America needed as allies: the intelligence networks of Saudi Arabia and Pakistan. Unquestionably, however, the entry of United States oil companies into oil-rich Azerbaijan was achieved with the assistance of a US-organized covert program using Arab-Afghan operatives associated with bin Laden. Oil was the driving force of US involvement in Central and South Asia, and oil led to US coexistence with both al-Qaeda and the world-dominating Afghan heroin trade.

This brings us to another extraordinary distortion in *The 9/11 Commission Report*. It says: "While the drug trade was a source of income for the Taliban, it did not serve the same purpose for al-Qaeda, and there is no reliable evidence that bin Ladin was involved in or made his money through drug trafficking."[13]

[That drug trafficking has supported al-Qaeda-connected operations has been energetically asserted by the governments of Great Britain and many other European countries, as well as the head of the US Congressional Task Force on Terrorism. Heroin trafficking has been a source of income in particular for al-Qaeda-related warriors in Tajikistan, Uzbekistan, Azerbaijan, Chechnya, and Kosovo. More recently, it has supported terrorist attacks in the Netherlands and Spain. US support for al-Qaeda elements, particularly in Azerbaijan and Kosovo, has dramatically increased the flow of heroin to Western Europe and the United States.]

The Examples of Azerbaijan and Kosovo

In the former Soviet Republic of Azerbaijan, Arab Afghans clearly assisted the effort of US oil companies to penetrate the region. In 1991, Richard Secord, Heinie Aderholt, and Ed Dearborn, three veterans of US operations in Laos and Nicaragua, turned up in Baku under the cover of an oil company, MEGA Oil.[14] MEGA never did find oil, but it did contribute materially to the removal of Azerbaijan from the sphere of post-Soviet Russian influence.

As the MEGA operatives in Azerbaijan, Secord, Aderholt, Dearborn, and their men engaged in military training, passed "brown bags filled with cash" to members of the government, and set up an airline after the model of the CIA's proprietary airline, Air America, which had been used for covert operations across Southeast Asia. The new airline was soon picking up hundreds of mujahideen mercenaries in Afghanistan.[15] (Secord and Aderholt claim to have left Baku before the mujahideen arrived.) Meanwhile, mujahideen leader Gulbuddin Hekmatyar in Afghanistan, who at the time was still allied with bin Laden, was "observed recruiting Afghan mercenaries [i.e. Arab Afghans] to fight in Azerbaijan against Armenia and its Russian allies."[16] At that time, heroin flooded from Afghanistan through Baku into Chechnya, Russia, and as far as North America.[17] It is difficult to believe that MEGA's airline did not become involved.[18]

The triple pattern of drugs, oil, and al-Qaeda was seen again in Kosovo in 1998, where the al-Qaeda-backed Islamist jihadis of the

Kosovo Liberation Army (KLA) received overt American assistance from the US government.[19] Though unmentioned in mainstream books on the war, both the al-Qaeda and drug backgrounds of the KLA are recognized by experts and to my knowledge never contested by them.[20]

Though the origins of the Kosovo tragedy were rooted in local enmities, oil and drugs were prominent in the outcome. At the time, critics charged that US oil interests wanted to build a trans-Balkan pipeline with US army protection. Although initially ridiculed, these critics were eventually proven correct.[21] BBC News announced in December 2004 that a $1.2 billion pipeline, south of a huge new US army base in Kosovo, had been given a go-ahead by the governments of Albania, Bulgaria, and Macedonia.[22] Meanwhile by 2000, according to DEA statistics, Afghan heroin accounted for almost 20 percent of the heroin seized in the United States—nearly double the percentage taken four years earlier. Much of it is now distributed by Kosovar Albanians.[23]

Sergeant Ali Mohamed and US Intelligence Links to the al-Qaeda Leadership

The 9/11 Commission Report describes Ali Mohamed as "a former Egyptian army officer who had moved to the United States in the mid-1980s, enlisted in the US army, and become an instructor at Fort Bragg," as well as helping to plan the bombing of the US embassy in Kenya (68). In fact, Ali Mohamed was an important al-Qaeda agent who, as the 9/11 Commission was told, "trained most of al-Qaeda's top leadership," including "persons who would later carry out the 1993 World Trade Center bombing." But the person telling the 9/11 Commission this, US Attorney Patrick J. Fitzgerald, misrepresented Ali Mohamed's FBI relationship. He told the Commission: "From 1994 until his arrest in 1998, [Mohamed] lived as an American citizen in California, applying for jobs as an FBI translator and working as a security guard for a defense contractor."[24]

Ali Mohamed was not just an FBI job applicant. Unquestionably he was an FBI informant, from at least 1993 and maybe 1989.[25] And almost certainly, he was something more. A veteran of the CIA-trained bodyguards of Egyptian President Anwar Sadat, he was able, despite being on a State Department watch list, to come to America around 1984, on what FBI consultant Paul Williams has called "a visa program controlled by the CIA." He was also able to obtain jobs, first as a security officer, then with US Special Forces.[26] In 1988, he took a lengthy leave of absence from the US army and went to fight in Afghanistan, where he met with Ayman al-Zawahiri (later bin Laden's chief deputy in al-Qaeda) and the Arab-Afghan leadership.[27] Despite this, he was able to receive an honorable discharge one year later, at which point he established close contact with bin Laden in Afghanistan.

Ali Mohamed clearly enjoyed US protection: In 1993, when detained by the RCMP in Canada, a single phone call to the United States secured his release. This enabled him to play a role, in the same year, in planning the bombing of the US embassy in Kenya in 1998.[28]

Congress should determine the true relationship of the US government to Ali Mohamed, who was close to bin Laden and above all to al-Zawahiri, who has been called by one writer the "main player" in 9/11.[29] (Al-Zawahiri is often described as the more sophisticated mentor of the younger bin Laden.)[30] In particular, Congress should determine why Patrick Fitzgerald chose to mislead the American people about Mohamed's FBI status.

In short, the al-Qaeda terror network accused of the 9/11 attacks was supported and expanded by US intelligence programs and covert operations, both during and after the Soviet Afghan War. Congress should rethink their decision to grant still greater powers and budget to the agencies responsible for fostering this enemy in the first place.

Sane voices from the Muslim world clamor that the best answer to terrorism is not war but justice. We should listen to them. By using its energies to reduce the injustices tormenting Islam, the United States will do more to diminish terrorism than it will do by creating any number of new directorates in Washington.

SIX

The "Strategy of Tension" in the Cold War Period

Daniele Ganser

Following the terrorist attacks of September 11, 2001, academics in Europe and in my native Switzerland with an interest in the details of the phenomenon anxiously waited for the official US investigation of the crime. Most realized immediately that the terror attacks on the US had great implications for Europe and the rest of the world also, and therefore had to be studied in detail. When *The 9/11 Commission Report* (sometimes called the Kean–Zelikow Report) was finally published in July 2004 — almost three years after the 9/11 attacks — many academics from the fields of contemporary history and international relations hoped to find in it the definitive account of 9/11.[1]

This hope was shattered a few months later with the publication of *The 9/11 Commission Report: Omissions and Distortions*, by David Ray Griffin.[2] "I suspect," Griffin wrote, "that many readers will be shocked, as I was, by the sheer number of the omissions and the audacity of the distortions."[3] Some academics in Europe with an interest in 9/11 read only the 571 pages of the official 9/11 report and, lacking further time or interest, had contented themselves with the account offered therein. Others, who had invested additional time and energy and also ploughed through the 339 pages of critique offered by Griffin, became deeply disturbed.

This difference led to a rather unfortunate divide among European academics interested in 9/11, one that persists today. A first group, those who had read the Kean–Zelikow report only, remained content that they had been told the truth about 9/11 by the Bush–Cheney administration and the official Kean–Zelikow

Commission, which by and large had confirmed the official line. A second group, after having read Griffin's analysis, could not help but, as he had predicted, be baffled by the audacity of the omissions and distortions. To this second group, in which I include myself, the Kean–Zelikow report was so seriously deficient and unbalanced that it could never be accepted as an accurate account of what really happened on 9/11.

An awareness that the Kean–Zelikow report is deficient does not immediately offer an insight into what really happened on 9/11. The crime therefore needs further investigation by academics across the world—urgent investigation, one might add, given the far-reaching consequences of the 9/11 attacks during the intervening years. This situation has forced all of us who specialize in secret warfare to go back to the 9/11 data, an ocean of data it really is, in order to figure out which theory best explains 9/11.

This chapter does not claim to be able to explain what really happened on 9/11. Neither does it go through all the conflicting 9/11 data available as of now. In fact, it deals only with data on secret warfare during the Cold War. Before we turn to this, however, it is necessary to mention briefly some of the contradictory 9/11 theories presently on offer.

Three Theories about 9/11

It is important to stress that all of the theories about 9/11 are conspiracy theories. A conspiracy is a secret agreement between two or more persons to engage in a criminal act. Conspiracies are nothing unusual or new in the field of historical research. At least since the assassination of Julius Caesar in classical Rome more than 2,000 years ago, conspiracies have been an element of the political fight for influence and power. As 9/11 was a criminal act which was definitively not planned and carried out by one single person alone but by at least two or more persons who agreed on the plan before it was implemented, 9/11 must be classified as a conspiracy. Once we realize that none of the theories can be dismissed on the grounds that it is a "conspiracy theory," the real question becomes: Which conspiracy theory correctly describes the 9/11 conspiracy? As of now, three conflicting theories dominate the discourse.

The first 9/11 theory is the so-called surprise theory. Offered by the Bush administration and the Kean–Zelikow report, it claims that Osama bin Laden conspired with Khalid Sheikh Mohammed,

Mohamed Atta, and other men to attack the US on 9/11. The surprise theory argues that 9/11 was a Muslim conspiracy. It concedes that there were rumors about a looming attack, but insists that the US intelligence community, including the NSA, CIA, FBI, DIA, and other intelligence services, along with the Pentagon, were unable to prevent the conspiracy from being implemented.

The second 9/11 theory on offer is the so-called LIHOP (Let It Happen On Purpose) theory. Like the surprise theory, it assumes that Osama bin Laden conspired with Khalid Sheikh Mohammed, Mohamed Atta, and other men to attack the US on 9/11. In stark contrast to the surprise theory, however, the LIHOP theory claims that persons within the US government deliberately allowed the attacks to be carried out in order to be able to start a number of wars that had been planned in advance. The LIHOP theory thus argues that 9/11 was a combined Muslim and Jewish-Christian conspiracy, in which the latter group outwitted the former.

The third 9/11 theory on offer is the so-called MIHOP (Make It Happen On Purpose) theory. It argues that criminal persons within the US government, in the Pentagon and the intelligence community, carried out the attacks themselves in order to be able to start a number of wars that had been planned in advance. The MIHOP theory thus argues that 9/11 was primarily a Christian or Jewish-Christian conspiracy, in which Muslims, if involved at all, were involved only in minor ways.[4]

Theologians have correctly pointed out that no true Christian, Jewish, or Muslim values—including love and respect for other human beings—can be found in the crimes of 9/11, and that it is therefore fundamentally wrong to link any of the three largest monotheistic religions of the world to the crime. If religion played a role in the fanatic crime at all, then it was misguided religion.

The Relevance of the History of Secret Warfare

Ordinary people with little knowledge of the history of secret warfare have found it profoundly disturbing even to contemplate the LIHOP and MIHOP theories. Why would any government in the world, they have asked, attack its own population or, only slightly less criminal, deliberately allow a foreign group to carry out such an attack? While brutal dictatorships, such as the regime of Pol Pot in Cambodia, are known to have had little respect for the life and dignity of their citizens, surely a Western democracy, the thinking goes, would not engage in such an abuse of power. And if criminal elements within a Western democracy, in North America or in Europe, had engaged in such a crime, would not elected officials or the media find out and report on it? Is it imaginable that criminal persons within a government could commit terrorist operations against innocent citizens, who support the very same government with the taxes they pay every year? Would nobody notice? These are difficult questions, even for academics who specialize in the history of secret warfare. But in fact, there are historical examples of such operations being implemented by Western democracies.

In this essay, I will report on some of the newest academic data about secret warfare during the Cold War. A secret military strategy that targets domestic populations with terrorism does indeed exist. It is called the "strategy of tension." And it was implemented by Western democracies.

The Strategy of Tension

It is probably fair to say that of the roughly six billion people who live on our planet today, far less than one percent has ever heard of the "strategy of tension." And only a very few of these could illustrate the strategy with specific historical examples. It is indeed a strategy of a shadow world, known only to a few military and intelligence officers (and some criminals) who have carried it out, a few police officers and judges who fought against it, and a handful of journalists and academics who have written about it.

In its essence, the strategy of tension targets the emotions of human beings and aims to spread maximum fear among the target group. "Tension" refers to emotional distress and psychological fear, whereas "strategy" refers to the technique of bringing about such distress and fear. A terrorist attack in a public place, such as a railway station, a market place, or a school bus, is the typical technique through which the strategy of tension is implemented. After the attack—and this is a crucial element—the secret agents who carried out the crime blame it on a political opponent by removing and planting evidence.

It must be noted that the targets of the strategy of tension are not the dead and the wounded of the terrorist attacks, as many might assume. The targets are the political opponents, who are discredited through the attack, and those who remain unharmed but learn of the attack, thereby coming to fear for their lives and those of their loved ones. Since the aims of the strategy are to discredit opponents and to create fear, the real targets are not the people who were killed, whether they number in the dozens or even thousands, but the millions of people who survive physically unharmed but emotionally distressed.

The strategy of tension forms part of what is called "psychological warfare" or PSYWAR. As the term indicates, this form of warfare does not attack human bodies, tanks, planes, ships, satellites, and houses in order to destroy them, but human psyches, human minds. Leaving aside the fact that philosophers, psychologists, neurologists, and theologians have never been able fully to agree on exactly what "the mind" is, we can for our purposes here define it simply as our human ability to think and feel. If a group can get access to our thinking and our feeling without our noticing, it can exercise great power over us. Once we notice that our psyches are being manipulated through psychological warfare, the technique loses some of its effect.

Psychological warfare played a central role in World War II and all the wars that followed. It was used by military leaders in Europe, the Americas, Asia, Australia, and Africa. It is sometimes popularly referred to as "propaganda," but propaganda is only one form of psychological warfare. The strategy of tension is a lesser known form. The US Department of Defense defines psychological warfare as: "The planned use of propaganda and other psychological actions having the primary purpose of influencing the opinions, emotions, attitudes, and behavior of hostile foreign groups in such a way as to support the achievement of national objectives."[5]

Psychological warfare can come in many different and seemingly unrelated forms—leaflets, posters, or television reports, all designed to shape the thinking and feeling of the target group. Or it can come in the form of a terrorist attack carried out by secret agents and blamed on a political opponent. Needless to say, strategy-of-tension terrorism that kills innocent people is a much more radical and brutal form of psychological warfare than dropping paper leaflets from a plane over enemy territory. But the two forms of psychological warfare are linked in their targeting of the mind—the emotions and thoughts of people.

I will now give some historical examples of strategy-of-tension terrorism. Arguably the best historical data available today on the strategy of tension come from Italy, where judges, parliamentarians, and academics together continue to make great efforts to understand and describe this secret strategy.

Judge Casson and the Peteano Terror

Italian Judge Felice Casson rediscovered the strategy during his investigation into a number of terrorist attacks Italy had suffered in the 1960s, 1970s, and 1980s. According to Casson, the best documented historical case in which the strategy of tension was implemented occurred in the Italian village of Peteano. There, on May 31, 1972, three members of the Italian paramilitary police, the Carabinieri, were lured to an abandoned Fiat 500 by an anonymous phone call and were killed when they opened the hood of the car, thereby triggering a bomb. For many years, this terrorist attack was blamed on the Red Brigades, a left-wing terror organization in Italy. But after Casson reopened the case, he found that the Catholic neofascist Vincenzo Vinciguerra, a militant anti-communist, had carried out the crime.

Casson also found to his great surprise that Vinciguerra had not operated alone, but had been protected by members of the Italian military intelligence service, today called SISMI (Servizio per le Informazioni e la Sicurezza Militare).[6] Judge Casson arrested Vinciguerra, who on trial in 1984 confirmed that it had been relatively easy for him to escape and hide because large segments of the Italian security apparatus, including the SISMI, had shared his anti-communist convictions and had, therefore, silently supported crimes that discredited the Italian left and especially the Communist Party, which was quite strong. After the bombing, Vinciguerra recalled, "A whole mechanism came into action.... [T]he Carabinieri, the Minister of the Interior, the customs services, and the military and civilian intelligence services accepted the ideological reasoning behind the attack."[7]

Casson found that by this crime and other attacks being blamed on the left-wing Red Brigades, the primary political enemy, the Italian Communist Party, was discredited. The directors of the military intelligence service and politicians argued after the crime that the "Communist danger" justified increased military spending and a reduction of civil liberties in the interest of state security. In this way, the strategy of tension, as executed through the Peteano terror, spread fear across Italy, discredited a political opponent, and allowed for the implementation of conservative security policies. It was very effective, for nobody knew at the time that the intelligence services had themselves supported the crime.

"As far as the intelligence services are concerned, the Peteano attack is part of what has been called 'the strategy of tension,'" Judge Casson explained in a BBC interview in 1991.

> The tension created within the country then served to promote conservative, reactionary social and political tendencies. While this strategy was being implemented, it was necessary to protect those behind it, because evidence implicating them was being discovered. Witnesses withheld information to cover right-wing extremists.[8]

Vinciguerra was a member of a private Italian fascist organization, Ordine Nuovo (New Order), which cultivated close relations with the SISMI. A fellow Ordine Nuovo member, Clemente Graziani, argued in a 1963 book that as Catholics it was their duty to fight the godless Communists by all means, including strategy-of-tension operations that, at first glance, might seem too brutal and immoral. The Communists also engaged in dirty tricks, he argued, and therefore would never be defeated if Ordine Nuovo for moral reasons shied away even from terrorism: "Terrorism obviously has the possibility to kill or let [be] kill[ed] also elderly people, women and children," Graziani noted. But, he continued:

> Operations of this kind have until now been considered to be contemptible and despicable crimes, and above all, useless crimes to win a conflict. The revolutionary warfare canon however subverts these humanitarian and moral principles. These forms of terrorist intimidation are today not only considered as acceptable operations, but are at times even absolutely necessary.[9]

Other Terrorist Attacks

Peteano was not an isolated tragedy in Italy, but part of a long series of terrorist attacks that had started in 1969. On December 12 of that year, four bombs exploded in public places in Rome and Milan, killing 16 and maiming and wounding 80 innocent civilians, with most of the deaths and injuries occurring in Milan's Piazza Fontana. After the massacre, according to the rules of the strategy of tension, the Italian military intelligence service SID planted bomb parts in the villa of well-known leftist editor Giangiacomo Feltrinelli in order to blame the terror on the Communists and other members of the extreme left.[10] Only years later was it revealed that Feltrinelli had absolutely nothing at all to do with the crime and that, in reality, the Italian extreme right, including Ordine Nuovo, had carried out the atrocity in order to promote the strategy of tension.

Major attacks came in 1974, a couple years after the Peteano tragedy. On May 28, a bomb exploded at an anti-fascist rally for which 3,000 had gathered in the Italian city of Brescia, killing 8 and injuring and maiming 102 people. To cover the traces of the right-wing bombers, the square was cleaned with water hoses before the investigating magistrates could reach the scene of the crime to secure the evidence. An Italian Senate commission later observed that "the investigations immediately after the massacre were characterized by such incredible mistakes that one is left speechless."[11] Then on August 4, a bomb exploded on a train, the Rome-to-Munich *Italicus Express*, killing 12 innocent civilians and injuring and maiming 48.

The most deadly attack came in 1980, on the afternoon of Saturday, August 2, a warm and sunny day that was also the first full day of the Italian national summer holiday. A massive explosion ripped through the second class waiting room at the Bologna railway station, killing 85 people in the blast and seriously injuring and maiming a further 200.

The Purpose of the Attacks

This series of terrorist attacks discredited the Italian Communists and spread maximum fear among the Italian population, as nobody really knew what was going on and who would be killed next. It was impossible to protect the entire transportation system, let alone all public places, and thus it was clear to all security experts at the time that democratic societies would always remain vulnerable to terrorist attacks. "You had to attack civilians, the people, women, children, innocent people, unknown people far removed from any political game," the neofascist Vincenzo Vinciguerra said after his arrest, explaining the strategy of tension in which he himself had participated.

> The reason was quite simple [he continued]. They were supposed to force these people, the Italian public, to turn to the State to ask for greater security. This is the political logic that lies behind all the massacres and the bombings which remain unpunished, because the State cannot convict itself or declare itself responsible for what happened.[12]

The Gladio Revelations

Italian Judge Felice Casson, who had rediscovered the strategy of tension, wanted to know why persons within the Italian government and intelligence services had supported the criminal strategy of tension. Following the arrest of Peteano bomber Vinciguerra, he decided to dig deep. "I wanted that new light should be shed on these years of lies and mysteries, that's all. That Italy should for once know the truth."[13] In the summer of 1990, Judge Casson requested permission from Italian Prime Minister Giulio Andreotti to search through the archives of the Italian military intelligence service (SISMI) in Rome.

The permission was given and Casson made a sensational discovery: He found that under the code name "Gladio" ("sword"), a secret army existed that had been set up by the Italian military intelligence service in close collaboration with the CIA in the years after World War II. This secret army was to function as a guerrilla unit in the event of a Soviet invasion and occupation of Italy.

The data found by Casson suggested that this mysterious Gladio army was linked to NATO and, in the absence of a Soviet invasion, seems to have manipulated Italian politics in a number of covert action operations during the Cold War in order to weaken the Italian Communists.

Casson confidentially informed an Italian parliamentarian commission of his far-reaching findings. The senators were greatly surprised and, on August 2, 1990, ordered the head of the Italian executive, Prime Minister Giulio Andreotti, "to inform the parliament within sixty days with respect to the existence, characteristics and purpose of a parallel and occult structure that is said to have operated within our secret service of the military with the aim to condition the political life of the country."[14]

On October 24, 1990, Andreotti handed a ten-page report entitled "The So-called 'Parallel SID'—The Gladio Case" to the Senate investigative commission under Senator Gualtieri. Andreotti's report confirmed that a secret army existed within the military intelligence service under the code name Gladio. Andreotti added that it was still active and operational. Unwilling to shoulder the far-reaching accusation of conspiracy alone, Andreotti insisted on the same day in front of parliament that "each chief of government has been informed of the existence of Gladio."[15] This announcement compromised, among others, former socialist Prime Minister Bettino Craxi (1983–1987) and above all Francesco Cossiga, a former prime minister (1978–1979), who in 1990 was acting president. The high-ranking magistrates were forced to take a stand. Craxi claimed that he had not been informed, until he was confronted with a document on

Gladio that he himself had signed as prime minister. Cossiga said that he was "proud of the fact that we have kept the secret for 45 years."[16]

In his report, Andreotti confirmed the findings of Casson and explained that Gladio was the Italian branch of a secret stay-behind army that had been set up after World War II by the CIA and SIFAR as part of an international network of clandestine resistance within NATO countries to confront a potential Soviet invasion. In case of invasion, the stay-behind armies would set up a resistance movement and operate behind enemy lines. These stay-behind armies were supervised and coordinated by two secret unconventional-warfare centers of NATO named the Allied Clandestine Committee (ACC) and the Clandestine Planning Committee (CPC). In Andreotti's words:

> Once the clandestine resistance organisation was constituted, Italy was called upon to participate... in the works of the CCP (Clandestine Planning Committee) of 1959, operating within the ambit of SHAPE [NATO's Supreme Headquarters Allied Powers Europe]...; in 1964 the Italian intelligence service also entered the ACC (Allied Clandestine Committee).[17]

Facing sharp protests from the Italian press, Andreotti claimed that the Italian military intelligence service in general, as well as the Gladio members in particular, had nothing to do with the terror from which Italy had suffered during the Cold War. He said that "the pre-selected subjects do not have a penal record, do not partake in active politics, nor participate in any sort of extremist movement."[18]

Peteano bomber Vinciguerra, who had been at the heart of the strategy of tension, disagreed with this account. Already during his trial in 1984, he had declared: "With the massacre of Peteano and with all those that have followed, the knowledge should by now be clear that there existed a real live structure, occult and hidden, with the capacity of giving a strategic direction to the outrages." The structure, he said, "lies within the state itself. There exists in Italy a secret force parallel to the armed forces, composed of civilians and military men, in an anti-Soviet capacity, that is, to organize a resistance on Italian soil against a Russian army."

Without revealing the name Gladio, Vinciguerra had clearly been speaking of the secret army many years before Prime Minister Andreotti confirmed its existence. Vinciguerra said in 1984 that what he was describing was "a secret organization, a super-organization with a network of communications, arms, and explosives, and men trained to use them." Vinciguerra insisted that this "super-organization, lacking a Soviet invasion, took up the task, on NATO's behalf, of preventing a slip to the left in the political balance of the country. This they did, with the assistance of the official intelligence services and the political and military forces."[19]

Former heads of the Italian military intelligence were shocked that Prime Minister Andreotti had revealed what many considered to be one of its best kept secrets. General Vito Miceli, chief of the Italian military intelligence service from 1970 to 1974, protested to the Italian press: "I have gone to prison because I did not want to reveal the existence of this super secret organization. And now Andreotti comes along and tells it to Parliament!"[20]

The Italian press was very critical of the Gladio revelations and the fact that the CIA had played a central role in the secret operation. The daily *La Stampa* commented:

> No raison d'état could be worth maintaining, covering up, or defending a secret military structure composed of ideologically selected members—dependent upon, or at least under the influence of, a foreign power—that allegedly serves as an instrument of political struggle. It cannot be defined as any less than high treason and an attack on the Constitution.[21]

The Italian Communist Party (PCI), convinced that they themselves, not foreign armies, had been the true target of the Gladio armies during the entire Cold War period, were especially outraged:

> With this mysterious Parallel SID, conjured up to head off an impossible coup by the left, we have seriously risked making a coup d'état by the right possible.... We cannot accept that... this super-SID was passed off as a military instrument destined to operate "in case of enemy occupation." The true enemy is only and has always been the Italian Communist party, i.e. an internal enemy.[22]

The Role of the CIA

In the United States, the story was ignored by the mainstream media. In one of the very few articles on the subject, the *Washington Post*—under the headline "CIA Organized Secret Army in Western Europe; Paramilitary Force Created to Resist Soviet Occupation"—reported that an unnamed intelligence officer familiar with Gladio had declared that it was "solely an Italian operation. We have no control over it whatsoever.... If there are allegations that the CIA was involved in terrorist activities in Italy, they are absolute nonsense."[23]

It is extremely difficult to research and clarify the details of strategy-of-tension operations, as nobody is willing publicly to confirm that he or she either ordered or participated in secret terrorist operations that killed innocent civilians, spread fear among a target group, and were wrongly blamed on a political enemy. If, as in the case of Italy, a number of different intelligence services are involved, including the Italian SISMI and the American CIA, then the matter becomes even more difficult, as the different services accuse and contradict each other.

In contrast to the anonymous US intelligence officer quoted in the *Washington Post*, who implicitly blamed the Italians for the terror in their country, researcher Philip Willan argues that blame belongs to the US government and its intelligence community:

> It is by no means easy to determine who was responsible for day to day tactical decisions in the running of the strategy of tension. But there can be little doubt that overall responsibility for the strategy lay with the government and the intelligence services of the United States.... [Q]uestions will remain about the adoption of methods that brought violent death to hundreds of innocent victims.[24]

During a television interview in Italy in 1990, Admiral Stansfield Turner, director of the CIA from 1977 to 1981, was unwilling to confirm this claim of Willan and strictly refused to answer any questions about Gladio. Out of respect for the victims of the numerous massacres, the Italian journalist conducting the interview insisted that Turner clarify the strategy of tension. But Turner angrily ripped off his microphone and shouted: "I said, no questions about Gladio!" whereupon the interview was over.[25]

Some retired, middle-ranking CIA officers were more outspoken about the secret strategies of the Cold War and illegal operations of the CIA. Among them was Thomas Polgar, who retired in 1981 after a 30-year career in the CIA. Questioned about the secret Gladio armies in Europe, Polgar confirmed that the stay-behind armies were coordinated by "a sort of unconventional warfare planning group linked to NATO." Polgar insisted that "each national service did it with varying degrees of intensity," adding that "in Italy in the 1970s some of the people went a little bit beyond the charter that NATO had put down."[26]

Members of the Italian parliament decided to dig deeper. Eight senators, most of whom belonged to the Democratic Left Party (PDS: Partito Democratico della Sinistra), which had replaced the

Italian Communist party after the collapse of the Soviet Union in 1991, continued to investigate Gladio and the strategy of tension. Under the chairmanship of Senator Giovanni Pellegrini, they heard witnesses, saw documents, and presented a 326-page report in 2000.[27] The former Communists concluded that during the Cold War the secret Gladio army had, together with the CIA, the Italian military intelligence service, and selected Italian neo-fascists, fought the Italian Communists and Socialists for fear that they would betray NATO "from within." The report said: "Those massacres, those bombs, those military actions had been organised or promoted or supported by men inside Italian state institutions and, as has been discovered more recently, by men linked to the structures of United States intelligence."[28]

According to the far-reaching findings of the Italian Senate, the strategy of tension had thus been implemented by members of both the American and Italian national security communities, including the CIA and the SISMI, which had linked up with extremists who had then planted the bombs. General Giandelio Maletti, former head of Italian counterintelligence, confirmed this account in March 2001, just a few months before the terrorist attacks of 9/11.

At a trial of right-wing extremists accused of being involved in the 1969 massacre in Milan's Piazza Fontana, General Maletti testified:

> "The CIA, following the directives of its government, wanted to create an Italian nationalism capable of halting what it saw as a slide to the left, and, for this purpose, it may have made use of right-wing terrorism.... The impression was that the Americans would do anything to stop Italy from sliding to the left," the General explained, and then added: "Don't forget that Nixon was in charge and Nixon was a strange man, a very intelligent politician, but a man of rather unorthodox initiatives."[29]

Investigations in the United States

In the US, apart from the often ignored but important work of Jeffrey McKenzie Bale,[30] not much research has been carried out on the topic of US-sponsored strategy-of-tension operations in Italy. Arthur Rowse, formerly on the staff of the *Washington Post*, was another of the very few Americans who took up the phenomenon. In the conclusion of a valuable article, he drew "the lessons of Gladio" in these terms: "As long as the US public remains ignorant of this dark chapter in US foreign relations, the agencies responsible for it will face little pressure to correct their ways." He added: "The end of the Cold War... changed little in Washington. The US... still awaits a real national debate on the means and ends and costs of our national security policies."[31]

The discovery of the NATO stay-behind army in Italy in 1990 and the ensuing debate about the strategy of tension had far-reaching international implications. As the details of the operation emerged, the *Times* (of London) concluded that the "story seems straight from the pages of a political thriller."[32] For only a short moment, the public at large was allowed a glimpse into a shadow world of terror, lies, and cover-ups. The British press concluded that Gladio, along with its strategy of tension, was "the best-kept, and most damaging, political-military secret since World War II."[33]

NATO's Response

By declaring that NATO coordinated the secret international networks, of which Gladio was but one branch, Andreotti had put great pressure on the European headquarters of NATO in Belgium. My subsequent research confirmed that secret stay-behind armies had existed in all the countries of Western Europe, operating under different code-names: in Denmark "Absalon," in Germany "TD BDJ," in Greece "LOK," in Luxemburg "Stay-behind," in the Netherlands "I&O," in Norway "ROC," in Portugal "Aginter," in Switzerland "P26," in Turkey "Counter-Guerrilla," and in Austria "OWSGV."[34]

NATO, the world's largest military alliance, reacted with confusion to the exposure of the secret network by issuing two contradictory comments. On November 5, 1990, after almost a month of silence, NATO categorically denied Andreotti's allegation concerning NATO's involvement in operation Gladio and the secret armies. Senior NATO spokesman Jean Marcotta said at SHAPE headquarters in Mons, Belgium, that "NATO has never contemplated guerrilla war or clandestine operations; it has always concerned itself with military affairs and the defense of Allied frontiers."[35] On November 6, however, another NATO spokesman explained that NATO's denial of the previous day had been false. This time NATO left journalists with a short communiqué only, which said that NATO never commented on matters of military secrecy and that Marcotta should not have said anything at all.[36] The international press protested against the ill-conceived public relations policy of the military alliance, with one British newspaper writing: "As shock followed shock across the Continent, a NATO spokesman issued a denial: nothing was known of Gladio or stay-behind. Then a seven word communiqué announced the denial was 'incorrect' and nothing more."[37]

In order to clarify NATO's position, I called NATO's Office of Security where Isabelle Jacobs informed me that it was unlikely that I would get any answers concerning sensitive Gladio questions, advising me to hand in such questions in writing via my embassy. Thus the Swiss mission at NATO in Brussels forwarded my Gladio questions to NATO, including: "Why has NATO senior spokesman Jean Marcotta on Monday, November 5, 1990 categorically denied any connections between NATO and Gladio, whereupon on November 7 another NATO spokesman had to declare Marcotta's statement of two days before had been false?" In May of 2001, Lee McClenny, head of NATO press and media service, offered a flat denial, saying: "I am not aware of any link between NATO and 'Operation Gladio.' Further, I can find no record that anyone named Jean Marcotta was ever a spokesman for NATO."[38]

Behind the scenes, however, NATO was forced to communicate more openly on the sensitive Gladio affair, as other sources revealed. Following the public relations debacle, NATO Secretary General Manfred Wörner briefed NATO ambassadors on stay-behind behind closed doors on November 7, 1990. A story in the Spanish press, commenting on this briefing, said:

> The Supreme Headquarters Allied Powers Europe (SHAPE), directing organ of NATO's military apparatus, coordinated the actions of Gladio, according to the revelations of Gladio Secretary General Manfred Wörner during a reunion with the NATO ambassadors of the 16 allied nations.

This story added that "Wörner allegedly had asked for time, in order to carry out an investigation with respect to the 'no knowledge at all' statement," which NATO had issued the previous day. "These precisions were presented in front of the Atlantic Council meeting on the level of ambassadors, which, according to some sources, was held on November 7."[39]

NATO Secretary General Manfred Wörner himself, this story continued, had been briefed by the highest-ranking military officer of NATO in Europe, US General John Galvin, the acting SACEUR (Supreme Allied Commander Europe).

During this meeting behind closed doors, the NATO Secretary General related that the questioned military gentlemen—precisely General John Galvin, supreme commander of the Allied forces in Europe—had indicated that SHAPE co-ordinated the Gladio operations. From then on the official position of NATO was that they would not comment on official secrets.[40]

NATO never publicly commented on the strategy of tension, whether NATO personnel or planning had been involved, nor offered any other details on the secret armies. "Since this is a secret organisation, I wouldn't expect too many questions to be answered, even though the Cold War is over," a NATO diplomat, who insisted on anonymity, reasoned in front of the press. "If there were any links to terrorist organizations, that sort of information would be buried very deep indeed. If not, then what is wrong with taking precautions to organize resistance if you think the Soviets might attack?"[41]

The parliament of the European Union was not amused that NATO refused to comment and, in a special resolution on the secret armies and the strategy of tension, declared sharply that "these organizations operated and continue to operate completely outside the law since they are not subject to any parliamentary control." The parliament then "called for a full investigation into the nature, structure, aims and all other aspects of these clandestine organizations." Such an investigation, however, was never carried out, as both NATO and its member states were concerned about a number of problems such an investigation could create. Yet the EU parliament made it clear that it "protests vigorously at the assumption by certain US military personnel at SHAPE and in NATO of the right to encourage the establishment in Europe of a clandestine intelligence and operation network." And there the matter rested.[42]

France

Italy, as I have mentioned, was not the only country in which stay-behind networks were involved in strategy-of-tension operations. Terror operations against the domestic population also took place in Belgium, Turkey, and Greece. As in Italy, the secret armies were trained and equipped by the CIA and its British counterpart, MI6, and operated as a top secret branch of the national military intelligence service. The details of the operations in these three countries are available in my book, *NATO's Secret Armies*.[43] In the present essay, I have space left only to give a brief discussion of operations in France.

The revelations of Italian Prime Minister Andreotti took Socialist François Mitterrand, the president of France from 1981 to 1995, by surprise. When questioned by the French press in 1990, Mitterrand made attempts to distance himself from the French secret army, claiming it had been closed down long ago. He said: "When I arrived I didn't have much left to dissolve. There only remained a few remnants, of which I learned the existence with some surprise because everyone had forgotten about them."[44]

Italian Prime Minister Andreotti, however, did not appreciate the way in which la Grande Nation tried to play down its role in the stay-behind conspiracy. He mercilessly declared to the press that the French secret army, far from having been closed down long ago, had recently—on October 24, 1990—sent representatives to a secret meeting of the NATO stay-behind council Allied Clandestine Committee (ACC) in Brussels. When this allegation was confirmed, it caused considerable embarrassment in Paris. Mitterrand refused any further comment.

Retired CIA officer Edward Barnes, who during the French Fourth Republic had worked for the CIA in France before leaving the country in 1956, was willing to provide some information. As the fear of the strong French communists persisted, Barnes explained, the French military intelligence service SDECE (Service de Documentation Extérieure et de Contre-Espionnage), under Henri Alexis Ribiere, set up a secret anti-communist army. "There were probably a lot of Frenchmen who wanted to be ready if something happened," Barnes argued. Recalling his own work in France, he said that a Soviet occupation was the primary motivation of the French secret army, while promoting anti-communist political activity in the country "might have been a secondary consideration."[45]

Terrorist Actions in Algeria

In the early 1960s, large segments of the French military and intelligence services started to disapprove strongly of President Charles de Gaulle's intention to allow Algeria, the former colony, to become an independent country. The secret army, perceiving De Gaulle's government as an enemy, evidently engaged in strategy-of-tension operations against it. Some "terrorist actions" against de

Gaulle and his Algerian peace plan had been carried out by groups that included "a limited number of people" from the French stay-behind network, admitted Admiral Pierre Lacoste, former director of the French military intelligence service (DGSE, formerly called SDECE), in 1990. Lacoste, who resigned in 1985 after the DGSE blew up the Greenpeace ship *Rainbow Warrior* while it was protesting French atomic testing in the Pacific, argued that despite its links to terrorism, France's stay-behind program was justified by Soviet contingency plans for invasion.[46]

One officer who promoted strategy-of-tension terror tactics during this period was Yves Guerin-Serac, a Catholic militant anti-communist. A specialist in secret warfare, he had served in Korea, Vietnam, and (as a member of the French 11th Demi-Brigade Parachutiste du Choc) in the war in Algeria. French intelligence service author Roger Faligot called this unit "the iron spear of the secret war in Algeria from 1954 to 1962."[47] By 1954, 300 men of this special force had arrived in Algeria. Most of them had extensive covert action and anti-guerrilla experience, having come directly from Vietnam after France's defeat at the battle of Dien Bien Phu had led France to give up its attempt to recolonize that country. The mission of Serac and his colleagues was crystal clear: To defeat the Algerian Liberation Front (FLN) in northern Africa by all means after France's humiliating defeats in World War II and Vietnam. This effort included strategy-of-tension operations designed to discredit the Algerian liberation movement.

After the defeat of the French and Algeria's declaration of independence in 1962, the secret war did not end for Guerin-Serac, who, together with other officers, felt betrayed by the French government and decided to continue their secret war. Serac knew exactly how a strategy-of-tension operation had to be carried out in order to discredit the communists and the members of liberation movements across the globe. In a November 1969 text, "Our Political Activity," Serac and other officers stressed that they had to infiltrate the enemy, then carry out atrocities in its name. They wrote:

> Our belief is that the first phase of political activity ought to be to create the conditions favoring the installation of chaos in all of the regime's structures.... In our view the first move we should make is to destroy the structure of the democratic state, under the cover of communist and pro-Chinese activities. Moreover, we have people who have infiltrated these groups and obviously we will have to

tailor our actions to the ethos of the milieu—propaganda and action of a sort which will seem to have emanated from our communist adversaries.... That will create a feeling of hostility toward those who threaten the peace of each and every nation, and at the same time we must raise up as defender of the citizenry against the disintegration brought about by terrorism and subversion.[48]

Italian judge Guido Salvini, who investigated the strategy of tension, found that Serac had indeed carried out the dark strategy-of-tension plans. He wrote:

In 1975 the group of Guerin Serac, together with the American Salby and militant French, Italian and Spanish rightists, organized a series of bomb attacks.... The bombs were planted at Algerian embassies in four different countries, France, Germany, Italy and Great Britain.... In reality the bombings were carried out by the group of Guerin Serac, who thus demonstrated his great camouflage and infiltration capabilities.... The bomb in front of the Algerian embassy in Frankfurt did not blow up, and was meticulously analyzed by the German police.... [I]t is important to notice the complex fabrication of the bomb. It contained C4, an explosive exclusively used by the US forces, which has never been used in any of the anarchist bombings.[49]

These statements by and about Guerin-Sarac provide undeniable evidence of the fact that secret armies in western Europe engaged in terrorist killings of innocent civilians to achieve political objectives. These secret armies, as we have seen, operated with guidance from the CIA and NATO, hence from US intelligence and military officers. I turn now to the question of strategy-of-tension operations in the United States itself.

The United States

In the United States, the strategy of tension was prominently advocated in the early 1960s by the highest ranking officer in the Pentagon—General Lyman Lemnitzer, chairman of the Joint Chiefs of Staff—as a pretext to convince the US public of the need to invade Cuba and overthrow Castro. Lemnitzer, who died in 1988, had been one of the senior officers sent to negotiate the Italian surrender in 1943 and the German surrender in 1945. After fighting in Korea, he became, in 1960, chairman of the Joint Chiefs of Staff. Following the CIA's failed Bay of Pigs invasion in 1961, leading generals in the

Pentagon, including Lemnitzer, argued that strategy-of-tension techniques should be used against the US population in order to create a pretext for war. Under the name "Operation Northwoods," they developed a set of combined strategy-of-tension operations designed to shock the US public and discredit Castro.

At the time, President John F. Kennedy and his secretary of defense, Robert McNamara, opposed such operations, which included killing US citizens and involved a large-scale manipulation of the American population. Lemnitzer's plan was, accordingly, not implemented.[50]

As with most strategy-of-tension operations, many years went by before the public learned of Operation Northwoods. Thanks to distinguished US researcher James Bamford, the formerly top secret Operation Northwoods documents became known to the public in April 2001, some months before the 9/11 terrorist attacks, when Bamford published his book *Body of Secrets: An Anatomy of the Ultra Secret National Security Agency*. This was 40 years after the Northwoods plans had been stamped "top secret" inside the Pentagon. The original documents are now available online.[51]

The Operation Northwoods documents specify how the Pentagon planned strategy-of-tension operations. Among other actions, the US officers suggested developing a fake "Communist Cuban terror campaign in the Miami area, in other Florida cities and even in Washington," faking a Cuban air force attack on a civilian jetliner, "sink[ing] a boatload of Cuban refugees (real or simulated)," and concocting a "Remember the *Maine*" incident by blowing up a US ship in Cuban waters and then blaming the incident on Cuban sabotage.

Ever since Bamford published the Operation Northwoods documents, those interested in the strategy of tension have wondered how far certain radical groups within the Pentagon were willing to go and what chance the US public and other nations had of discovering and stopping such plans. Bamford wondered whether Operation Northwoods was the most corrupt plan ever created by the US government, or whether the Gulf of Tonkin incident of 1964 — the incident that provoked America's full-fledged war in Vietnam, which led to the deaths of 56,000 US soldiers and 3 million Vietnamese — had been a typical strategy-of-tension operation designed and carried out by the Pentagon. "[I]n light of the Operation Northwoods documents," Bamford concluded, "it is clear that deceiving the public and trumping up wars for Americans to fight and die in was standard, approved policy at the highest levels of the Pentagon."[52]

Conclusion

The two main arguments against the view that the attacks of 9/11 were influenced by the US government and its military, in either a LIHOP or MIHOP scenario, have been a priori arguments. One of these is that civilized Western governments in general, and the US government in particular, would never do such a heinous thing. The other main a priori argument is that if the attacks of 9/11 were carried out by forces within America's own government, this fact could not have remained secret for this long. The information in this chapter shows both of these arguments to be dubious at best.

SEVEN

9/11, Texas A&M University, and Heresy

Morgan Reynolds

"Every violation of truth is not only a sort of suicide in the liar, but is a stab at the health of human society."
—Ralph Waldo Emerson, 1841

There is an amazing intersection between 9/11, the state of Texas, the Bush family, and Texas A&M University. It reminds me of the JFK assassination plot, another intersection of Texas and national conspiracy.

In June, 2005, my suspicion that 9/11 was a false-flag operation committed by the US government in consort with selected outsiders became widely known after UPI, the *Washington Times*, and the Drudge Report picked up the story. A principal reason that my article—"Why did the Trade Center Sky Scrapers Collapse?"[1]—garnered such "near-mainstream" attention was that I served for 16 months as chief economist at the US Department of Labor in 2001–2002. I was, therefore, a Bush appointee during George W. Bush's first term. And I was the first official from the Bush administration to declare the official 9/11 account bogus.

Among the lessons I learned in coping with the many reactions to my article, some intense, was the response of the academic community when the official conspiracy theory of 9/11 was challenged, primarily a deafening silence, with a few notable exceptions. Only one colleague in my department, for instance, called me on the telephone to ask what was going on. During the course of our conversation I told him that he was a scholar and a gentleman for trying to get my side of the story. My university, Texas A&M University, the oldest public institution of higher learning in the Lone Star state, where I had been an active faculty member for 28 years, went beyond a cool silence and quickly weighed in with this statement:

> The following is a statement from Texas A&M University regarding recent news reports about the collapse of the World Trade Center on 9/11.
>
> Dr. Morgan Reynolds is retired from Texas A&M University, but holds the title of Professor Emeritus—an honorary title bestowed upon select tenured faculty, who have retired with ten or more years of service.... Any statements made by Dr. Reynolds are in his capacity as a private citizen and do not represent the views of Texas A&M University. Below is a statement released yesterday by Dr. Robert M. Gates, President of Texas A&M University:
>
> "The American people know what they saw with their own eyes on September 11, 2001. To suggest any kind of government conspiracy in the events of that day goes beyond the pale."[2]

Dealing with Heresy in Texas

Universities are supposedly about the life of the mind, but it would be hard to craft a more anti-intellectual statement than that of Robert Gates. The official A&M statement might have stopped with the first part, predictable enough and not especially oppressive for today's higher education establishment.[3] But Gates went much further. The first part of Gates's statement says that people "know what they saw with their own eyes." What does that mean? The clear implication is that we have no need to investigate further: first impressions are final impressions. CNN and the government told us what we saw, what to believe. The media always separate the real from fake on TV. So we should accept what we were told and move on.

Maybe I am too suspicious about government and its deceptions and a step slow to boot, but I am still trying to figure out what happened with four reported airliner crashes, all of which yielded little or no wreckage and none of which were investigated by the NTSB, not to mention many other mysterious aspects of that blood-soaked morning.

But even if people properly understood what they saw that morning, the implication from Gates is that we should not ask such questions as: Why did this happen? Who did it? How did they pull it off? What happened to the CIA and other intelligence services? Why was the entire northeast undefended by our air force that murderous morning? How could three steel skyscrapers collapse so neatly at nearly free-fall speed? After these spectacular crimes, why did officials destroy evidence?[4] Why were thorough investigations resisted if officials have nothing to hide? Why has not a single bureaucrat or disgraced warrior been disciplined? And the most important question about the official account of 9/11: Where is the proof? Proof is evidence that can be verified and therefore trusted, in contrast with the inaccessible and uncorroborated pabulum dished out by the 9/11 Commission.[5] The Bush administration's view is that evidence to back up the official conspiracy doctrine of 9/11—that a rag-tag band of 19 young Arabs plus a few cave dwellers in Afghanistan pulled off these atrocities, unaided—is unnecessary in our post-9/11 world. Government need not meet the standard of proving the case in criminal court. No, the government can just declare that 9/11 "means war." The US and British governments promised to produce a "white paper" to prove that Osama bin Laden and his suicidal band of Islamic fanatics committed these atrocities. But these promises have been flushed down the memory hole. While the FBI puts bin Laden at the top of its international most wanted list, he is not actually wanted for 9/11 because, as the FBI chief of investigative publicity shockingly admitted in June 2006, "The FBI has no hard evidence connecting Bin Laden to 9/11."[6]

To doubt government doctrine is heresy or, as Gates puts it, "To suggest any kind of government conspiracy in the events of that day goes beyond the pale." But the first questions the police ask when investigating a crime are: *Cui bono*—Who benefits? Who had the motive? Who had the means? Who had the opportunity? Certainly the US government benefited immensely from 9/11 and cannot therefore be dropped from any rational list of suspect organizations. Would it be the first time in history that a government provoked or staged an attack on its own people to stimulate the juices of war? Hardly (as the chapters in this volume by Daniele Ganser and Ola Tunander show). By extension, I guess, questions and answers about the initiation of the Mexican-American war, the sinking of the USS *Maine*, the sinking of the *Lusitania*, the Reichstag fire, the attack on Pearl Harbor, the Bay of Pigs conspiracy, Operation Northwoods, JFK's assassination, Gulf of Tonkin disinformation, Nixon's Watergate conspiracy, Reagan's Iran-Contra conspiracy, the first President Bush's Kuwaiti baby incubator hoax, the present administration's Iraqi WMD fraud, along with countless other cases of skullduggery since Nero burned Rome to blame the Christians, are verboten.[7] Given this long history, there is no basis for an a priori claim that our government cannot be suspected of lying to us about 9/11.

To raise that possibility, Gates suggests, puts one "beyond the pale," which means "[o]utside the normal limits of good behavior, what is acceptable." The expression comes from the 16th century, when "the pale" was the name for the limited area of English government around Calais or Dublin, and the people who lived beyond it were considered "uncivilized barbarians."[8] In Gates's formulation, it is as if "the pale" is the university and my questioning the official 9/11 story is beyond its province. But in fact, such questioning is what the university is founded on. Consider these portions of the mission statement of the institution he guides:

> Texas A&M University is dedicated to the discovery, development, communication, and application of knowledge in a wide range of academic and professional fields. Its mission of providing the highest quality undergraduate and graduate programs is inseparable from its mission of developing new understandings through research and creativity.... Texas A&M assumes as its historic trust the maintenance of freedom of inquiry and an intellectual environment nurturing the human mind and spirit.... In the twenty-first century, Texas A&M University seeks to assume a place of preeminence among public universities while respecting its history and traditions.[9]

A&M is dedicated to the discovery and development of knowledge? Developing new understandings? Research and creativity? Freedom of inquiry? An intellectual environment? Really? The statement by Gates serves none of these purposes. In fact, Gates's anti-research message reached the A&M faculty loud and clear. It was another signal to steer wide of white-hot topics such as depleted uranium, stolen elections via electronic vote fraud, and, most of all, 9/11.

In a better world, with a university managed more or less in accord with its founding principles, perhaps a meeting of the Board of Regents would have been called to consider the president's remarks. Instead, there is reason to suspect that they agreed with Gates. One A&M board member of interest is Lowry Mays, namesake of the A&M Business School and former CEO and current chairman of the board of Clear Channel Communications.[10] Clear Channel owns and operates 1,225 radio stations and 39 TV stations. This media giant, aptly termed "radio's big bully," also dominates concert venues and touring promotions.[11] Concentrated corporate media, of course, have acted as a government megaphone, largely blocking out criticism of the official 9/11 account and the lies that led our troops into the disastrous war in Iraq. Clear Channel, a Texas-based company that is "tight" with George W. Bush, lowers its hammer on political dissent as it pleases. Among its credits, the company has arranged pro-war rallies, targeted the Dixie Chicks after lead singer Natalie Maines criticized President Bush, and terminated "shock jock" Howard Stern, allegedly for "indecency," but more likely because Stern came out against Bush.[12] Stern even had 9/11 skeptics as guests and "told his 13 million listeners that he did not believe a commercial airliner hit the Pentagon; a cruise missile, he said, was a far more plausible explanation."[13] Mays is a Bush insider whose value system probably does not rank freedom of inquiry, open debate, logic, and evidence near the top. Clear Channel is a powerful example of why the internet, satellite radio, and alternative media must be kept as free as possible from central political control.

A&M's administration claims that it strives mightily for an environment in which "each person's individuality and contributions are respected." The school also has its Aggie code of honor: "An Aggie does not lie, cheat, or steal or tolerate those who do."[14] A lie includes "anything meant to deceive or give a wrong impression." Gates endorses the Aggie code 100 percent because, he says, "Choosing to join the community obligates each member to a code of civilized behavior.... We should all aspire to conduct ourselves with respect for others, the highest ethical standards and personal integrity."[15] Yet his statement, in which he declares my analysis of 9/11 "beyond the pale," seems designed to deceive by implying that what happened on 9/11 is entirely settled and that there is no reason to suspect US government complicity. Gates leads by example and in this case the lesson for Aggies is that there is no need to challenge a serious analysis by pointing to deficiencies of logic and evidence. It is sufficient simply to denounce it. I fail to see any respect for "individuality and contributions" in that tactic.

The general problem, of course, goes far beyond the personalities at Texas A&M or the unique culture of Aggieland. Universities are an integral part of the establishment and therefore independent-minded scholars face serious disincentives if their interests should stray "beyond the pale." Brigham Young University physicist Steven Jones, for example, has had to reach an accommodation with his dean to continue his research on what brought down three buildings at the World Trade Center on 9/11. Professor Jones has received various communications from outside the university promising rewards if he changes his research agenda and punishments if he does not. Universities are big businesses, and growing revenues from government grants, legislative appropriations, and corporate contracts are key. Noble purposes still play a role but rarely dominate when they conflict with more money.

2020 Vision at A&M and the Space Command

A few years ago, Texas A&M initiated Vision 2020, the University's "roadmap for attaining its quest to be recognized as a consensus 'top 10' public university by the year 2020."[16] With leaders like Gates in charge, I fail to see how A&M can achieve this.

Ironically, A&M's Vision 2020 was initiated in 1997 by then-President Ray Bowen. In quite a coincidence, the US Space Command published "Vision for 2020" in February of 1997. As David Ray Griffin points out in the present volume, the mission statement at the head of this document reads: "US Space Command—dominating the space dimension of military operations to protect US interests and investment."[17] There is no mention of freedom, democracy, and human rights, but plenty about "full spectrum dominance," which will involve merging "space superiority with land, sea, and air superiority" and doing it all to protect US commercial interests. Weaponization and dominance in space would include the power "to deny others the use of space." As if to emphasize its aggressive intent, the logo of one of the program's divisions is: "In Your Face from Outer Space."[18] At a minimum, should not the Defense Department revert to its previous name, the War Department?

The link between the crimes of 9/11 and the increased militarization of space is tighter than you might at first believe. At a press conference on 9/11 itself held by Secretary of Defense Donald Rumsfeld, the chair of the Senate Armed Services Committee was berated in these words: "Senator Levin, you and other Democrats in Congress have voiced fear that you simply don't have enough money for the large increase in defense that the Pentagon is seeking, especially for missile defense.... Does this sort of thing convince you that an emergency exists in this country to increase defense spending?"[19] The attacks of 9/11, understood as a new Pearl Harbor, were used by Rumsfeld to force Congress to increase the military budget, especially for the US Space Command.

Rumsfeld, moreover, was not alone in this lust among the DoD leadership. General Richard Myers, who was the acting chairman of the Joint Chiefs on 9/11, was previously head of the US Space Command. Widely known as "General Starwars," he evidently supervised the writing of "Vision for 2020." In addition, General Ralph E. Eberhart, who as commander of NORAD was in charge of the defense of North America on 9/11, was also the commander of Space Command.[20]

These three men at the top of DoD, entrusted to "support and defend the Constitution of the United States against all enemies, foreign and domestic," inexplicably failed totally and catastrophically to defend America that day.[21] The British, while not required to fall on their swords, at least have a tradition of high officials resigning in the event of abysmal failure on their watch. We are apparently quite different here, with conspicuous failure richly rewarded. But was the Rumsfeld-Myers-Eberhart 9/11 performance really a failure? It can be regarded as an example of "failing upward," given the immense budget increases for the military, including the Space Command, that followed, along with the initiation of an endless war on terror, the invasion of two weak Muslim nations, and plans for more. How much of the new funding bonanza has spilled over to space-grant schools like A&M I know not.[22]

Who is Robert M. Gates?

While I do not want to launch an ad hominem attack on Gates, we can hardly overlook his extraordinary credentials, experience, and qualifications. Why is this man president of a major state university? His appointment tells us a lot about the military-industrial complex, the global domination project (to use Richard Falk's term[23]), and the present and future of American universities.

Gates had a 26-year career as an intelligence professional, including 9 years on the National Security Council under four presidents of both major parties.[24] After starting at the CIA in 1966 as an intelligence analyst, he was the only entry-level CIA employee to rise to director. (He was appointed to that position by George H.

W. Bush in 1991.) The Bush family puts a premium on personal loyalty, and Gates is clearly a Bush family loyalist. Gates's own memoir, *From the Shadows*, whose subtitle proclaims himself "the ultimate insider," fawns over the first President Bush.[25] When Gates observed the Soviet Union's collapse from his CIA perch in 1991, this "joyless victory" perhaps led Gates to think about how to create a new enemy to sustain the enormous budgets of the CIA and the military-industrial complex. If he had special insight into the 9/11 hoax, this fact might partly explain his eagerness to "silence" an A&M faculty skeptic.[26]

Gates was first nominated to be the director of Central Intelligence in 1987 by President Ronald Reagan, who was known as the Great Delegator (which may mean that Gates was really nominated by George H. W. Bush assisted by James Baker), at the height of the controversy over the criminal sale of arms to Khomeini and transfer of money to the Contras. But Gates, facing rejection, withdrew.[27] Tom Polgar, a CIA station chief and staffer on the Senate Select Committee on Iran-Contra, wrote in an op-ed piece: "My objections to Gates center on his performance during the Iran-contra affair.... Throughout it, Gates acted as if he was in a complete fog or was interested primarily in keeping the truth from being aired in public or from reaching Congress."[28] During Iran-Contra, Gates was CIA deputy director for intelligence, then the deputy director of Central Intelligence (hence the number two man), and finally the acting director. Gates was close to Iran-Contra figures and in a strong position to know about what was going on. Although Gates was an early target of investigations, Independent Counsel Lawrence E. Walsh ultimately decided not to prosecute Gates for perjury without stronger evidence. It appears that Gates tried to protect the Agency by leaving aggressive criminal activity to Col. Oliver North and company, but that Gates dissembled when he claimed to suffer from "recall failures" while testifying before the grand jury. In his Final Report of August 4, 1993, Walsh wrote:

> Notwithstanding Independent Counsel's disbelief of Gates, Independent Counsel was not confident that Kerr's testimony, without the support of another witness to his conversation with Gates, would be enough to charge Gates with perjury or false statements for his testimony concerning the timing of his knowledge of the diversion.... The question was whether there was proof beyond a reasonable doubt that Gates deliberately lied in

denying knowledge of North's operational activities. A case would have depended on the testimony of [John] Poindexter. [Alan] Fiers would not testify that he supplied Gates with the details of North's activities. In the end, Independent Counsel concluded that the question was too close to justify the commitment of resources. There were stronger, equally important cases to be tried.[29]

Gates gives us his take on Iran-Contra in his memoirs. It contains, of course, no admission of guilty conduct on his part. He just did not know much, he claims, saying:

> What I describe below I learned only in the course of the Iran-Contra investigations.... I knew very little about the fund-raising and virtually nothing about the NSC's operational role.... I was caught in the middle.... The details of all this were known only to a handful of people at CIA headquarters. I was not among them.... I had no knowledge of Casey's close working relationship with North. (311, 391, 392, 415)

Being out of the loop on the main covert operation of the era does not fit the definition of the "ultimate insider," deputy director for intelligence since 1982, deputy director of central intelligence from April 1986 through March 1989, a man whose office adjoined Bill Casey's, and who shared his chief of staff (410). Gates admits some regret about his failure to act against criminals during the Iran-Contra Affair (416–417), but if he had actually known nothing, there would be no cause for regret. Gates was close to then Director Casey and asserts that "With respect to the Iran arms-for-hostages operation, Casey was involved from the beginning and... the only senior official who wholeheartedly backed the idea from the outset"(401). Despite Casey's deep involvement, Gates argues that Casey did not know about the diversion of funds to the Contras from the Iran operation. Knowing how Washington works, I consider this idea, which enhances the odds that Gates was in the dark, far-fetched. More plausible accounts suggest otherwise.[30]

What to make of Gates's Iran-Contra behavior? At the very least, Gates did not live up to the Aggie Code. He, in effect, defended a government of (lawless) men, not a government of laws. The Boland amendment, with its restrictions on the executive, is indisputably binding law.[31]

The most glaring defect of Gates's sanitized screenplay about Iran-Contra is the absence of George H. W. Bush, whose presidential library and museum (along with the Bush School of Government and

Public Service) are at Texas A&M. On Christmas eve of 1992, Bush, defeated for reelection, pardoned six former government employees implicated in Iran-Contra, most prominently former Secretary of Defense Caspar Weinberger. Weinberger was scheduled to stand trial for lying to Congress about his knowledge of arms sales to Khomeini and concealing 1,700 pages of his personal diary detailing discussions with other officials about these matters. Because Weinberger's notes referred to Bush's endorsement of the secret shipments to Iran, thereby contradicting Bush's claims that he had only peripheral knowledge of the arms deal and aid to the Contras, Bush's pardon had the happy effect of thwarting an expected order to appear before a grand jury or be indicted.

A *New York Times* editorial on Christmas, entitled "Mr. Bush's Unpardonable Act," charged: "Mr. Bush remains implicated in Iran-Contra and in that sense he has shamelessly pardoned himself."[32] A furious Lawrence Walsh, likening the pardons to Nixon's Saturday Night Massacre, charged: "The Iran-contra cover-up, which has continued for more than six years, has now been completed." Bush responded that the Walsh probe constituted an attempt to criminalize a policy dispute between the legislative and executive branches, although in his diary he confessed: "The pardon of Weinberger will put a tarnish, kind of a downer, on our legacy."[33] In addition to Weinberger, Bush pardoned Duane R. Clarridge, Clair E. George, Robert C. "Bud" McFarlane, Elliott Abrams, and Alan G. Fiers Jr.[34]

Gates defends the absurd official tale about 9/11, according to which, in the words of the 9/11 Commission, "This immeasurable pain was inflicted by 19 young Arabs acting at the behest of Islamist extremists headquartered in distant Afghanistan."[35] But his status as an "ultimate insider," especially within the world of US intelligence, means that he surely knows better, much better. During Gates's CIA watch in the 1980s, the Agency created al-Qaeda, the Taliban, and Osama bin Laden as anti-Soviet, pro-western assets. Although Gates would never admit it, he has to know that, in the words of Webster Tarpley, "High-profile international terrorism is not spontaneous: it is artificial and synthetic."[36]

The evidence provided by Tarpley and many other writers, including some in the present volume, suggests that 9/11 is not about the sociology of the Middle East but about false-flag state terrorism on the part of the United States and one or more of its allies. The

Bush–bin Laden connection goes back to the 1970s.[37] Osama will prove elusive as long as he remains a "necessary enemy"[38] in the present American version of what Daniele Ganser and Ola Tunander, in this volume, call "the strategy of tension."

Given the background of Robert M. Gates, it is hard to believe that he does not know this. His attempt to stifle any serious questioning of the official story about 9/11 can, accordingly, be suspected of being part of the cover-up.

Academics and Technical Experts on 9/11

9/11 has clearly become the linchpin of US domestic and foreign policy. Overwhelming evidence backs up this claim.[39] For example, on September 30, 2005, Secretary of State Condoleezza Rice said at Princeton University:

> But if you believe, as I do and as President Bush does, that the root cause of September 11th was the violent expression of a global extremist ideology, an ideology rooted in the oppression and despair of the modern Middle East, then we must speak [sic] to remove the source of this terror by transforming that troubled region. If you believe as we do, then it cannot be denied that we are standing at an extraordinary moment in history.[40]

It is a revealing statement, an unintended psychological projection of this administration's madness. September 11th was indeed, as Rice says, the "violent expression of a global extremist ideology." But the villains most likely were not those that she would have us believe. We stand at an extraordinary moment in history to be sure, witnessing an administration drunk on its own "global extremist ideology," supposedly "transforming that troubled region" and running amuck in the world. Or consider this statement by neoconservative columnist Charles Krauthammer, in which the fear-card is played to the hilt: "For all the Vietnam nostalgia at the Washington march," Krauthammer wrote in October 2005, "things are different today. In Vietnam it could never be plausibly argued that Ho Chi Minh was training commandos to bring down skyscrapers in New York City. Today, however, Americans know that this is precisely what our jihadist enemies are pledged to do."[41] As administration officials declared that day, 9/11 was an "opportunity," an opportunity to reshape the world—including the US itself.

Why have so few academics and technical experts, such as

physicists and engineers, raised questions about the 9/11 gruel that government has pushed? Why so little investigation and research about this pivotal event in world history? The question almost answers itself with people like Mr. Gates in charge of major research institutions. Partly it is about intimidation, fear, self-censorship, careerism, and assorted incentives and disincentives.

Following the shock of 9/11, research academics and technical experts quickly learned to keep their hands off the subject. The experience of Van Romero, the vice president for research at the New Mexico Institute of Mining and Technology, where he was previously in charge of its research on the effects of explosives on buildings, is illustrative. Romero was quoted by the *Albuquerque Journal* as saying, on 9/11 itself: "My opinion is, based on the videotapes, that after the airplanes hit the World Trade Center there were some explosive devices inside the buildings that caused the towers to collapse." Ten days later, Romero had changed his tune: "Certainly the fire is what caused the building to fail."[42] No new analysis was offered to support this denial that explosives were involved. Proving that hypocrisy pays, Romero has thrived, snaring $15 million in federal money for anti-terrorism and being declared one of the top lobbyists in the country—indeed, a "superstar."[43] It would appear that Romero's change of tune was based on a deeper analysis not of the evidence but of his prospects for success as a lobbyist for governmental funds.

The message telegraphed to academics and scientists by the Romero incident shortly after 9/11 was later reinforced by the dismissal of environmental engineer Kevin Ryan. Ryan was the site manager of Environmental Health Laboratories, a division of Underwriters Laboratories, which had certified the steel components used in construction of the WTC towers for their ability to withstand fires.[44] In November of 2004, Ryan wrote a letter to Dr. Frank Gayle, a metallurgist at the National Institute of Standards and Technology (NIST). Ryan's letter challenged the preliminary NIST metallurgical findings on the WTC collapses, saying: "This story just does not add up. If steel from those buildings did soften or melt, I'm sure we can all agree that this was certainly not due to jet fuel fires of any kind, let alone the briefly burning fires in those towers."

Explaining his reasons for this statement, Ryan said:

[S]teel components were certified to ASTM E119.... [T]he steel applied met those specifications. The time temperature curves for this standard require the samples to be exposed to temperatures around 2,000°F for several hours.... [E]ven un-fireproofed steel will not melt until reaching red-hot temperatures of nearly 3,000°F.... [T]he buildings should have easily withstood the thermal stress caused by pools of burning jet fuel.)

Therefore, the suggestion by one expert "that 2,000°F would melt the high-grade steel used in those buildings makes no sense at all." Ryan even pointed out that Gayle himself suggested "that the steel was probably exposed to temperatures of only about 500°F (250°C), which is what one might expect from a thermodynamic analysis of the situation."

These findings were ignored, Ryan pointed out to Gayle, as the official summary effectively claimed

> that these low temperatures caused exposed bits of the building's steel core to "soften and buckle." Additionally this summary states that the perimeter columns softened, yet your findings make clear that "most perimeter panels (157 of 160) saw no temperature above 250°C degrees." To soften steel for the purposes of forging, normally temperatures need to be above 1,100°C,

four times higher. Ryan thereby rejected NIST's implication that such low temperatures were able not only to "soften the steel in a matter of minutes, but lead to rapid structural collapse."[45]

The absurdity of the official story about the WTC collapses being caused by fires weakening WTC steel is further exposed by another fact: "Corus Construction Corporation performed extensive tests in multiple countries in which they subjected steel-framed carparks, which were uninsulated, to prolonged hydrocarbon fueled fires," writes Jim Hoffman, "and the highest temperatures they recorded in any of the steel beams or columns was a mere 360°C. At that temperature, structural steel loses only about 1 percent of its strength."[46] Besides the fact that steel conducts heat extremely well, so that the heat from the fire in any one part of one of the towers would have quickly been diffused throughout the rest of the building, the towers had redundant strength on the order of 600 percent.[47] Another problem with the official story is that if the fires were hot enough to cause massive steel columns to buckle, some of the aluminum façade should have melted, given the fact that aluminum melts at less than half the temperature required to melt steel.

For these and many other reasons, the official theory about the collapse of the WTC buildings is physically impossible. But the effect of Ryan's speaking out was that he was fired. And what of the less courageous? Aside from the academics in the present volume and a few others, the academy, despite the security for many of tenure, has thus far not been much of a force for truth about 9/11, leaving it up to independent writers, researchers, and the alternative media to carry on the battle for truth and justice. With the academic silence on 9/11, there's "just us," as one wag put it.

Conclusion: Desanctifying the State

Honest analysis of the events of 9/11 is an example of what Murray Rothbard calls the "noble task of Revisionism," that is, "to de-bamboozle: to penetrate the fog of lies and deception of the State and its Court Intellectuals, and to present to the public the true history of the motivation, the nature, and the consequences of State activity."[48] Anyone who penetrates the fog of state deception to the truth, the reality behind the false appearances, effectively desanctifies the state in the eyes of the previously deceived public. That is why the establishment reacts sharply to discredit revisionists with credentials and prestige who get close to the truth about 9/11 and other gigantic hoaxes. If the truth about these matters were revealed and widely embraced, it would prove ruinous to the regime.

To desanctify our state in our time, we need to expose the fact that it is motivated by purposes not unlike those of regimes we have (rightly) been taught to despise. Hitler's Nazi state, claiming that it sought only *lebensraum* (room to live), sought suzerainty over resources in economic backwaters, as did fascist Japan. Today, the pugnacious and impulsive George W. Bush, leader of a well-endowed, continental-size nation, seeks "democracy" overseas—that is, global domination, which involves control over oil supplies in economic backwaters, secure pipelines, and related capital investments throughout central Asia, all the way to the Mediterranean. The leaders of other large nations, whether or not their countries are endowed with oil and natural gas, hardly look with favor on "the global domination project." Hence, the stage is primed for major war.

The main pretext for this global domination project has been the attacks of 9/11. Every time the Bush administration is confronted with facts showing that it has broken laws, engaged in torture, or committed other outrages, it deflects these criticisms, in effect justifying its actions, by appealing to 9/11, saying that "it changed everything," so that the president, to carry out his charge to protect the American people, cannot be hamstrung by pre-9/11 niceties.

To have any hope for a sane, peaceful, and better world, therefore, we must desanctify 9/11, showing that, far from being an attack by rag-tag terrorists that showed American to be so vulnerable that they must now give up their outmoded ideas about civil liberties and torture, it was a false-flag attack carried out by forces within our own government, aided by selected outsiders. Surely there can be no higher duty for academics and other intellectuals at this time than to expose the big lie of 9/11, thereby undermining the primary pretext for the global domination project.

Despite all the clampdowns,[49] hoaxes, and ruses by the Bush administration, time is not on the side of the perpetrators of 9/11. As emotion fades, what remains is an absurd conspiracy theory to "explain" these crimes. Ask people in everyday life if they are satisfied with the official 9/11 explanation. I have found that very few are. Many suspect foul play, some kind of inside job. But the controlled media will not reveal this fact.

While history never repeats itself exactly, it rhymes, and the model is the JFK assassination. The rogue network behind this operation was never busted and it has carried on to the present. Less than one in five polled believe the Warren Commission "lone nut" theory, and a similar opinion is destined for the Kean–Zelikow cover-up about 19 young Arabs. This development, of course, could have breathtaking implications for public perception about the scope of rot in this nation.

Meanwhile, the 9/11 perpetrators hope to run out the clock. Yes, 9/11 researchers are having difficulty figuring out exactly what happened on 9/11 in important respects. But they have made magnificent progress showing the falsity of the official story, such as the official accounts of the destruction of the WTC and the strike on the Pentagon. There's more to come in debunking official doctrine on 9/11. If the perpetrators are not indicted and convicted during their lifetimes, truth will disgrace them at the bar of history, ex-CIA director presidents of major universities notwithstanding.

Given the increased danger to our world by the global domination project, however, it is important that the truth about 9/11 be exposed sooner rather than later. The exposure could come about quite quickly if a large number of college and university professors from all over the country would take their unique position in our nation's civic life seriously and assert their freedom to investigate, across a variety of disciplines, the grave events of 9/11 and its cover-up. Scholars for 9/11 Truth was founded in December 2005, and has made remarkable progress along these lines.[50] With the present essay I hope to encourage more academics across the land to come forward and not be intimidated by colleagues, boards of trustees, or presidents, who, like Robert Gates, appear less interested in the truth than in protecting the powers that be.

EIGHT

Global Ambitions and Geopolitical Wars: The Domestic Challenge

Richard Falk

There are many continuities between the global ambitions of the Clinton and Bush presidencies, including a shared commitment to sustaining American global preeminence in relation to diplomacy, economic globalization, global military and cultural reach, and the post-Cold War resolve to seize the moment to anchor global governance for the indefinite future in the military-political-financial prowess of Washington/New York.

But there were also some notable differences in style and substance between these two grandiose images of the American global future. Above all, the Bush neoconservative entourage insisted on the need for aggressive warfare and territorial hegemony to realize its global ambitions, while the Clintonites were more willing to allow market forces shaped by neoliberalism to do most of the job, although they were ready to rely on military dominance if challenged. Beyond this, the Bush approach to world order rested on a shift of vital concerns away from Europe and toward the Middle East, and to a lesser extent Southeast Asia, while the Clintonites rested their hopes on sustaining the Atlanticist alliance and Asian engagement that had prevailed in the Cold War and could now be harnessed to cooperate in promoting, under American leadership, a highly beneficial unfolding of economic globalization. Both approaches sought legitimacy through their advocacy of democracy, but the Bush neocons associated their program of democratization with intervention and regime change in antagonistic target countries of geopolitical importance, while the Clinton quasi-liberals favored humanitarian diplomacy and muscular multilateralism at the margins of world politics. Finally, the Bush presidency was cruder in its reassertion of American exceptionalism, especially an insistence on its prerogatives of unilateral war-making and related exemption from emergent standards of legal accountability, while the Clinton presidency gave lip service to an international legal order in which equals were treated equally, while exploring more discreetly its own byways of exception, perhaps most vividly signaled by Madelaine Albright's reference to America as "the indispensable nation."[1]

Neil Smith argues that "American imperial ambition is not new either with the neocons or the post-cold war world but... has been episodic throughout US history." Of both the Clinton and Bush endorsement of imperial ambition, Smith writes that "the Clinton and Bush administrations represent two sides of a single historical moment, namely the zenith of a third moment of US global ambition. In victory and defeat, both were committed to a successful endgame of globalization."[2]

Part of the discrepancy between the Bush and Clinton approaches arises from a split within American capitalism, with finance capital more associated with the non-territorial economistic approach ascendant during the Clinton presidency, and energy-driven territoriality shaping the outlook of the Bush presidency. Simplistically expressed, Wall Street versus Houston. It is obvious that Houston hyper-capitalism on a global scale in the 21st century needs to exert control over the energy reserves of the world, inclining its version of grand strategy toward war and intervention. Wall Street views the trade and capital flows as essentially occurring in a boundaryless world market economy. Despite this, ideological affinities led the main operatives on Wall Street to prefer the Bush administration, mainly because its policies on taxation, welfare, and inheritance were so favorable to the super-rich.

The Israeli factor powerfully reinforced these dispositions in ways that have induced costly wars and self-destructive diplomacy. Both the Clinton and Bush presidencies were overwhelmingly supportive of Israel, insulating the country from international pressures within the United Nations and without, especially associated with the maintenance of the illegal and cruel occupation of Palestinian territory. But the Bush advisors carried this bipartisan pro-Israeli foreign policy a step further, exhibiting responsiveness to the priorities of the far right in Israel, epitomized by the Likud Party. Such influential figures in the Bush entourage as Richard Perle and

Paul Wolfowitz did little to obscure the links between their endorsement of regime change for Iraq, brought about by military means, and the Likud preoccupation with the elimination of the Saddam Hussein leadership in Iraq. At this writing, there is an increasing concern about Israeli pressures to strike suspected Iranian nuclear facilities and the Bush willingness to pursue such a reckless and unlawful policy, possibly relying on nuclear warheads to ensure the destruction of heavily guarded underground sites in Iran.[3]

Interpreting 9/11

It is against this background of geopolitics and pancapitalism that the events of 9/11 are best understood.[4] Despite some pre-9/11 bravado on the part of the Bush White House, principally taking the form of repudiating several widely respected international treaties, the foreign policy of the early months of the Bush leadership was essentially Clintonesque. But we also know that the neoconservative consensus was geopolitically restless, seeking to implement the approach advocated within the Pentagon by Wolfowitz and others as early as 1992 and elaborated at great length in "Rebuilding America's Defenses," a study published in the fall of 2000 by the Project for the New American Century (PNAC), a neocon organization.[5] This restlessness was epitomized by the now notorious acknowledgment in the study that without "a new Pearl Harbor," it would not be possible to obtain the revenue and mandate from the American people to realize global ambitions as delineated by the neocon consensus. In this respect, it was the prudential climate of American "democracy" that stood in the way of pursuing this visionary variant of global ambition. The events of 9/11 dramatically removed this obstacle, overnight creating unified and essentially mindless support in Congress, the media, and the public for a total embrace of the entire agenda of Bush geopolitics of war and imperial encroachment, including tightening the noose of government around the American citizenry beneath the banner of "homeland security."

It is inevitable that this neoconservative recognition of the need for a new Pearl Harbor and the events associated with the 9/11 attacks arouse suspicion. In fact, the surprising element is that despite this fact, and a series of other serious discrepancies between the official version of 9/11 and the evidence, the level of suspicion has been so low and, as a practical matter, relegated to the outer margins of public opinion inhabited by "conspiracy theory" and other supposedly outlandish views of reality.[6]

This management of suspicion is itself suspicious, manifesting a phenomenon that might be described as the enfeeblement of democracy in America. Of course, this capacity to convert suspicion into "conspiracy theory" has a rather long lineage in American experience, which stretches back at least to the sinking of the USS *Maine* to jumpstart the Spanish American War in 1898. More recent instances other than Pearl Harbor itself include the Kennedy assassination of 1963 and the assassinations of Martin Luther King and Robert Kennedy in 1968. Here, then, is the issue: Momentous suspicious events bearing on the legitimacy of the process of governance in the United States have been consistently shielded from mainstream inquiry by being reinscribed as the wild fantasies of "conspiracy theorists." As a result, the issue never gets resolved and lingers in domain of limbo, beclouded by suspicion, but unresolved so far as opinion-makers are concerned—and thus ignored. The stakes associated with the misapprehension of 9/11 are so high that many have made a major effort, at risk to their reputation and possibly their personal safety, to explore these grounds of suspicion in various arenas.

There are two lines of explanations to account for the discrepancies, both of which have deep implications for the future.

The weak hypothesis: The 9/11 attacks occurred as reported by the mainstream media, offering providential political support for the neoconservative worldview, which was quickly actualized by initiating a war against Afghanistan and planning a war against Iraq. In the face of these responses, the constitutional and public order of American society exhibited virtually no capacity or willingness under the stress, trauma, and manipulation following the 9/11 attacks to oppose or even seriously question the embrace of a fiscally and politically catastrophic foreign policy. In this weak view, even if the leadership was not complicit due to an active engagement with the 9/11 attacks, there seems ample evidence of an institutional unwillingness to heed warnings or to risk the exposure of negligence, or something worse, by clearing up discrepancies between official versions of the events and independent scrutiny.[7]

This weak hypothesis is itself a terrible indictment of the condition of American political culture, exhibiting no independent capacity to guard itself against indigenous tendencies toward right-wing political and religious extremism, orientations that contradict the American political design as a republic and abandon its roots in Enlightenment traditions of reason and secularism. A political democracy that adopts a war policy without airing critical views in Congress and the media betrays its identity and does not deserve to be regarded as a democratic society.

The strong hypothesis: The 9/11 attacks would not have been consummated without some activist degree of complicity on the part of operatives prominent in the Bush administration, a viewpoint given high credibility by the explorations of independent intellectuals and scholars, most effectively and comprehensively by David Ray Griffin in his two books on this topic.[8] It is also a position that intrigues the imagination, given the frustrations experienced by the early months of this new neoconservative presidency, the first ever, and seemingly not even truly elected in 2000. There is little doubt that 9/11 firmly entrenched neoconservative approaches and personnel all over the government, especially in the White House and Pentagon. Until this added leverage, the Bush foreign policy was being stymied at the water's edge and lacked much hope of holding onto the reins of power without the onset of a national emergency. Bush's popularity while president was in steady decline in the period prior to 9/11.

It should also be noticed that several of the most influential figures in the neoconservative "revolution" considered themselves disciples of the political theorist Leo Strauss, who encouraged the belief that a responsible political leadership needed to deceive the citizenry to the extent necessary to produce benevolent policies.[9] That is, deception is actually required to achieve virtuous leadership in a liberal democracy, because the public cannot be trusted with the truth.

To the extent that this attitude is prevalent within the US government, it divorces the practices in American democracy from any need to gain the trust of the citizenry. If this is the case, debate is hobbled and virtually irrelevant, as the leadership knows what is best and is prepared to do it. Already we have documented disclosures that the Pentagon has taken steps to overcome objections to the American occupation of Iraq by paying Iraqi journalists, and even mullahs, to plant stories in the Iraqi media that vindicate the American presence in the country. Such conduct represents further grounds for suspicion with respect to official presentations of controversial events, especially when the event provides the basis for a line of policy that was not previously viable politically.

Should some version of this strong hypothesis turn out to be further verified and taken by influential arbiters of reality as accurate, as an increasing number of people here and abroad appear to believe, then it will exhibit the great vulnerability of American constitutionalism to fundamental subversion from within by the most extreme and ethically depraved members of its own political community. It also should give rise to a movement demanding the radical restructuring of constitutional roles within the United States, a process of great importance to the rest of the world, given the American leadership role.

It appears to me on the basis of the available evidence that one of these two lines of explanations of American conduct since 9/11 corresponds with the realities of the situation, but there is also a slight possibility that the cover story, that is, the official explanation, is partially or substantially correct. In that eventuality, which I am positing as remote, the overall assessment is only marginally more reassuring. In this mode of understanding, we assume that the 9/11 attacks were more or less authentically reported in good faith, that the systemic failures to heed various warning signals and to follow normal precautionary procedures resulted from massive bureaucratic snafus, and that the Bush leadership was and is convinced that the al-Qaeda network was directly responsible for the attack and continues to exist, and that a combination of linked and unlinked terrorist groups pose a continuing major security threat to the United States. Beyond this, let us even grant the accuracy of the central contention that the al-Qaeda headquarters were located in southern Afghanistan and that the Taliban leadership then in control of the country showed no willingness or capacity to turn over Osama bin Laden, as well as the rest of the al-Qaeda leadership operating from Afghan bases, and that it refused to end the use of Afghan territory as a training ground and launching pad for transnational terrorism on a grand scale. Given those assumptions, waging war against Afghanistan seemed at the time a plausible, if not entirely warranted, instance of defensive necessity justifying stretching the norms of self-defense in international law to accommodate the American claims.[10] The situation in Afghanistan, given this set of perceptions, presented a credible threat that had shown the capacity and will to inflict severe harm on the United States. Any politically plausible American leadership would in the aftermath of 9/11, under these assumptions and circumstances, have been likely to mount a military response aimed at Afghanistan.

For instance, if the electoral returns had been counted in such a way as to produce a Gore presidency in 2000 and then 9/11 had occurred, the response would in all likelihood have been recourse to "war" and a reliance on the Pentagon to shape the tactical campaign. But note some likely differences in implementation: The tactics would have aimed to destroy the al-Qaeda network as quickly and effectively as possible, with no diversion of resources and attention to Iraq. In fact, to concentrate fully on the terrorist challenge, an imaginative diplomatic initiative in accordance with realist thinking would have been to normalize relations with Iraq, despite the oppressive leadership of Saddam Hussein. In this context, the intervention in Afghanistan, if it had occurred, would have probably led to a greater commitment of American resources, especially manpower, to the establishment of security throughout the country and to the economic-political reconstruction of that long-devastated country. In these conditions, American-led occupation would have resembled, in intention and likely effects, more closely the post-World War II occupations of the defeated Axis powers. One of the factors that hampered this kind of effective occupation by the United States, given the Bush approach, was the priority accorded by the Secretary of Defense, Donald Rumsfeld, to leading a "revolution" in American military forces, relying far more on high technology and "shock-and-awe" tactics and weaponry, and much less on boots on the ground.

Objections to this American response by way of war against Afghanistan could reasonably be put forward, especially in retrospect. It might have been possible to reach the same or better anti-terrorist results through diplomatic pressures and threats and by treating the 9/11 attacks as massive crimes against humanity, calling for enhanced global cooperative law enforcement rather than as an occasion warranting recourse to war. The purported intention to liberate the Afghan people from an oppressive regime was hardly credible. Until mid-2001, the United States was shielding the Taliban regime from sanctions and seeking to facilitate a pipeline deal between UNOCAL and the Afghan government. It was in this period of normal, yet not formal, diplomatic relations with Washington that the worst Taliban abuses occurred. It seems also the case that it was the Northern Alliance leadership supported by Washington that originally was responsible for admitting al-Qaeda and bin Laden to Afghanistan after the latter was expelled from the Sudan.[11] The actual politics and tactics of the war disclose a failure to focus on the terrorist challenge in a serious manner from the outset and seem to be more congruent with an opening move in the grand strategy of the Bush team as depicted in PNAC's "Rebuilding America's Defenses," officially inscribed in US policy in the canonical 2002 *National Strategy of the United States of America*, as well as reflecting the innovative approach to war-fighting so ardently championed by Rumsfeld. What was earlier described as an energy-driven, Israeli-influenced geopolitics, with a Middle East focus, became a credible project for world domination immediately after 9/11. Anti-terrorism was at most a sideshow, but it was valuable as a means to mobilize and discipline the American citizenry. This war mentality, configured around the menace of a non-territorial enemy that could be anywhere and everywhere but also nowhere, overwhelmed American traditions associated with the Rule of Law and constitutional restraint, validating encroachments on domestic freedoms in the name of homeland security and periodically heightening fears of new attacks with its manipulation of color-coded threat levels.[12]

It is confirmatory of this view that Rumsfeld and the military leadership, with the support of the president, were already discussing an invasion of Iraq on September 12, 2001! This is so significant because Iraq, as an enemy, seemed entirely remote from "the war against terrorism" and could only be given a temporary spin as connected to 9/11 by weaving a fabric of falsehoods and deceptions, including the "cooking" of intelligence advice.[13] The selection of Iraq as an imminent threat of great magnitude was grossly and deliberately misleading, devastated as the country was by the 1991 Gulf War (a UN report at the time described the country as driven back to the Stone Age) and twelve years of punishing sanctions that exacted an extraordinarily heavy cost for the Iraqi civilian population, including the death of several hundred thousand Iraqis. Iraq was the ideal choice of adversary from the perspective of the American neoconservative grand strategy: an illegitimate dictatorial regime with no friends abroad and many enemies at home; a country with a weakened capacity to defend its territory, making it a predictable pushover on the battlefield; and a strategic site with the world's second largest proven oil reserves and a central location for establishing military bases, exerting control over the entire Middle East, and satisfying Israeli demands for regime change in Baghdad. Also relevant here is the extent, under-studied in the anti-imperialist literature, to which Rumsfeld's controversial effort to engender a "revolution" in military doctrine and practice operated as a necessary adjunct to Houston geopolitics, which depended on the territorial control of vital energy reserves in the Middle East and Central Asia.

In this respect, it is interesting to note that the Clintonites, including Hillary Clinton and John Kerry, favored sending more American troops in Iraq, relying on more traditional military superiority to sustain global ambitions, but regarded the war in Iraq as more incidental to their view of a market-oriented grand strategy. Their attitude toward Iraq as of this writing in early 2006 is to question the initiation of the war, to regard it as a mistake, but to join with the Bush leadership in insisting that the outcome must be a "victory" for the United States.

It is also the case that the Clintonites are no more ready than the Bush neoconservatives to heed the legitimate grievances of the Arab world, starting with the harsh Israeli occupation of Palestine and the bloody American occupation of Iraq, and, by so heeding, explore the possibilities of shifting Islamic resentments from extremist violence in the direction of negotiated accommodations. In this crucial respect, however 9/11 is viewed and whichever part of the American political establishment is governing, whether rightists or liberals, the underlying encounter between the United States and the Islamic world would almost certainly persist as a cause of inter-civilizational tension, conflict, and violence.

If this mainstream perception of 9/11 as more or less authentic is accepted, the developments since that date are still shocking in the extreme with regard to the political health of American constitutional democracy. The Congress and the media were accomplices in leading the country into an aggressive and dysfunctional war against Iraq, which could not be justified by either defensive necessity or humanitarian emergency under international law, which failed to gain approval in the United Nations Security Council despite feverish and misleading American efforts, and which deeply worried and antagonized traditionally friendly governments and world public opinion. As such, this war has diminished America's legitimacy and leverage as global leader, essentially changing the perception of the United States from "the sole surviving superpower" to that of "the rogue superpower," widely viewed as acting in a manner that is undermining the stability of the ecological, economic, and political future of humanity, generating an entirely avoidable "clash of civilizations," and obstructing processes of global problem-solving. There was also scant show of support for protecting Arab minorities from abuse in the United States and for upholding civil liberties and human rights more generally, with security exceptions only to the extent truly needed.

In part, this pattern exhibits an acquiescence, if not more, on the part of the Clintonites, acknowledging that 9/11 proved that the neoconservatives were essentially right all along in their central contention that it would be impossible to realize American ambitions after the Cold War without recourse to a militarist geopolitics in the Middle East and elsewhere, that a market-driven strategy on its own would not get the job done. It is possible to interpret the hostility of Wall Street to the Clinton presidency, despite his enthusiasm for globalization and a turn toward a market-oriented geopolitics, as a recognition that globalization, to succeed in the face of growing populist and Third World opposition around the world, depended on establishing a global empire, whether light or heavy, and that this required a militarist American foreign policy if it was have any prospect of success. As in the Clinton years, the territorial interests of American workers continue to be jeopardized by trends in the world economy, and the Bush pro-business outlook has done little to arrest this trend, despite its greater attachment to territoriality and sovereignty.[14]

With or without 9/11, the American political system seems incapable of adjusting to the altered conditions of Westphalian twilight.[15] In this contrarian sense, 9/11 changed nothing—nothing, at least, relating to the wider structural challenges associated with establishing a sustainable, equitable, and legitimate world order. In this regard, the failures to address global warming and other ecological dangers in a responsible fashion is as indicative of bankrupt global leadership as is a grand strategy that relies on war to establish a new kind of global empire in the early 21st century, which I have elsewhere called "the global domination project."[16]

The Psycho-Politics of 9/11

Nevertheless, the doubts about the authenticity of the official versions of 9/11 are fundamental and cannot be wished away. True, even without 9/11 and without the neoconservative agenda, needed and beneficial world order adjustments would not have been undertaken by the political forces currently in control of American society at this point. Unless these forces are effectively displaced, these adjustments will not be made in years ahead, even if the deck chairs are reshuffled, and a catastrophic future for the world will be made all but inevitable.

But given the tainted legitimacy of a political system that either allowed 9/11 to happen, in a supreme display of callousness and opportunism, or conspired to make it happen, there is a dark, paralyzing secret harbored in the deepest recesses of the governing processes.[17] The failures of the 9/11 Commission to allay these anxieties, but on the contrary its contribution to increasing the credibility of these anxieties, supports the conclusion that the entire elite structure of authority was unable and unwilling to confront the realities of 9/11, even in an investigative mode of truth-telling. The acute fear that the dark secrets will somehow be exposed also generates strong inhibiting pressures on the citizenry, which are exhibited in many ways, including exaggerated threat perception of enemies within and without, and reliance on the magicians' gift of diverting a perplexed audience from the real dangers. That is, until the dark secret is either revealed or effectively explained, the entire political order will lack the moral agency to perceive the challenges confronting society, much less manifest the capacity to respond successfully.

In this sense, probing the mysteries of 9/11 is a crucial precondition for addressing the structural deficiencies of a globalizing world in desperate need of a humane form of global governance. These mysteries are difficult, almost beyond comprehension, to penetrate because of the many layers of insulation that continue to surround uncomfortable political realities. Never before has it been as imperative to struggle for a true rendering of the 9/11 reality, and never have the incentives been greater to prevent such a rendering.

NINE

9/11 and the 9/11 Wars:
Understanding the Supreme Crimes

John McMurtry

Above the Law: Freedom of the National Security State

In May 2004, leading Americans and the international community were indignant at the tortures of Iraqi prisoners by US occupying forces when undeniable pictures were published. Yet did anyone in the media of record or anyone else in a position of public trust observe the sinister continuity of the torture regime with the long train of lies and crimes of the Bush cabal since they stole the 2000 presidential election?[1] Did anyone recognize that the US invasion of Iraq was "the supreme crime" under international law, the crime which the judges at Nuremberg described as "only differing from other war crimes in that it contains within itself the accumulated evil of the whole"?[2]

In fact, since September 11, 2001, presidential decrees have overridden one law after another, including the US-signed Geneva Convention of 1949 on the treatment of prisoners.[3] Anyone who objected was "lending support to terrorists." Prisoners never charged or tried under any due process of law—hooded, shackled and limb-trussed in abuse that would qualify as cruelty to animals—were paraded in front of tv cameras with no public condemnation. Canadian "human rights specialist" at Harvard and subsequent Liberal Party leadership candidate Michael Ignatieff urged fellow Canadians on public television to join the US in enforcing "human rights" across the globe. CBS blocked a *60 Minutes* report first publicly revealing the years-old torture regime because the pictures of tortured victims were "not very patriotic" to show.[4] The uppermost concern of critics expressing public shock was not the years of torturing innocent people since 2001. It was the "tarnishing of America's image."

The ruling assumption throughout was that the United States has the natural right to be above the law. In the explicit declaration of the September 2002 National Security Strategy document:

> We will take the actions necessary to ensure that our efforts to meet our global security commitments are not impaired by the potential for investigations, inquiry, or prosecution by the International Criminal Court (ICC), whose jurisdiction does not extend to Americans and which we do not accept.[5]

The national press did not disagree. It cheer-led the criminal foreign invasions. The cross-continental reign of terror was glorified as "our troops liberating Iraq" and "fighting the remnants of Saddam's dictatorship." American repudiations of international laws of every kind continued and escalated. The Bush administration in one way or another unilaterally sabotaged the operations of the Convention for the Prevention of the Crime of Genocide, the Kyoto Protocol, the Rights of Children, the Landmines Treaty, the Convention against Racial Discrimination, the Comprehensive [Nuclear Bomb] Test Ban Treaty, the monitoring and testing requirements of the Chemical and Biological Weapons Treaties, the Covenant for Economic, Social and Cultural Rights of Nations, and the proposed Treaty on the Limitation of the Military Use of Outer Space. No expert commentary joined the dots in public. No official opposition appeared. Something deeper than class or nation was at work in the cross-border complicity. To be above the law—including laws applied by the US to prosecute others—was proclaimed as "America's leadership of the Free World," and no Democrat or ally identified the supreme crime, or the mass murder under law, that was in fact occurring in Iraq. The UN Secretary-General illustrated the group-mind compliance by praising a longtime leader of US war crimes, John Negroponte, as "a wonderful ambassador [in Iraq]."[6]

As with the facts of 9/11 itself, denial was the norm, image the public issue, and stable extension of US corporate-military crime the given order.

The administration's criminal occupation of Iraq continued with renewed UN support on June 8, 2004. Everything was vindicated by 9/11. The fact that a similar justification was used decades earlier by the Third Reich was unspeakable. Yet the parallels were undeniable. Behind one corporation-friendly state was the precipitating Reichstag Fire of February 27, 1933, to declare war on all who stood in the way. Behind the successor war state was the destruction of the World Trade

Center to allow the same in different degree. Both industrial super states were supported by familiar transnational corporations working both sides.[7] Both claimed "terrorism" by shadowy others as the ground of "self-defense" by emergency legislation and criminal wars of invasion. No one seemed to notice that the scenario proposed by the Project for the New American Century, many members of which became key members of the Bush administration, was unfolding as planned—"full spectrum US dominance" across the world. The desired "catastrophic and catalyzing event" to ensure that the process was not a long one was 9/11.[8]

Global Market Empire:
Official Complicity with US War Crimes across Borders

There was no public discussion of the idea that 9/11 was a "catastrophic and catalyzing event" to expedite desired geostrategic control over vast regions of once publicly owned oilfields that were no longer within or protected by the Soviet Union. No one appeared to notice that, amid all the disasters of the Iraq occupation, the master strategy had strikingly achieved all of its declared pre-9/11 objectives. It remained unthinkable that the major results of 9/11—the seizure, control, and restructuring of the routes and sources of the vast and publicly owned oil resources of Central Asia ("the Afghanistan War") and the Middle East ("the Iraq War")—could have been the reasons for 9/11. Even former foes of the Iraq invasion, France and Russia included, did not publicly perceive the fact that the war itself was "the supreme crime under international law." The war-criminal occupation was provided unanimous approval of the UN Security Council on October 16, 2003, and again on June 8, 2004, with media congratulations around the world for "the emerging consensus on Iraq."[9] The complicity was now global.

Financial, logistical, and moral assistance for the approved occupation was now demanded from "those concerned about the people of Iraq" by the Bush administration. "The full and free independence of Iraq" proclaimed on June 30, 2004, allowed, in fact, none.[10] US-appointed governors were not granted any control over the armed forces occupying the country, and the original agreed-upon choice by the UN envoy (Lakhdar Brahimi) for the position of prime minister (the anti-Saddam scientist, Hussein Shahristani) was reversed. In his place, with none in the UN remembering the fact, emigré Iyad Allawi, a former killer for

Saddam who was backed by the CIA, was installed as the representative of an organization created by the CIA and Britain's M16.[11] The ever bloodier occupation was called "rebuilding free Iraq." Canada, whose Prime Minister Jean Chretien had bravely refused to join the invasion before being ousted by a corporate media and party campaign led by his pro-US successor, Paul Martin, quietly supplied 15,000 military personnel and 20 warships to occupy Afghanistan and the Persian Gulf.[12] Full approval by the UN Security Council was agreeably granted "after disagreements were resolved by US flexibility." No exposure of the continuing war crimes was acceptable in international media and diplomatic circles.

The armed forces of Israel and the United States all the while grew bolder. They murdered the resistance at will, blew up village houses and families, and continuously enforced a scene from hell on civilian populations in the name of "stopping the terrorists." None of this was perceived as itself terrorist. "The international community's greatest threat" was in this way—as usual—publicly projected onto the victims who resisted. Where does the circle of complicity stop?

"Not for oil" was an unofficial repudiation of the US-led invasion of Iraq that arose from the world's peoples demonstrating in the streets, an historic uprising of life consciousness far ahead of the elite of the New World Order. But not just Middle East oil was involved. In Iraq, a sudden and total expropriation was planned, though seen only in glimpses. Publicly controlled banks, industrial infrastructures, electricity and water supplies, and food production and delivery systems were all time-scheduled for dismantling, control, and marketization by US-led and -subsidized corporations.[1] The full-spectrum confiscation was called the Comprehensive Privatization Plan, a history-turning document not mentioned in the media or parliaments. The Comprehensive Privatization Plan—itself a war crime—was to be complemented by "forgiveness of Iraq's debt," now that it was under US control. Texas bank owner James Baker III, the Bush family's point man for the stolen 2000 US election, was the same person selected to obtain agreement from European and Russian banks and officials for "debt forgiveness" of Iraq under US control.[14]

The stage was set for what the September 25, 2003, *Economist* called "a capitalist dream." The pattern was familiar in outer fact, but the logic of murderous expropriation was not. Unseen through the ruling lens, there was no limit to the US's confiscations of public wealth in the name of the "defense of freedom," from both American taxpayers and the Iraqi and Central Asian peoples. From the US populace came the over $1-billion-a-day armed forces supplied and serviced by US multinational corporations in semi-monopoly or no-bid conditions, which guarantees super profits to be paid into the future. From the Iraqi and Central Asian peoples, natural and built resources were systematically transferred by armed force to foreign control by US-selected transnational corporations. All the while, the media referred to the armed resistance of Iraqis and Afghanis to the occupation of their countries as "terrorism."

That the genocide of a socialist society was going on was unspeakable in acceptable public discourse. Yet as UN Coordinator of Humanitarian Aid Denis Halliday observed, the destruction of civilian infrastructures and the bombing of villages was "in keeping with the definition of genocide in the UN convention."[15] Instead, the ground rules of discourse were that "Saddam" was "a brutal dictator who had to be replaced" and that his "invasion of Kuwait" and the "Islamic terrorists' attack on America" were "the background causes of Iraq's difficulties." That Saddam himself was paid, armed, and directed by the US from obscurity into war against Iran until his 1991 invasion of Kuwait (which the US did not oppose until after it had started) were facts that did not register.[16] Worse, nor did the deaths of over 1,000,000 Iraqis since 1991 by US-led bombings, depleted uranium contamination, and sanctions against repairs of free public water and electricity systems paid for by still publicly owned oil.[17]

Clashing opinions, perpetual news, and academic detail-work all moved within the reference points and coordinates of one meta-program of belief. Isolated facts of mass death were reported by medical witnesses at work behind the scenes. But they appeared and disappeared with no more effect on the ruling mindset than if they had not happened.

The attacks of 9/11 fed perfectly into the conditioned structure of thought that supported genocidal imperialism as "defending our freedom against the Enemy." The bombing, invasion, and occupation of Afghanistan was an act of "necessary self-defense" against "terrorist training camps attacking the US" — terrorist camps that were also first financed, armed, and directed by US intelligence forces.[18] Two years later, "America's New War" to invade and occupy Iraq by armed force in place of UN inspections was propelled by a glaring big lie that no mainstream news source at the time would name as a big lie—Iraq's weapons of mass destruction.

In fact, no one in official culture connected the wars to the call by the Project for the New American Century for "full spectrum dominance" across the globe. No voice audible in the mainstream recognized the war crimes as an issue. No analyst in the mainstream press connected the pattern to the global corporate capitalization of the remaining world.

The Group-Mind that Binds

Iraq was thus "liberated by America" with George Bush and an "absolutely convinced" Tony Blair leading history from their "*cojones* meeting"—"to do what I think is right."[19] "We must hold the course," "win the peace," "not turn our backs"—all official figures in both countries agreed through the lens of the regulating mindset. New leadership would replace old, but the set-points of meaning and purpose were fixed. The systematic genocide of a region-leading economic order and looted cradle of civilization was an act of benevolence to bring "the free market and democracy to another people." As evidenced from the early geostrategic plan to the massively destroyed art treasures and health records in the invasion, the actual people whose lives were being sacrificed and whose economy was being dismantled for foreign profit were hardly given a thought.[20]

The supreme crime, which "accumulates withinitself the evil of the whole," remained unmentioned—as blocked out as the cause of 9/11, which set the supreme crime in motion. Deeper than the presidential cabal's operations lay a ruling meta-program of belief across the ruler–ruled division. Let us call it "the ruling group-mind." Its thrall is strange to theory because it is housed within classes, countries, and cultures, a silent regime of collective thought-system that is not rooted in locale, practice, or productive prestige.[21] It structures the mind itself beneath professional and cultural variation—from New York to Shanghai to Rio de Janeiro.[22] Yet not even psychiatry penetrates its meaning because it cannot speak from a couch. The meaning of the ruling group-mind cannot be elicited from any individual. Marx reified the ruling group-mind's regulating principles as economic "laws of motion," but these cannot explain why people both identify with and reject them.

Until it is laid bare to consciousness, the ruling group-mind may operate within and across societies and selves. Its transcendental set-points may cross borders as a regulating ground of value and meaning. The Canadian Public Broadcasting Corporation of my own country, for example—which is in the pay of no US multinational and accepts orders from no one outside—continuously produced its stories prior to March 20, 2003, within the normalized line of "Saddam's dictatorship" and "the war against terror and weapons of mass destruction." Even as the supreme crime of US military invasion remained unnamed, it was proclaimed as "inevitably" unfolding like a phenomenon of nature with no accountability to law or public interest. A silent clamp-down invisibly awaited anyone who called the accepted meaning into question.

To test the hold of this ruling group-mind across borders, I accepted an invitation to appear on CBC Sunday News right before the US invasion of Iraq, to debate a well-known US geostrategic planner and co-manager of the Project for the New American Century, Thomas Donnelly. I did not remain within the assumed parameters of discussion. I explained that the United States was engaged in launching a criminal war against the Iraqi people and continuing its genocidal destruction of the people's socialized infrastructures of water supplies, electricity, food distribution, and public healthcare and education. To the predictable group-mind reflex of "what about Saddam's brutal dictatorship" and "use of biological weapons against his own people," I pointed out that the US had armed and supported Saddam and his regime in these actions from the beginning. I suggested, in fact, that Donnelly ought to be arrested under the relevant Canadian Criminal Code section, the Crimes Against Humanity Act, for advocating war crimes and crimes against humanity with no justification of self-defense and in sabotage of ongoing and accurate UN weapons inspections. He responded with grimaces and slogans of praise for America's love of freedom since the "US liberation of Europe." Behind the eminent advocate of the murderous invasion was a belief program that could not relate to any reference body beyond itself.

CBC management did not approve. The meta-program continued in operation. The "arrest" phrase was deleted from the 30-minute delayed broadcast. The research reporter who had arranged the debate would not return my inquiries on the debate's feedback, but would only refer to other matters, and was soon no longer on the CBC's major public affairs program. The experimental as well as control conditions yielded a consistent result. Nothing could be seen that did not conform to the understanding of the US as a benevolent power leading the way to a free world and market, even the murderous theft of the resources of faraway countries for private corporate control. Neither fact nor argument could enter the organizing framework of understanding]

Far from the Washington political center and across an international border, during a groundswell of uprising against the coming US invasion, the deep lines of disconnect were at work—the omnipresent on-off switches of the ruling group-mind. Its invisible lines of force are what make us "not know what is going on," although the evidence shows mass murder and is known. Even the *Guardian Weekly*, which had published my correspondence for many years, refused to print it after I named "the supreme crime" about to unfold.

9/11 Denial:
Explaining the Phenomenon across Left–Right Divisions

Four years before 9/11, US National Security Committee advisor to President Carter, Zbigniew Brzezinski, wrote what US geostrategists were already thinking across Republican-Democrat divisions after the collapse of the Soviet Union: "[The United States needs] unhindered financial and economic access [to] Central Asia's natural resources," he advised, "[especially] the enormous economic prize of the natural oil and gas located in the region." But, he continued, it will be "difficult to fashion a consensus on foreign policy issues, except in the circumstances of a truly massive and widely perceived direct external threat."[23] That "truly massive and widely perceived threat" was, of course, provided by 9/11.

Why have such facts, with such clear through-line of purpose and effect, been ignored in public and media discussion? The consensus has, in fact, crossed the poles of left–right division. Even Z-Net has been gatekeeping against the connected meaning.[24] The taboo was encoded into identity structure across ideological oppositions. Any fact exposing the official story was a "conspiracy theory" or, to Z-Net, a "distraction." Given the known pre-9/11 search by US geostrategic planning for a publicly saleable reason to invade central Asia and Iraq, 9/11's occurrence was disconnected from what it provided the ideal pretext for—as explained before 9/11 by the Project for the New American Century as well as Brzezinski. No one denied that legitimation for a militarily imposed new control over the world's main supplies of oil was on the minds of US war planners. The fact was just "disappeared." Each war for oil was wholly disconnected from the known plans to control the region's oil sources by 9/11 deniers across the US political spectrum.

The documented details that expose 9/11 denial will not be repeated here, because this volume and others have already reported them. They are impressively massive in confirming—and are not balanced by any facts disconfirming—the long open pathway to the attacks and the blocking of all independent inquiry since. Even when one faultless sequence of anomalies and coincidences worked continuously in one direction to one vast payoff matrix—the gold at the end of the rainbow of strategic calculation—still the endlessly repeated charge of "conspiracy theory" blocked out all informed questions. For decades, US administrations had claimed an "international communist conspiracy" with little or no evidence for such a vast plot. Suddenly, the rules of meaning were completely reversed. Now even a substantiated hypothesis of a criminal conspiracy within one administration was taboo to consider. Everything before and after 9/11 that substantiated the forbidden meaning was disconnected from or distorted.

When such a chain of denial and distortion is itself blocked out all around and delinked at every joint, the breakdown of normal cognition needs to be explained. US geostrategic mass murder justified by false pretexts of attack was long on the record. Countless thousands of people—sometimes millions, as in Vietnam—had been sacrificed in the past to achieve far less. What could still block informed questions about 9/11? Why would everyday and elite perception across doctrinal and interest conflicts assume that the Bush administration's strategic cabal would not be involved in the construction of 9/11 when it gave the US transnational corporate empire unprecedented domestic and foreign powers? Recall that this same group had arranged for the overturn of state laws to seize the US presidency and then waged a murderous war in Iraq, which was led by many of the same officials who, in a prior Republican administration, presided over death squads and secret deals that destroyed countless lives.

To those who believe that it was not planned, I would ask: What would have been done differently any step of the way if it had all been planned? The real difficulty here is to find any compelling evidence against the hypothesis—for example, some loss or harm to any of the Bush executives who reaped vast rewards by the 9/11 attack. There is no such evidence.

Political history since 9/11 deepened the mystery of the collective mind-lock against the facts of complicity—or worse. Despite subsequent years of spectacular lying about Iraq by the Bush administration, the mass media, foreign affairs respondents, and opposition critics blinkered out the accumulating evidence for a strategically constructed 9/11 attack—the anonymously blocked FBI investigations before 9/11, the ignored intelligence warnings from many foreign state agencies beforehand, and the immediately prior Washington visit of the CIA-advised Pakistani intelligence (ISI) paymaster of one of the alleged lead hijackers.[25] Most remarkably, the laws of physics themselves were disregarded. The instant and inexplicable collapses of the World Trade Center buildings in uniform demolition style could not be explained by fire (plus, in the case of the Twin Towers, the impact of the airplanes) without contradicting the laws of engineering physics.[26]

Here more paradigmatically than the unrecognized war crime itself, a structure of denial and projection decoupled elite and public consciousness from the evidence as if it did not exist. We know Church authorities would not look through Galileo's telescope to examine the astronomical facts. In our contemporary case, the ruling group-mind crossed societies, and the this-worldly facts that it turned away from showed a Bush-administration agenda that deeply opposed the interests of almost everybody else. The dominant refusal of people to see facts against their own interests cannot be explained by existing theories. Only an intersubjective mindset across classes and parties can explain the phenomenon of mass denial.[27]

I take this opportunity to distinguish this intersubjective mind-lock, or ruling group-mind, from the micro concept of "groupthink" associated with the work of Irving L. Janis.[28] He proposes a model for a "defective" decision outcome by a small, isolated group of homogenous and cohesive members in a stress situation—something like the US national security decisions taken by Kennedy's administration that culminated in the Bay of Pigs invasion of Cuba. While there are common operations at work here (principally, moral certitude of cause, stereotyping of opposition, and collective rationalization), "groupthink" in this committee sense is a micro-symptom of the disorder I explain here. How can we define this far deeper and wider syntax of the ruling group-mind, which can hold a whole society or even civilization in thrall? At the risk of being formalistic, I define the disorder as the a priori regulation of everyday and elite consciousness by a normative syntax of perception, understanding, and judgment that is closed to life-and-death facts and presupposed across classes to be certain.

The top-level, secret, and ultimately failed decisions that Janis and co-researchers examine are, I contend, downstream expressions of this more systematic cultural pathology—just as a publicly supported criminal war of aggression is the downstream effect of a normal regime of thought that selects for and approves it, blocking out any standard of value other than operational failure. Janis's model itself may be a symptom of this normalized cognitive disorder by selecting for case study only what is seen to fail, thus excepting even ecogenocides if they are successfully operationalized. The culture of America certainly indicates the signs of a ruling group-mind as a collective thought disorder. On the most general plane, there is the society-wide preoccupation with acts of violence and killing at all levels of the culture—from continuous violent entertainments of sports and everyday spectacles to a robot cop for governor of the most populated state to triumphal carpet bombings of defenseless societies timed for mass consumption on the evening news. The defining pathology of the ruling group-mind is that its operations are indifferent to the destruction of other people's lives. It is a life-blind regime of collective consciousness, which lies behind the world's most lethal external problems.

Who Benefits? The Unthinkable Question of 9/11

As we have seen, "conspiracy theory" is the stigma term to fence off the taboo zone of 9/11. Forbidden thoughts are erased by calling them names. But let us go deeper. Would it not be geostrategically rational—that is, in the economic and foreign policy terms assumed as given by these event managers—to exploit the greatest opportunity in history to establish the "full spectrum dominance" that was planned long before 9/11? Would not the managed risk of being able to control investigations for the next four or eight years and to denounce any accuser as "unpatriotic" and "betraying America" be worth it for the historic prize? Why would this once-in-a-lifetime opportunity not have been considered a possible scenario when history tells us that US national security planning has never really eschewed mass-murderous options? In fact, from the known strategic war-gaming standpoint, wouldn't it be irrational to forfeit a chance to put the greatest treasure in the world under firm US control, with fewer American lives lost than a few months of traffic accidents?

"You are the Haves, and the Have Mores. You are my base," is George W. Bush's known salute to those who have the most. The corporate market structure of consciousness, we know, selects what facts are seen and not seen, in accordance with one deciding value alone: Does it profit us, and can we sell it? Every thinking person knows this. Why, then, has the most elementary query after any crime—*Cui bono*? (Who benefits?)—been totally suspended in public discourse about 9/11? The fabulous payoffs that 9/11 has netted to the oil and military corporations and executives dominating the Bush administration are so immense and so cost-free to them that it is like a very large elephant in the room. Yet even the most self-evident questions have been blinkered out as unspeakable.

The payoffs of 9/11 and the 9/11 Wars to this regime's constituency and chief executives have not been adequately forensically examined. The obvious motives for the deadly event have slipped from public memory. The facts are too disturbing. Yet the vast treasure for the Bush cabal and their corporate constituency was far greater and less risky than any planned by the National Socialist Party of 1930s Germany and its big business backers in America and Europe. The staggering payoffs, which still flow to the beneficiaries, include open access to the world's formerly untouchable and greatest wealth resources; a new command position over public financing for subordinate militaries and police apparatuses across the globe; privatization of the world's richest publicly owned and state-controlled oilfields and the social infrastructures they support; the newly declared right to suspend the historical basis of rule by law, habeas corpus, to protect the reigning order against subversion; legitimation of a president who was not actually elected; diversion of the public eye from the regime's known corrupt supporters and from the setting of energy policy by the most criminally fraudulent corporate leadership in American history; unprecedented new powers for price leveraging of oil supplies; an ongoing cornucopia of lavish contracts for military services for a "war without end"; new police powers across borders to imprison, without right of legal defense, anyone deemed to obstruct an international corporate meeting; and—at the crest of glory instead of ignominy—unlimited new rights of men with draft-dodging pasts to command everyone else.[29]

The problem of the collectively unthinkable runs deep into the psyche. "I can't believe..." is the sign pointing back to the mind-block behind it. These on-off switches of the regulating meta-program of belief are by no means confined to the corporate elite or those benefiting from the war regime. They are the set-points of thought across classes and interests that bond the collaborators as one "Fatherland," "patriotic America," or "Free World." They organize perception itself to conform, and to screen out all that does not. Once these set-points of consciousness are fixed by dividing lines of war, a fateful consequence follows: feeling and awareness are disconnected from facts and relations that conflict with the regulating assumptions of popular identity. In response to the extreme pressures of forcing reality to conform to manufactured delusions, the group and its members become increasingly submerged within a preconscious field of hysteria, denials, and projections. In the case of 9/11 and the 9/11 Wars, two war-criminal invasions of other societies and police-state laws across the world were supported or acquiesced in by the broad US public—with no questions arising in Congress or the press except about the costs to the US invader.

The 9/11 Wars as "Our Freedom": The Logic of Collective Crime

We can see, if we do not turn away, the monstrous pattern across pretexts and wars—a ruling group-mind led by corporate America, harnessed to the US military juggernaut and a bottomless consumer maw that only desires more.[30] This is the underside of "our freedom." All its creatures serve one transnational regime—the globalizing corporate system that occupies within and without with no limit of growth or concern for life. This global capitalism is based on a centuries-old paradigm that has so ossified as to now seem a law of nature—or, for some, a law of God. With war fever as its moving passion, this meta-program becomes mechanically ecogenocidal in its self-concept as the one and only Superpower. The atomized masses of America are made one in a salvational fantasy of triumph over the Enemy.

There is a clear pattern to the madness that expresses this ruling group-mind. What is selected to remove or destroy always advances the global corporate order's subjugation of formerly independent societies and resources, however false the justifications and however defenseless the victims may be. One form of Other is always selected for attack and appropriation—any autonomous, public or civil sector that can be privatized for profit, and any individuals, movements, or societies obstructing this conversion. All who oppose are "communists," "terrorists," or their "sympathizers," and are therefore subject to threats, torture, or death. When the global marketization of peoples happens by "peaceful means," it works by strategic electoral marketing and fiat trade treaties. When it is by armed force, it is preceded by a casus belli for armed crusade against the Enemy. This was 9/11's function.

Since all who are bearers of the ruling group-mind agree by assumption on what "freedom," "growth," and "future prosperity" mean, the only question left is how to get there. The commanding assumptions of belief appear to their creatures as a moral structure of necessity to which "all must adapt to survive." It is not an exaggeration to say that all of planetary existence is now included as an actual or potential object of these "global market laws" of the US imperium—from the genes of first people's seeds to the ocean floors and the skies above. America's military supremacy across the borders of the world is the high-tech investment vector and enforcement arm of the ever-expanding "globalization" of foreign money-capital rule. All conditions of life are progressively converted into its subservient functions as the meaning of "development," "freedom," and "civilization." The 9/11 Wars are the militant forward edge of this march of world rule, and those who purvey and believe its meta-narrative are the complicit functionaries of its advance.

Trade, investment, and political-legal treaties have been the system's mode of transnational advance since 1988, with thousands of articles of prescription codified in such administrative instruments as NAFTA and the WTO, which are armored against any elected legislature debate by their international treaty form. Media and infotainment programs of every kind are its communications relations. But behind all levels of the US-led global corporate system is a syntax of belief that silently selects and excludes what elites and populations think, decide, and expect throughout.[31] It is the internal order of the outer mechanism of destruction.

Populations were thus hypnotized into a set-point of militant or acquiescent compliance. Complex systems do not continue intact unless all their subsystems collaborate. With the media as the speech and sign system of the regulating group-mind, the "9/11 attack on America" permitted what was before impossible. It allowed an illegitimate administration to transmute into America's patriotic champion at war, above accountability and the rule of law. "Defending America from another terrorist attack" became a political blank check for corporate corruption of government expenditures with impunity, war criminal acts and threats across the Islamic and alternative third world, and attacks on civil rights and commons at home. Nothing was fated, but all was undertaken as if it were. The opposing 2004 Democratic platform itself proclaimed the "Post-9/11 World" in which US state-terrorist measures, technologies, inspections, and controls were "not nearly enough."[32] A narcissism of small differences strutted on the stage. All joined in round-the-clock proclamations of the "war against terror" while, hardly seen, the real state terror and corporate despoliation of the planet's conditions of life proceeded at stepped-up levels.

In this way, the disasters of the failed global capitalist experiment were projected onto the "threat of terrorism" of opponents instead. This reversal of cause and effect worked. The public sectors whose collective actions could alone stem and meet the larger world problems were now drained by the military costs of over a billion dollars a day to clear the Middle East and Central Asia of obstacles to the New World Order. The 9/11 Wars and simultaneous multi-hundred-billions of tax cuts to the wealthy bankrupted the social state at the same time. As the fanaticism of the global capitalist crusade grew ever more evident, the recognition of its cognitive disorder was increasingly silenced in the media, textbooks, and classrooms. Market panaceas were now proposed for the war-devastated Middle East, which lacked even intact public water systems.

The United Nations Development Program (UNDP) itself stepped to the same drumbeat as the new global market crusades. It co-sponsored a US-circulated plan for "G-8-Greater-Middle-East Partnership" to prescribe "an economic transformation similar in magnitude to that undertaken by the formerly communist countries of Central and Eastern Europe." Improved life means or livelihoods were not included in either of these capitalist revolutions. Catastrophic declines of real living standards in "the formerly communist countries of Central and Eastern Europe" were ignored. The reduced nutrition of the majority, defunding of free education and health-care provision, and a radically new insecurity of livelihood for workers and pensioners were simply purged from the mind. Economic "reform" in the Middle East was, instead, a fig leaf for the military occupation of the rich oil region for US control. The new market miracle of "micro-finance" was proclaimed. "A mere $100 million a year for five years will lift 1.2 million entrepreneurs out of poverty," it was promised, by "$400 loans to each."[33]

In the historical background, David Rockefeller long ago expressed the lead vectors of the US world empire for a post-nation future. "A supernational sovereignty of an intellectual elite and world bankers," he advised in a statement leaked from the June 1991 Bilderberg annual meeting, "is surely preferable to the national autodetermination practiced in past centuries."

The Religion of America that Justifies All

In the enthusiastic foreground of market worship, tens of millions of poorer and working-class devotees paid evangelicals for the high returns of God's grace, while the most devout awaited Armageddon and the Rapture. For market science itself, the magic of the Invisible Hand infallibly transfigured the limitless desires of market selves into the providential outcome of "the public welfare." The 9/11 Wars were thus launched in a moral universe in which the intersection of divine plan and history was set. America, God's contemporary chosen nation, moved rapidly to fulfill its grand mission—to liberate peoples everywhere to the promised land of "market freedom and democracy." The material plan was full-spectrum US military and corporate dominance with no outer or inner perimeter. The ruling-group-mind transfigured meaning was "the last best hope of humankind."

The conversion of all life organization and conditions into commodities and the turning of money into more money for those who have it was not seen as a problem, because it was already known to be without alternative. Thus ever more of earth's existence was converted into variations of "market growth"—from privatized water systems across the world to the engineered chemicals and genes of future Frankenfoods and obesity, from the oilfields of poor countries to virgin air and cyberspace.[34] Peoples variously rebelled against the instances—in Cochabamba, the Niger Delta, the European food market, and the anti-Star Wars movement—but the ruling meta-program of belief repelled any meaning beyond itself. "Grow or die" was the motto of reproduction and increase, the new evolutionary mechanism on earth.

The fall of the Soviet state was this ideology's "end of history."

9/11 marked a second and less visible turning point toward universal corporate-market rule. That is, it legitimated as "self-defense" pre-emptive armed attack on any movement or force that was opposed—whether unarmed "violence-threatening protestors" in domestic public spaces, or "suspected terrorists" in civilian populations of the militarily occupied world. Behind all the variations of times and conditions, one inner logic determined every step of the post-1988 global market crusades, first by transnational trade and investment treaty-fiats inalterable by elected legislatures and, since 9/11, by the machinery of war.

What before 9/11 was a world becoming aware of the life-despoiling mechanics of the global corporate system and its one-sided decrees binding societies to its agenda was, after 9/11, a reverse "war against terrorism." Disconnection from every real problem of collapsing life-support systems that humanity faces was in this way licensed as a patriotic necessity of the American religion. Any and all societies, parties, or governments that seek any other economic organization are "despotic" and must be eradicated "to defend freedom." Optimal states of expectation—as subsequent history confirms—thus predictably followed in train after the invasion of Iraq in March 2003. War-criminal occupation was perceived as liberation through the lens of the ruling group-mind. In this view, the occupation promised more efficient market relations of production and distribution to the locked-in resources and peoples involved, new private capital formations and freedoms, opportunities for spectacular market growth where before there was none, relief of consumers from the inefficient Arab monopoly of oil, a competitive price system to properly deploy and allocate resources instead of an "Islamic or socialist prison" keeping the people in "backward dependency on handouts and subsidies," and "historic new vistas for foreign capital and local entrepreneurs to lead both Afghani and Iraqi societies out of the dark ages to development and freedom." Annunciations of "the first Islamic market miracle" were on the lips of believers before the electricity was back on.

In ascendant market logic—as F. A. Hayek and his disciple Margaret Thatcher proclaimed from before the beginning of the neo-classical revival—"there is no such thing as society." There is only "the extended capitalist order" upon which human existence depends. Thus when Deputy Secretary of Defense Paul Wolfowitz expected flowers of welcome thrown in the streets in a Paris-like welcome of the liberators, he was simply expressing the ruling market group-mind of which he was a war-planning functionary. He was not alone in his structure of thinking. Two decades of "shock treatment" neoliberalism are the background to the Iraq shock treatment by war. Raising up from backwardness and ignorance is the great deliverance that the neoliberal crusades of the capitalist religion imagine. The complete incapacity of the market-state invaders of Iraq to provide even collective security from attack, or the most basic infrastructures of water and electricity—let alone food and employment or healthcare or education—was not anywhere related to the ruling economic paradigm in terms of whose magical thinking one disaster after another had happened across borders and continents for 20 years—from Argentina to Russia to Indonesia.[35]

"Selling the goods" has many meanings. To universalize God's laws of global freedom and prosperity under money-capital rule is America's providential function. If the ruling calculus does not compute life lost or gained but only priceable assets and gains, and its national-security calculus does not recognize law as binding on actions "to protect US interests and investments abroad," then why not an attack like 9/11 to win the great prize? If the most systemic and global destructions of life in our time (ecological collapse and the obesity-starvation cycle, for example) can continue to escalate even after the consequences are known, then why not 9/11 and a far bigger payoff matrix to the chosen nation?

If the US geopolitical calculus is based on advance of US corporate market interests alone and there are no US-recognized constraints of law on these "national security interests," then why not proceed with the divine mission? If 9/11 was planned by a former lead ally of US national security planners, Osama bin Laden, who had led the "moral equivalents of the founding fathers," as Ronald Reagan called them, then why would 9/11 not be game-planned as a geostrategic option by the warriors of God? We need to bear in mind here that all such strategic planning pivots around the "payoff matrix," the meaning of "rationality" in US economic-military planning since the Cold War against "godless communism" began.[36] Sacrifice of lives to achieve noble objectives has been built into the higher calculus from the start.

America is, after all, the world's savior state—"the leader of the Free World," serving "a higher destiny" to liberate all peoples. "This great country of ours," "the greatest country in the world," "the leader of freedom-loving peoples everywhere," and "the last best hope of humankind" are choral epithets of America's self-description as the anointed superpower of the world. "The idea of America," echoes the last liberal great hope, John Kerry, at the height of his campaign to dislodge a "polar opposite" George Bush as president, "is, I think proudly and chauvinistically, the best idea we've developed in this world."[37]

The self-conception of America as supreme on earth in matters of significance is obligatory in public policy formation and expression of acceptable opinion in America. Backed by "the greatest military power the world has ever seen," the divine sign to believers in the religion of America, the commander-in-chief always decides with God's blessing. No major decision fails to invoke the divine sanctification. Accordingly, bipartisan declarations of certitudes about America's higher calling, supreme power, and benevolence of will are daily incanted as articles of public faith. None may be doubted without accusations of treason.[38]

Such a religion is idolatrous in principle, of course, but this meaning is not possible for believers to recognize. Propelled by a conviction of overriding natural right and with mass-homicidal weapons to enforce its convictions, this fundamentalism overrides natural limits of world ecosystems and regards the most extreme inequality in history as "America's greatness."[39] In this way, the global market's Invisible Hand comes to work as an Old Testament Yahweh. America's God is a jealous God, tolerating no opposition. Fateful historical consequences follow from this closure of belief system to the feedbacks of reality. If the religion of America legitimates limitless money-capital growth and the marketization of all that exists, then it follows that its wars, too, are divinely sanctioned.

"In God We Trust" is appropriately the invocation of solidarity on all American money, just as the words "under God" were inserted into the Pledge of Allegiance to "fight communism" in the 1950s (in violation of the constitutional separation of Church and State prescribed by the Republic's founders).[40] The meaning of "democracy" is not now, as Jefferson or Lincoln thought, self-government by the people. It is the gospel of the religion of America, whose collective self-worship follows one simple algorithm of meaning. This inner catechism of Superpower faith regulates all acceptable public thought in post-9/11 America:

(1) America is the moving line of goodness and freedom in the world; therefore

(2) All who oppose America are the enemy and evil; therefore

(3) The free and the good of America must triumph over the evil enemy to protect the world; therefore

(4) America must always be supreme in its armed force and willing to use it; therefore

(5) America's commander-in-chief must achieve what God's might requires; therefore

(6) America and its president can never commit war crimes against others.

The religion of America is evident once exposed. But as psychiatry has long observed, the unconscious may be fanatically compulsive when not seen. The meta-theme is as old as tyranny. An all-powerful, all-knowing, and jealous Supreme Power rules the world in accordance with an invisible design, and it is the US. The life-and-death ultimatum to all is: "You are either with us or with the terrorists."

The American Republic admits of far higher and saner possibilities. But the future has been foreclosed by public belief in the 9/11 spectacle of attack, which "has changed the whole world." Half a decade later, with the massacres and public debts still mounting, a defining opposition within America has emerged—between those who worship armed force, national supremacy, and money rewards, and those who know better. For the fanatic armies of the imperial God, 9/11 is their sacred holocaust to justify anything—continuous war crimes against third-world peoples, militarization of public wealth, life-blind despoliation of the world's environment, obscene inequality and unprecedented corruption in high places, and cumulative suppression of democratic dissent at home and abroad. For those who are able to think past the pathological loops of this meta-program, the pieces connect into emergent meaning. With or without 9/11 as a pretext for "war without end," the post-1991 global capitalist experiment has failed as a form of economic organization that serves human life and conditions on our planet.

TEN

The War on Terror and the Pax Americana

Ola Tunander

For the Bush administration, terrorism has replaced communism as the "new evil." On September 20, 2001, President George W. Bush, in a much publicized speech, promised to eliminate terrorism "and destroy it where it grows."[1] The US-led anti-terrorist "coalition of the willing" was presented as a coalition for the 21st century, replacing the institutional structures of the Cold War.[2] A new world order is emerging, with the US taking center stage as global protector, defining the world order as a Pax Americana.

Since the fall of the Berlin Wall, and particularly in recent years, the focus of European states has been on non-military domestic issues of the European Union, but the United States, with its superior military might, has been preoccupied with military conflict. Many Europeans have been attracted to the idea of a multipolar world order, coordinated by international organizations and based on the principles of international law and peaceful competition between economic powers in Beijing, Tokyo, Brussels, Washington, Moscow, and New Delhi. For US leaders, by contrast, such a system is far from satisfactory: A central role for the United Nations and international law makes no sense to them as long as this world order is not backed up by military force. From the early 1990s on, accordingly, a number of US analysts have argued that the US should strengthen its current military hegemony. They have favored a unipolar world order under US leadership, arguing that international peace should be based on the establishment of a Pax Americana.[3]

Prior to September 11, 2001, it was impossible for the US leadership to take the necessary steps for establishing this new world order. In the wake of 9/11, however, the US was able to make military intelligence and might the very axis of the world system, replacing the Cold War and the post-Cold War order of the 1990s with the "War on Terror." The emergence of a potential multipolar economic-political order was blocked by the creation of a more militarized and unipolar Pax Americana. And, with its military superiority and intelligence hegemony, the US has played the role of global protector while transforming other states into something akin to US protectorates. The threat of terrorist attacks within their own territories forced these other states to follow the lead given by US intelligence and even to participate in US-led wars. In this light, the wars in Iraq and Afghanistan can be understood as directed not primarily against those two particular states, or even against terrorists operating from within their borders, but rather against other major powers, which now have to accept a militarily—rather than economically and politically—defined world order, one that subsumes their sovereignty under a Pax Americana.

Defining the Problem of Terrorism

While terrorism has been primarily perceived within European countries as a civilian matter, not as a task for defense ministers, it is seen very much as a military issue within the US.[4] The US's War on Terror has been manifested primarily as a series of coordinated military operations that "takes the battle to the enemy, wherever they are" to wipe out terrorists that might potentially use nuclear or biological weapons to kill not just 3,000 civilians, as on 9/11, but "potentially millions of people," to quote US Secretary of Defense Donald Rumsfeld.[5] According to Condoleezza Rice, 9/11 was an "earthquake" that "has started shifting the tectonic plates in international politics."[6] Indeed, Rumsfeld has said, Washington now views the world "through the prism of September 11."[7]

To most Europeans, by contrast, terrorism is an "all-too-familiar historical legacy, which cannot be attacked with methods of war," to quote former British ambassador Alyson Bailes, now the director of the Stockholm International Peace Research Institute.[8] For Europeans, accordingly, terrorism may have changed its face as a result of the attacks in New York, Washington, Madrid, and London, but it is not the single defining element—perhaps not even the primary element—for understanding the current era. While the enormous force of modern weapons of mass destruction, the vulnerability of today's communication systems, and the global reach of the latter have certainly changed the way we look at threats to our security, this is just one side of the security coin.

Terrorism is often presented by scholars in the following ways: first, as a tactic used by marginal groups or networks that lack major military capabilities (asymmetric threat); second, as a potent weapon that can be used to inflict considerable damage on the complex societies and vulnerable communication systems of the contemporary world (risk society); third, as an expression of the processes of globalization and communication that have moved "faraway threats" closer to Europe and the US; and fourth, as an exceptionally dangerous threat because of the possibility that terrorist groups might gain access to nuclear and biological weapons, which would drastically alter the equation of force. All this makes terrorism more relevant both to Europe and the US, because the potential use of nuclear weapons by small peripheral groups could render a terrorist attack as devastating as any traditional war. Additionally, terrorism is sometimes understood as an instrument for mobilizing marginal groups and for coercing states into changing their policies. Terrorism is considered a violent mix of diplomacy and propaganda that reinforces the strength and morale of the marginal group. The phenomenon, however, is much more complex than this.

Indeed, historically speaking, terrorism has also been used as a psychological tool for creating fear within the state, to discredit enemies and political opponents, and to cause people to turn not against the state but rather to the state for protection and security. For example, recent research by Daniele Ganser, among others, shows that much of the terrorism that took place during the Cold War was primarily carried out by major powers as a way of exercising domestic control within particular states.[9] Terrorism has thus been a dual force, and in many cases terrorist groups have involved a range of different players, often with very different interests.

While terrorism is a political instrument used for various purposes, it is also an indicator of the kinds of conflicts and rhetoric that are prevalent in the world. The terrorism of the Cold War was often presented as secular and leftwing, while today's terrorism is described as primarily religious and Muslim, representing a change in political perceptions. The ideological face of today's terrorism is certainly different from that seen previously, but the contemporary phenomenon may very well be as complex as the terrorism of the Cold War.

Terrorism provokes the institutions of the democratic state and reinforces demands for security that leave no space for political choice. In other words, terrorism becomes an instrument for limiting the range of the public sphere and for "securitizing" what was formerly part of the democratic and legal process.[10] What was formerly an issue of political choice is now presented as an issue of life and death, with no alternatives available. And, just as the individual turns to the state for protection from terrorism, so will the smaller state turn to the hegemonic power—at this point, the US—to guarantee its security. Terrorism has thereby become the road to Pax Americana. It has become a way of carrying out politics outside the arena of the democratic state in order to limit the democratic state's room to operate. Terrorism has become a form of extra-legal politics conducted by major powers, by individual states themselves, and by the critics of both, whether these be Islamist, nationalist, or socialist.

Terrorism as "Asymmetric Warfare"

Most people think of "regular terrorism" in terms of weaker elements fighting stronger ones, as a form of "asymmetric threat." We commonly speak of the grievances born in war, violence, and counter-violence that, in a globalized world, enter Europe or the US.

Let us look at a couple of examples to illustrate this. In September 1970, the Popular Front for the Liberation of Palestine (PFLP) hijacked four airliners to focus the world's attention on the plight of the Palestinians and to disrupt a pending peace process—the Rogers Plan, named for then Secretary of State William Rogers—which was being conducted over the heads of Palestinian organizations. King Hussein of Jordan used the opportunity provided by the high-profile hijackings to launch a major assault on Palestinian organizations in Jordan. This September campaign, which came to be known among Palestinians as "Black September," had been in the pipeline for more than half a year. For the Jordanian king, therefore, the hijackings provided a convenient pretext for carrying out what he saw as a necessary expulsion of Palestinian organizations from the Jordanian kingdom.

The events in Jordan ultimately gave their name to a prominent

Palestinian terrorist group, Black September, which would later be responsible for the massacre of the Israeli Olympic team in Munich in 1972, providing a potent reminder that previous exposure to violence and war is typical for many individuals participating in terrorist organizations. Accordingly, while some people speak of graduating from Harvard or Yale, Venezuelan terrorist Ilich Ramirez Sanchez, better known as "Carlos," claimed that he "graduated in Jordan 1970."[11] The events of "Black September"—the Jordanian bombing of Palestinian refugee camps—turned 21-year-old Carlos into a terrorist.

Similarly, one might argue that Osama bin Laden "graduated" in Afghanistan a decade later. Originally, bin Laden had been recruited as a young man by Saudi Chief of Intelligence Prince Turki bin Faisal to support the Islamist rebels in Afghanistan, and 22-year-old Osama arrived in the latter country a few days after Soviet troops entered it in late 1979. His brother Abdullah has said that "the war changed [Osama] completely."[12]

A decade later in the 1990s, a young British citizen at the London School of Economics, Omar Saeed Sheikh, saw a film about the brutal conflict taking place in Bosnia. Subsequently, in April 1993, 20-year-old Sheikh traveled to Bosnia, where he saw "a 13-year-old Muslim girl who'd been raped and murdered by Serbs. Years later, Sheikh would tremble at the memory."[13] To paraphrase Carlos, Omar Saeed Sheikh graduated in Bosnia 1993. (Indeed, the London *Times* has described Sheikh as a "British Carlos."[14])

We should note that while it might be argued that some cultures and classes are more willing to embrace violent solutions than others, the above examples provide little support for that hypothesis. Carlos came from a wealthy socialist family in Venezuela; Osama bin Laden from an extremely wealthy family with intimate relations to the king of Saudi Arabia; and Omar Saeed Sheikh from a less wealthy London East End family from Pakistan. But all of these world-famous terrorists have in common the experience of war during their formative years.

Consequently, preliminary conclusions might include the following points about "regular terrorism": First, it is often born out of grievances in war. Second, it is used as a military tactic by a weaker party in fighting a hegemonic enemy. Third, it is used to disrupt "unfair" negotiations and agreements that do not take the views of weaker parties into consideration. Fourth, it is used to back negotiations with force. Fifth, it is used to strengthen the morale of the weaker party by signaling to a hegemonic enemy that resistance is still possible. For example, after Hezbollah in 1983 used a car bomb in an attack on US Marine barracks in Lebanon, which resulted in the death of 241 Americans, US forces were withdrawn. It was a successful asymmetric attack and a propaganda victory as much as a military victory. Similar operations were conducted, allegedly by bin Laden, in Riyadh and Khobar in 1995–1996, in an attempt to force the US to withdraw from Saudi Arabia.

Such episodes fit the standard picture of "asymmetric warfare" operations, with the weaker trying to force the stronger to retreat. Many commentators have attempted to interpret recent terrorist attacks in New York, Washington, Madrid, and London in a similar fashion.

Regular Terrorism and Intelligence Organizations

Returning to the famous terrorists discussed above, we find that, in addition to their grievances and their experience of war, Carlos, Osama bin Laden, and Omar Saeed Sheikh have something else in common: They had all been working for or collaborating with agents from various security or intelligence services. Indeed, although Carlos was at one stage the "most wanted man in the world," he was able to live more or less a normal life in Beirut. People who knew him described him as amiable and good-humored, adding, however, that he boasted openly and recklessly of his various "adventures" with anyone who would listen. In Beirut, Carlos visited cafés and restaurants without either cover or bodyguards, disregarding basic rules of discretion, and he was constantly monitored by the Lebanese, Syrian, and Israeli services.[15] In some operations, he collaborated with agents from other Arab countries.[16] Interestingly, however, although Mossad hit squads killed a number of Black September and PFLP activists, they never touched Carlos, even though he would have made an easy target. Perhaps he was seen as a symbol of terrorism that could be used to discredit the Palestinian cause. In line with this suggestion, we should note that former Mossad agent Victor Ostrovsky claimed that Carlos's liaison officer to Beirut, Michel Moukharbel, had already been recruited by Mossad in June 1973. According to Ostrovsky, Moukharbel informed Israel of Carlos's exact whereabouts almost every day. At the same time, he and Carlos ran operations together.[17]

Similarly, Osama bin Laden was, prior to 9/11, certainly monitored by various intelligence and secret services, and his organization had most likely been penetrated by a number of agents or informants. *Jane's Intelligence* reported in September 2001 that bin Laden received regular medical treatment for his kidney disease at the Peshawar military hospital and that US agencies were fully informed about this.[18] In the war against the Soviets, he and his Service Bureau had been a major receiver of US support; after that war, in the early 1990s, one of bin Laden's close associates, the Egyptian Ali Mohamed—who trained al-Qaeda activists in how to carry out bomb attacks and trained bin Laden's bodyguards after an attempt on the latter's life—was at the same time a US Army special forces reserve officer, who went to Afghanistan with high-level US backing. While still an FBI informant, Ali Mohamed was directly involved in the preparations for the bombing of the US embassy in Nairobi in 1998 that left 250 people dead and several thousands wounded. He was a US asset who had even tried to infiltrate Hezbollah on behalf of the CIA.[19]

Omar Saeed Sheikh, whom bin Laden referred to as "his special son," is responsible for killings and kidnappings and has been presented as one of the men behind the 9/11 operation.[20] At the time, however, he was working for General Mohammad Aziz Khan of the Pakistani intelligence service, the ISI. Sheikh was protected by the ISI and was frequently seen at local parties hosted by senior Pakistani officials.[21] Like Carlos, he lived openly and was described as "a nice guy, well-mannered and educated."[22] US intelligence has described him as an ISI asset,[23] while a story in a US newspaper said that "[t]here are many in Musharraf's government who believe that Saeed Sheikh's power comes not from the ISI, but from his connections with our own CIA."[24]

Seemingly, then, no serious form of terrorism is able to neglect the intelligence game. This becomes even more obvious when one examines Black September leader Ali Hassan Salameh, believed to have carried out the attack against the Israeli athletes in Munich in 1972. He was at the very top of Mossad's assassination list,[25] but he turned to the CIA, and his security forces protected US embassy personnel during the civil war in Lebanon in 1975–1976. In late 1976, Salameh was received as a hero at CIA headquarters in Langley. Mossad would not manage to kill him until 1979,[26] in an assassination that was probably intended to damage PLO–CIA ties.

Abu Nidal was even more in the hands of intelligence services—those of the Iraqis, the Syrians, and the Libyans—and his organization was evidently penetrated by several Mossad agents. One was senior leader Ghassan al-Ali, who was responsible for choosing targets for Nidal's bombings and assassinations. From 1975 on, Nidal's group took over from Mossad's own assassination teams, as the systematic killing of Palestinian leaders by Israeli teams in the first half of the 1970s gave way to systematic killings carried out by the Nidal organization.[27]

It seems, then, that "regular terrorism" has difficulty surviving without some kind of intelligence service protection or involvement. In many cases, terrorists linked to an insurgency are able to continue their activities while being monitored at every step by intelligence services, which permit them to carry out bombings in order to discredit the insurgency.

The Use of Terrorism against "Terrorism"

In his *Theory of the Partisan*, Carl Schmitt described the irregular fighter or anti-state insurgent as a "partisan," arguing that in "the vicious circle of terror and counter-terror, the combat of the partisan is often simply a mirror-image of the partisan battle itself."[28] Schmitt drew on the example of French General Raoul Salan, head of the Organisation d'Armée Secrète (OAS), which in 1961 began a long campaign of terror against the Algerian insurgency. Salan introduced the ideas of "revolutionary war" to combat the insurgency through the adoption of its own "terrorist tactics."[29] From the early 1960s, the OAS used ruthless methods to undermine the legitimacy of the insurgency. These methods included "false-flag" attacks on French citizens—attacks made to look as if they were carried out by the insurgents.

Historically, such false-flag terrorism has been as important as so-called regular terrorism. In the early 20th century, for example, the Okhrana, the Russian security service, infiltrated anarchist organizations and carried out bomb attacks that were blamed on the anarchists in order to strengthen the legitimacy and role of the security apparatus. One Russian security agent, Evno Azev, penetrated the Social Revolutionary Party in the early 20th century, later working his way up to become its commander for terrorist activities. He was responsible for the murder of Vyacheslav Plehve, the Russian minister of the interior. The terrorist activities of the

Social Revolutionary Party were, therefore, actually run by the Russian security service,[30] which was able to use this group's ruthless killings to discredit the radical opposition.

In 1954, Israeli military intelligence planted bombs in British and American cultural and information centers in Cairo, laying the blame for these attacks on Egyptians, in order to poison the relations of Egypt with the UK and the US. This particular operation was run by Colonel Benjamin Giivi of Israeli military intelligence, along with Moshe Dayan and Shimon Peres. It also reportedly involved Israeli Defense Minister Pinhas Lavon, who later had to leave his position (this scandal has become known as the "Lavon Affair"). It was not publicly recognized that the bombings had been part of an Israeli operation until six years later.[31]

Later in the 1970s and 1980s, Israel's Mossad recruited Palestinians and North Africans in the Abu Nidal organization to assassinate PLO leaders and to carry out a brutal bombing campaign in the name of "Fatah" in order to discredit Palestinians in general and the Palestinian insurgency in particular.[32] Mossad tried to fight the Palestinian insurgency by stepping up the violence and taking it to a new level, using "terrorism against terrorism."

The first major terrorist attack in postwar Europe, the 1969 Piazza Fontana bombing in Milan, left 16 dead and more than 80 wounded. Simultaneously, three bombs exploded in Rome, wounding another 14 people. In the wake of these attacks, 27 anarchists were arrested.[33] The mass media hysterically proclaimed their guilt, and anarchist Pietro Valpreda was subsequently imprisoned for three years. As pointed out in Daniele Ganser's chapter, however, it was discovered in 2001 that this operation had actually been carried out by agents from the fascist Ordine Nuovo in collaboration with Italian military intelligence (SID) and the CIA. It was also learned that the equally ultra-fascist Avanguardia Nazionale, under Stefano delle Chiaie, had carried out the bombings in Rome.[34] Indeed, a confidential SID document states that the bombs had been planted by Mario Merlino masquerading as an anarchist and "acting on the orders of the known Stefano delle Chiaie."[35] In 1974, after these fascists had been forced to leave Italy, the police arrested the top leadership of the Red Brigades, which opened the way for SID and Secret Service infiltrators to function as their replacements.[36] They radically raised the level of violence to discredit the left. Indeed, the arrest of the leftwing leadership came to represent a "watershed between the relatively mild and relatively idealistic Red Brigades of the early years and the blind terror of the later years."[37]

Similar operations were carried out in other countries, sometimes to test the security at military bases.[38] But through their presentation as terrorist attacks, they were transformed into psychological operations (PSYOPs) to convince governments, the general public, and local military forces that they had been lulled into a false sense of security.

Former US Secretary of Defense Caspar Weinberger has stated that in the 1980s the US had units that were specifically tasked with playing the role of enemy forces. These units secretly attacked Western defenses worldwide, in order, said Weinberger, to test their capabilities and improve their state of readiness "regularly" and "frequently." Referring to US/UK covert submarine operations in Swedish waters in the 1980s, Weinberger said:

> [I]t was necessary to test frequently the capabilities of all countries, not only in the Baltic [Sea]—which is very strategic, of course—but in the Mediterranean and Asiatic waters and all the rest.... And it was not just done in the sea. It was done on air defences and land defences as well... and all this was done on a regular basis and on an agreed upon basis.[39]

In collaboration with local security elites, the US "security state"—or "deep state" (see below)—tested and reinforced the defensive capability of Western states worldwide. In Italy, the same US officers (David Carret and others) ran not only the operations aimed at "testing the readiness" of Italian coastal defenses (Delfino Attivo and Delfino Sveglio) but also the simultaneous terrorist campaign to raise awareness and alter the mindset of the Italian population.[40]

After the Hezbollah attack against US Marines in Beirut in 1983, Rear-Admiral James Lyons, Deputy Chief of Naval Operations for Plans, Policy, and Operations, set up a "terrorist unit," the Red Cell, recruited from his own naval special forces unit (SEAL Team Six). The Red Cell attacked naval bases worldwide, planting bombs, wounding US personnel, and taking hundreds of hostages. According to Lyons, real terrorism provides "no second chance." Therefore, it was necessary to set up "terrorist teams" to provide US forces with "physical" experience of the terrorist threat in order to "change the mindset" and "raise the awareness" of security forces so that they would be able to prevent an even more devastating attack.[41] By challenging the security system of the Western world, state-run terrorist units were able to provide physical experience to change the mindset, something administrative measures are unable to do. It is clear that the US had developed a security system that included both sides of the coin: defensive security forces—sometimes lulled into false security—as well as secret offensive forces introduced to challenge the former to increase their readiness.

A similar argument has been made after the 9/11 attacks. These attacks, by challenging the Western security system, are said to have stimulated this system to introduce measures aimed at preventing an even more destructive attack. In October 2001, Donald Rumsfeld commented that the only way to deal with terrorism "is to take the battle to the terrorists, wherever they are"[42]—the argument being that one cannot simply wait defensively for terrorists to use weapons of mass destruction, because any response would be simply too late: There is "no second chance." A catastrophic terrorist event was thus portrayed as the ideal vehicle for transforming US security forces so that they would be able to prevent a nuclear or chemical attack, one that might "kill hundreds of thousands" or "potentially millions of people," in Rumsfeld's words.[43]

Similarly to the "terrorist attacks" of the Red Cell, then, the terrorist attack of 9/11 might have been seen as a "necessary measure," but on a much larger scale, to increase US readiness and to improve the country's security against a potential terrorist attack involving nuclear weapons. From this point of view, "necessary security measures" cannot be developed by the use of administrative measures and will demand limited terrorist attacks to restructure the security system against terrorism. Some further preliminary conclusions can be drawn: First, terrorist activities could as easily be the hegemonic power's countermeasures against an insurgency as actions taken by the insurgency itself. Second, this kind of state-run terrorism often makes use of false-flag operations, raising the level of violence in order to discredit the insurgency whose legitimacy is most dangerous to the hegemonic power. Third, such terrorist operations often target the state's own population and security forces to test their readiness and capabilities as an indirect way of increasing the security against terrorism. Fourth, false-flag terrorism in the domestic environment can be used as a pretext for offensive military operations, whereby the state aims to go after the alleged terrorists "wherever they are." Fifth, terrorist operations at home are sometimes launched to restructure the nature of the domestic society in order to prepare it for a potentially even more devastating terrorist attack.

Terrorism as a Pretext for War

On September 20, 2001, President Bush promised to eliminate terrorism "and destroy it where it grows." One has to go to war and overthrow regimes harboring terrorists. But Deputy Defense Secretary Paul Wolfowitz reportedly told the 9/11 Commission that if the Department of Defense had gone to Congress before 9/11 and asked to invade Afghanistan, it would not have been taken seriously.[44] This view was echoed in the testimony of Secretary Rumsfeld, who said: "After... the embassy bombings in East Africa and the attack on the *Cole* [in 2000] reasonable people have concluded that the value of [a defensive] approach had diminished," meaning that states like Afghanistan that harbor terrorists will have to "pay a price." But "before September 11th [a US president could not go] before the Congress and the world and [say] we need to invade Afghanistan and overthrow the Taliban.... [U]nfortunately history shows that it can take a tragedy like September 11th to waken the world to new threats and to the need for action."[45]

Already in September 2000, a document put out by the Project for the New American Century (signed by Wolfowitz and several other future members of the Bush administration) had emphasized that what they saw as a required transformation of the US military would be a long process "absent a catastrophic and catalyzing event—like a new Pearl Harbor." Such a catastrophic event would justify increased defense spending, described as a precondition for reaching the strategic goal: the creation of a Pax Americana.[46] In January 2001, the Rumsfeld Commission, arguing for increased military activity in outer space, suggested that perhaps a "space Pearl Harbor" would be "the only event able to galvanize the nation and cause the US Government to act."[47] Wolfowitz (Rumsfeld's deputy) and Lewis "Scooter" Libby (Vice President Cheney's chief of staff) argued within days that an attack against Iraq was necessary in spite of the fact that no link between Iraq and the attacks of 9/11 had been demonstrated.[48] These men had presented arguments for a war against Iraq on a number of occasions from 1992 onwards.[49] The 9/11 attacks provided a suitable pretext for carrying out this war.

In 1992, in a Defense Policy Guidance draft,[50] Libby and Wolfowitz had argued that control of Persian Gulf oil was vital to prevent powers like China, Europe, and Japan from developing into rivals to the US. The interventions of those powers might not immediately threaten the US, but in the long term they might be able to grow into powers that could challenge US authority.[51] According to Libby and Wolfowitz, the US should use military force to control "access to vital raw materials, primarily Persian Gulf oil, proliferation of weapons of mass destruction and ballistic missiles, [and] threats to US citizens from terrorism."[52] All these arguments supported a US invasion of Iraq. However, there was no justifiable basis for such an invasion; Iraq certainly was not going to launch a conventional attack against the United States. An invasion of Iraq could only be justified as a response to an unconventional (terrorist) attack, whether a "regular" or a "false-flag" terrorist attack. A regular terrorist attack against the United States would have been hard to guarantee. This fact provides the basis for a strong argument for the second option.

This argument is in line with pretexts proposed for a war against Cuba in 1962. As Ganser's chapter points out, official documents from that year, which were declassified in 2001, have revealed that the US Joint Chiefs of Staff, under the chairmanship of General Lyman Lemnitzer, proposed the use of Cuban exiles to carry out a terrorist campaign, including the planting of explosives in US cities, to justify an invasion of Cuba. By the use of terrorist attacks, world opinion "should be favorably affected by developing the international image of the Cuban government as rash and irresponsible, and as an alarming and unpredictable threat to the peace of the Western Hemisphere."[53]

"US Cubans" were trained in the use of explosives and underwater demolition at Harvey Point Defense Testing Activity, a CIA camp in North Carolina. Since the 1960s, thousands of CIA agents, special forces personnel, and foreign nationals—including Cuban exiles, Israelis, Nicaraguan Contras, Palestinians, and Arab Islamists—have passed through the CIA's "terrorist" course, in which they received training in using homemade fertilizer-based explosives, self-made napalm, Molotov cocktails, and plastic explosives.[54] CIA veteran Robert Baer has described how he learned to blow up things, such as cars and buses, using US C-4, Czech Semtex, and a few other foreign plastic explosives: "We blew up one bus using three sacks of fertilizers and fuel oil.... We were also taught some of the really esoteric stuff like E-cell timers, improvising pressurized airplane bombs.... By the end of training, we could have taught an advanced terrorist course."[55] In any case, the Joint Chiefs' idea in 1962 was to use a US bombing campaign against the US's own people as a pretext for war against Cuba.

There have also been examples of third-party terrorism aimed at convincing one side to launch a war against another. Initially, for example, it was believed that the bomb that exploded on April 5, 1986, in the Berlin Le Belle disco, which was frequented by US officers, had been detonated by Libyan terrorists. The attack wounded 230 people and killed two US servicemen and a Turkish woman. Soon after the attack, the Reagan administration accused Libyan leader Muammar Qaddafi of responsibility for the bombing. Ten days later, the US launched a massive air attack on Libya.

It now seems clear, however, that the La Belle bombing was carried out by Mossad agent Mohammed Amairi and his colleague "Mahmoud" Abu Jaber, together with Musbah Eter, a CIA informant in the Libyan embassy.[56] This operation was conducted a month after Mossad and Israeli naval special forces had installed a "Trojan"—a communications device—on Libyan territory. This device transmitted false Libyan messages that were then picked up and decoded by Western intelligence and became the false evidence used to justify a major US attack on Libya.[57] Similar to the Lavon Affair in 1954, this incident now appears to have been an Israeli attack on US interests in order to create tension between the US and an Arab state.

To summarize: First, a terrorist operation with its roots in various conflicts can be used by a major power to justify a military attack that was already planned. Second, a security service may monitor a terrorist group and let it prepare and launch a terrorist attack in order to create a pretext for a military response. Third, a security service or intelligence service may plant explosives, or it may penetrate or even take over an existing terrorist group, then have that group use explosives, in order to manufacture a pretext for a military attack. Fourth, an intelligence service from a third country may launch a false-flag terrorist attack in order to start a war between two other countries. Fifth, intelligence or security services of major powers may prefer a parallel use of all or several of the former techniques in order to make any investigation difficult while guaranteeing operational success. To rely on a regular terrorist attack alone is often too risky, because such an attack may well be postponed for a year or more, which would obstruct relevant war preparations. A regular terrorist attack may also lack the force and precision necessary to justify a military counterattack.

Terrorism as a Vehicle for a Pax Americana

As mentioned above, recent trials and parliamentary investigations in Italy have established that bombing campaigns in the 1960s and 1970s in that country were not run by various anarchist, communist, or other left-wing groups, as was generally believed at the time, but were instead arranged by the right-wing organization Ordine Nuovo. These attacks were carried out by NDS action squads (NDS = Nuclei di Difesa della Stato [Nuclei for the Defense of the State]), in accordance with the now notorious "strategy of tension," which Ganser discusses at length.

The general ideas behind this strategy were presented at a seminar in May 1965 at the Alberto Polio Institute for Military Studies in Rome.[58] The following year, Aginter Press, an international fascist intelligence network, was established in Lisbon to implement the strategy, with support from the CIA as well as the Portuguese security service PIDE. This network included a unit specializing in the infiltration of anarchist and pro-Chinese groups. Its operatives would use their status as "correspondents" of this "press" as a cover for carrying out bombings and assassinations. An Aginter Press document from 1969, which was discovered in Lisbon in 1974, proposed both "selective terrorism," which would "eliminat[e] certain carefully selected persons" (including political leaders), and "indiscriminate terrorism," including "randomly shooting down people with firearms" and detonating explosives in public squares or buildings, in accordance with the strategy-of-tension bombing campaign.[59]

Subsequently, while masquerading as left-wingers, Italian NDS squads carried out a bombing campaign that resulted in the deaths of hundreds of people, in direct collaboration with the CIA and "US factions" of the Italian intelligence and security services. Later, Carlo Digilio, who had worked for the CIA in Italy, recounted in court hearings how the bombing campaign had been linked to a US plan to bring about a state of emergency in Italy in order to exclude the political left from government.[60] Italian Chief of Counter-Intelligence

General Gianandelio Maletti confirmed in court that "the CIA wanted through the birth of an extreme nationalism and the contribution of the far right, particularly Ordine Nuovo, to stop Italy sliding to the left." He said that US intelligence instigated terrorism and had provided the explosives for the 1969 Piazza Fontana bombing in Milan.[61] Digilio also described how he passed on details of planned bomb attacks to his CIA contact, Captain David Carret, who had told him that the bombing campaign was part of a US plan to create a state of emergency in order to exercise control over Italian domestic politics.[62]

The activities of the US in Italy during the Cold War resemble what the Turkish military elite might describe as the correction of the course of democracy by the "deep state," or what some call the "fine tuning" of democracy.[63] This "deep state"—what Carl Schmitt called the "sovereign"[64]—may raise the "security temperature" through the use of "indiscriminate terrorism:" bombings in public squares to make people trade freedom for security. Indeed, fear of bomb attacks has an enormous psychological impact on people, persuading them to turn to the state for protection and channeling their anger and fear against a perceived enemy. In the event of such attacks, the mass media often respond hysterically, blaming whomever the authorities claim to have been responsible. Such an instrument is thus ideal for calibrating government policy—that is, "fine tuning" democratic politics and "securitizing" issues that were formerly open to public debate, bringing the democratic political sphere more in line with the political vision of the "sovereign." Most important is the exercise of control over domestic politics in a way that could not be achieved through legal means.

In this way, during the Cold War, US elites played a game of fear and protection to set the agenda, to influence local governments, to calibrate mass media, and to veto policies and discredit individuals in conflict with US interests. The bombing campaign made people turn for protection to the state, which turned to the US for support. Any dissident state would soon feel the consequences of the terrorist campaign and would adapt to US policy.

Terrorism, accordingly, can be used globally in accordance with the strategy of tension to restructure the world order and its global security system. US intelligence and military forces have taken center stage as the global protector, because these forces are the only ones that are able to intervene worldwide to protect others from a major terrorist threat. Terrorism has seemingly been used on a global scale to introduce a Pax Americana.

In the 1990s, Europeans looked upon capital cities around the globe—Beijing, Tokyo, Brussels, Washington, Moscow, and New Delhi—as centers in a multipolar world order governed by international law. With the end of the Cold War, military force no longer seemed to be the defining element in the civilized "cosmos." But then the events of September 11, 2001, were used to launch the War on Terror and to highlight the role of military force. Ongoing terrorist attacks forced a number of other states to permit US counterterrorism operations to take up residence within their own state borders. The CIA was granted access to one country after another, because local security services were not viewed as having appropriate capacities. The US thereby took the stage to weed out regimes harboring terrorists and to protect its allies from an elusive terrorist enemy seen to be threatening the civilian order, and state after state was turned into a US protectorate. A new pattern was emerging. The US's superior military strength and intelligence hegemony could only be translated into power and real global strength if there were ongoing conflicts—wars and terrorist attacks—that threatened the multipolar power structure of the economic-political world order.

The vision of a unipolar Pax Americana, clearly expressed in the document put out in 2000 by the Project for the New American Century, presupposes ongoing military conflicts or terrorist attacks that are able to define the global system in primarily military-political terms. While the economic-political power structure—represented by the US, the EU, Japan, China, India, and Russia—has no single leader, the same is not true for the military-political structure. By presenting the world in terms of terrorism and military threats, the US has been able to profit from its military-intelligence hegemony to transform the global system into a unipolar world order. Immediately prior to the 1991 war against Iraq, Charles Krauthammer noted in *Foreign Affairs* how quickly the myth of a multipolar world had exploded: At the first shots, Germany and Japan hid under the table. "The true geopolitical structure of the post-Cold War world," Krauthammer argued, was "brought sharply into focus by the Gulf crisis: a single pole of world power that consists of the United States at the apex of the industrial West.... Iraq [has] revealed the unipolar structure of today's world."[65]

This observation was brilliant: The war, which since 9/11 was turned into a "permanent war," has become an instrument to introduce a unipolar Pax Americana.

But the neoconservative ambition to establish such a world order through a permanent War on Terror has led to a backlash. This strategy is certainly creative, but the focus on military strength and unilateral use of force—rather than on permanent institutions able to guarantee legitimacy, like NATO and the UN—has provoked tension with several European states and even tension in the US between power elites who believe in a Pax Americana of some sort.[66]

We might thus draw the following tentative conclusions: First, the kinds of indiscriminate bombings we experience today were frequently used during the Cold War, not by "regular terrorists" but by factions of the state—the "sovereign" or the "deep state"—to create fear, to discredit an opponent, and to justify emergency measures that would force the public to trade freedom for security in accordance with the strategy of tension. Second, during the Cold War this kind of terrorism was used particularly by the US to create a paranoid security climate, to control other states domestically, and to keep the US sphere of interest intact. Third, military campaigns in Afghanistan and Iraq had been proposed by central actors in the Bush administration prior to 9/11, campaigns that would have been difficult to justify without a major attack on the US. Fourth, the neoconservative proposal for establishing a Pax Americana presupposed a militarized world order that only could be justified by a major military or terrorist attack able to replace the civilian multipolar system with a unipolar one, with the US "at the apex of the industrial West." Fifth, the events of 9/11 and similar attacks have apparently been used on a global scale to introduce such a Pax Americana, because US intelligence and military forces are the only ones able to intervene worldwide to protect others from a major terrorist threat.[67]

Pax Americana as a unipolar power structure is defined by military strength and intelligence hegemony, and all other countries have to follow suit. From a European, Chinese, or Japanese perspective, however, every US war, wherever fought, is directed against the economic-political multipolar power structure that would give Europe, China, and Japan a more significant position in the world. US wars thereby transform a potential multipolar power structure into a unipolarity, degrading other states into US protectorates in the process. The military power gap between Europe and the US does, to some extent, explain a psychological difference. More importantly, however, the power gap is translated into a major political clash between the US and the others, with a majority of Europeans regarding the US—or the US and Israel[68]—as the greatest threat to world peace.

Terrorism today seemingly has two major root causes: Muslim grievances against Western and particularly US military presence, and the US hegemonic interest in replacing a multipolar world order with a militarized unipolar Pax Americana. Both US-instigated terrorism and Islamist anti-US terrorism function as supplementary instruments for raising the level of violence, which in practical terms replaces a more civilian multipolar system with a more militarized unipolar world order. If these two forms of terrorism were exposed as dual vehicles for establishing a Pax Americana, each would lose its legitimacy. The terrorism of anti-Western Islamism will lose its legitimacy in the Muslim world when exposed as a US instrument to restructure the world order, while the US policy will lose its legitimacy in the Western world when exposed as a terrorist project in the guise of Islamist operations. Consequently, any possibility of transcending the era of terrorism would seem to presuppose the exposure of the US intelligence game together with the role of Islamist terrorism in this game.[69]

ELEVEN

Parameters of Power in the Global Dominance Group: 9/11 & Election Irregularities in Context

Peter Phillips with Bridget Thornton and Celeste Vogler

The leadership class in the United States is now dominated by a neoconservative group of people with the shared goal of asserting US military power worldwide. This "global dominance group," in cooperation with major military contractors, has become a powerful force in world military unilateralism and US political processes. This research study is an attempt to identify the general parameters of the key actors supporting a global dominance agenda and how collectively this group has benefited from—and perhaps encouraged—the events of September 11, 2001 and the irregularities in the 2004 presidential election. This study examines how interlocking public-private partnerships, including the corporate media, public relations firms, military contractors, policy elites, and government officials, jointly support a US military global domination agenda. We ask about the most powerful military-industrial complex in the world the traditional sociological questions: who wins, who decides, and who facilitates action.

A long thread of sociological research documents the existence of a dominant ruling class, which sets policy and determines national political priorities. This ruling class in the US is complex and inter-competitive, maintaining itself through interacting families of high social standing with similar lifestyles, corporate affiliations, and memberships in elite social clubs and private schools.[1]

The American ruling class has long been determined to be mostly self-perpetuating,[2] maintaining its influence through policy-making institutions such as the National Manufacturing Association, National Chamber of Commerce, Business Council, Business Roundtable, Conference Board, American Enterprise Institute, Council on Foreign Relations, and other business-centered policy groups.[3] These associations have long dominated policy decisions within the US government.

C. Wright Mills, in his 1956 book *The Power Elite*, documents how World War II solidified a trinity of power in the US that comprised corporate, military, and government elites in a centralized power structure motivated by class interests and working in unison through "higher circles" of contact and agreement. Mills described how the power elite were those "who decide whatever is decided" of major consequence.[4] These higher-circle decision-makers tended to be more concerned with inter-organizational relationships and the functioning of the economy as a whole than with advancing their particular corporate interests.[5]

The higher-circle policy elites (HCPE) are a segment of the American upper class and are the principal decision-makers in society. While having an overall sense of "we-ness," they tend to have continuing disagreements on specific policies and necessary actions in various socio-political circumstances.[6] These disagreements can block aggressive reactionary responses to social movements and civil unrest, as in the case of the labor movement in the 1930s and the civil rights movement in the 1960s. During these two periods the more liberal elements of HCPE tended to dominate the decision-making process and supported passing the National Labor Relations and Social Security Acts in 1935, as well as the Civil Rights and Economic Opportunities Acts in 1964. These pieces of national legislation were seen as concessions to the ongoing social movements and civil unrest and were implemented without instituting more repressive policies.

On the other hand, during periods of threats by external enemies in World Wars I and II, the HCPE were more consolidated. In these periods, more conservative/reactionary elements of the HCPE were able to push their agendas more forcefully. During and after World War I, the United States instituted repressive responses to social movements through the Palmer Raids and the passage of the Espionage Act of 1917 and the Sedition Act of 1918. After World War II, the McCarthy-era attacks on liberals and radicals and the passage in 1947 of the National Security Act and the anti-labor Taft–Hartley Act were allowed and encouraged by the HCPE.

The Cold War led to a continuing arms races and a further consolidation of military and corporate interests. President Eisenhower warned of this increasing concentration of power in his famous 1961 speech to the nation, in which he said:

> Our military organization today bears little relation to that known by any of my predecessors in peacetime, or indeed by the fighting men of World War II or Korea.

> Until the latest of our world conflicts, the United States had no armaments industry. American makers of plowshares could, with time and as required, make swords as well. But now we can no longer risk emergency improvisation of national defense; we have been compelled to create a permanent armaments industry of vast proportions. Added to this, three and a half million men and women are directly engaged in the defense establishment. We annually spend on military security more than the net income of all United States corporations.

> This conjunction of an immense military establishment and a large arms industry is new in the American experience. The total influence—economic, political, even spiritual—is felt in every city, every Statehouse, every office of the Federal government. We recognize the imperative need for this development. Yet we must not fail to comprehend its grave implications. Our toil, resources, and livelihood are all involved; so is the very structure of our society.

> In the councils of government, we must guard against the acquisition of unwarranted influence, whether sought or unsought, by the military industrial complex. The potential for the disastrous rise of misplaced power exists and will persist.[7]

The HCPE attitude toward military expansion after World War II was significantly different from its attitude after World War I. In the 1920s, the HCPE were uncomfortable with war profits and the power of the arms industry. After WWII, which was followed by the Cold War, the Korean War, and then the Vietnam War, the HCPE supported continued unprecedented levels of military spending.[8]

The top 100 military contractors from WWII acquired over three billion dollars in new resources between 1939 and 1945, representing a 62 percent increase in capital assets. Five main interest groups—Morgan, Mellon, Rockefeller, Dupont, and Cleveland

Steel—controlled two thirds of the World War II prime contractor firms and were key elements of the HCPE who sought to continue high levels of military spending.[9] Economic incentives, combined with Cold War fears, led the HCPE to support an unprecedented military readiness, which resulted in a permanent military industrial complex. From 1952 to the collapse of the Soviet Union, the United States maintained defense funding in the 25–40 percent range of total federal spending, with peaks during Korea, Vietnam, and the Reagan presidency.[10]

The breakup of the Soviet Union undermined the rationale for continued military spending at high Cold War levels, and some people within the HCPE, while celebrating the victory over communism, saw the possibility of balanced budgets and peace dividends in the 1990s. In early 1992, Senator Edward Kennedy called for the taking of $210 billion dollars out of the defense budget over several years and spending $60 billion on universal health care, public housing, and improved transportation.[11] By the spring of 1992, however, it was clear that strong resistance to major cuts in the military budgets had widespread support in Washington. That year the Senate, in a 50–48 vote, was unable to close Republican and conservative Democrat debates against a proposal to shift defense spending to domestic programs.[12] In 1995, Defense Secretary Les Aspin (who during his tenure under Clinton made minor cuts to Pentagon budgets) argued that spending needed to remain high, especially for intelligence on "targeting terrorism and narcotics."[13] By 1999, editorials bemoaning the loss of the peace dividend were all that was left of major cuts to military spending.[14] And, at the same time that liberal elements of the HCPE were pushing for a peace dividend, a neoconservative group was arguing for using the decline of the Soviet Union as an opportunity for US military world dominance.

Foundations of the Global Dominance Group

Leo Strauss, Albert Wohlstetter, and others at the University of Chicago working in the Committee on Social Thought have been widely credited for influencing the neoconservative agenda through their students, Paul Wolfowitz, Allan Bloom, and Bloom's student Richard Perle. Adbuster summed up neoconservatism as:

> The belief that Democracy, however flawed, was best defended by an ignorant public pumped on nationalism and religion. Only a militantly nationalist state could deter human aggression.... Such nationalism requires an external threat and if one cannot be found it must be manufactured.[15]

The neoconservative philosophy emerged from the 1960s era of social revolutions and political correctness, as a counterforce to expanding liberalism and cultural relativism. Numerous officials and associates in the Reagan and George H. W. Bush administrations were strongly influenced by the neoconservative philosophy, including John Ashcroft, Charles Fairbanks, Dick Cheney, Kenneth Adelman, Elliot Abrams, William Kristol, and Douglas Feith.[16]

Within the Ford administration, there was a split between Cold War traditionalists, seeking to minimize confrontations through diplomacy and détente, and neoconservatives, advocating stronger confrontations with the Soviet "Evil Empire." The latter group became more entrenched when George H. W. Bush became director of the CIA. Bush allowed the formation of "Team B," headed by Richard Pipes along with Paul Wolfowitz, Lewis Libby, Paul Nitze, and others who formed the Committee on the Present Danger to raise awareness of the Soviet threat and the continuing need for a strong and aggressive defense policy. Their efforts led to strong anti-Soviet positioning during the Reagan administration.[17]

Journalist John Pilger recalled an interview with neoconservative Richard Perle during the Reagan administration.

> I interviewed Perle when he was advising Reagan; and when he spoke about "total war," I mistakenly dismissed him as mad. He recently used the term again in describing America's "war on terror." "No stages," he said. "This is total war. We are fighting a variety of enemies. There are lots of them out there. All this talk about first we are going to do Afghanistan, then we will do Iraq.... [T]his is entirely the wrong way to go about it. If we just let our vision of the world go forth, and we embrace it entirely and we don't try to piece together clever diplomacy, but just wage a total war... our children will sing great songs about us years from now."[18]

The election of George H. W. Bush as president and the appointment of Dick Cheney as secretary of defense expanded the presence of neoconservatives within the government and, after the fall of the Berlin Wall in 1989, allowed for the formal initiation of a global dominance policy.

In 1992, Cheney supported Lewis Libby and Paul Wolfowitz in producing the Defense Planning Guidance draft, which advocated US military dominance around the globe in a "new order." The report called for the United States to grow in military superiority and to prevent new rivals from rising up to challenge us on the world stage. Using words like "unilateral action" and military "forward presence," the report advocated that the United States dominate friends and foes alike. It concluded with the assertion that America can best attain this position by making itself "absolutely powerful."[19]

The Defense Policy Guidance draft was leaked to the press and came under heavy criticism from many members of the HCPE. The *New York Times* reported on March 11, 1992, that

> Senior White House and State Department officials have harshly criticized a draft Pentagon policy statement that asserts that America's mission in the post-cold-war era will be to prevent any collection of friendly or unfriendly nations from competing with the United States for superpower status.

An administration official familiar with the reaction of senior staff at the White House and State Department characterized the document as a "dumb report" that "in no way or shape represents US policy." Senator Robert C. Byrd, Democrat of West Virginia, called the draft Pentagon document "myopic, shallow and disappointing."[20] Many within the HCPE were not yet ready for a unilateral global-dominance agenda. So with Bill Clinton's election to the White House in 1992, most neoconservative members of the HCPE were out of direct power during the next eight years.

The HCPE within both major political parties tend to seek to maintain US world military power. Both political parties cooperate by encouraging Congress to protect US business interests abroad and corporate profits at home. To better maintain defense contractors' profits, Clinton's Defense Science Board called for a globalized defense industry, obtained through mergers of defense contractors with transnational companies, which would became partners in the maintenance of US military readiness.[21]

James Woolsey, Clinton's director of the CIA from 1993 to 1995, a man described as a hard-liner on foreign policy, wanted to continue a strong defense policy.[22] But the Clinton administration stayed away from promoting global dominance as an ideological justification for continuing high defense budgets. Instead, to offset profit declines for defense contractors after the fall of the Berlin Wall, the Clinton administration aggressively promoted international arms sales, raising the US share of arms exports from 16 percent in 1988 to 63 percent in 1997.[23] And it was under Clinton's watch that the US Space Command's 1996 report, "Vision for 2020," called for "full spectrum dominance" by linking land, sea, and air superiority to satellite supremacy along with the weaponization of space.[24]

Outside the Clinton administration, neoconservative HCPE continued to promote a global dominance agenda. On June 4, 1994, a neoconservative "Lakeside Chat" was given at the San Francisco Bohemian Club's summer encampment to some 2,000 regional and national elites. The talk, entitled "Violent Weakness," was presented by a political science professor from UC Berkeley. The speaker focused on the way in which increased violence in society was weakening our social institutions. Contributing to this violence and the resulting decay of our institutions, this professor argued, are bisexualism, entertainment politics, multiculturalism, Afrocentrism, and a loss of family boundaries. The professor claimed that, to avert further deterioration, we need to recognize that "elites, based on merit and skill, are important to society and any elite that fails to define itself will fail to survive.... We need boundaries and values set and clear! We need an American-centered foreign policy... and a president who understands foreign policy." He went on to conclude that we cannot allow the "unqualified" masses to carry out policy, but that elites must set values that can be translated into "standards of authority." The speech was forcefully given and was received with an enthusiastic standing ovation by the members.[25]

During the Clinton administration, neoconservatives within the HCPE were still actively advocating military global dominance. Many of the neoconservatives and their global dominance allies found various positions in conservative think tanks and with Department of Defense contractors. They continued close affiliations with each other through the Heritage Foundation, American Enterprise Institute, Hoover Institute, Jewish Institute for National Security Affairs (JINSA), Center for Security Policy, and several other conservative policy groups. Some became active with right-wing publications such as the *National Review* and the *Weekly Standard*. In 1997, they received funding from conservative foundations to create the Project for the New American Century (PNAC).

HCPE advocates for a US-led "New World Order," along with Reagan/Bush hard-liners and other military expansionists, founded

PNAC in June of 1997. Their statement of principles called for guiding principles for American foreign policy and the creation of a strategic vision for America's role in the world. PNAC set forth its aims with the following statement:

- we need to increase defense spending significantly if we are to carry out our global responsibilities today and modernize our armed forces for the future;

- we need to strengthen our ties to democratic allies and to challenge regimes hostile to our interests and values;

- we need to promote the cause of political and economic freedom abroad;

- we need to accept responsibility for America's unique role in preserving and extending an international order friendly to our security, our prosperity, and our principles.

- Such a Reaganite policy of military strength and moral clarity may not be fashionable today. But it is necessary if the United States is to build on the successes of this past century and to ensure our security and our greatness in the next.[26]

The statement was signed by Elliott Abrams, Gary Bauer, William J. Bennett, Jeb Bush, Dick Cheney, Eliot A. Cohen, Midge Decter, Paula Dobriansky, Steve Forbes, Aaron Friedberg, Francis Fukuyama, Frank Gaffney, Fred C. Ikle, Donald Kagan, Zalmay Khalilzad, I. Lewis Libby, Norman Podhoretz, Dan Quayle, Peter W. Rodman, Stephen P. Rosen, Henry S. Rowen, Donald Rumsfeld, Vin Weber, George Weigel, and Paul Wolfowitz. Of the 25 founders of PNAC, 12 were later appointed to high-level positions in the George W. Bush administration.[27]

Since its founding, PNAC has attracted numerous others who have signed policy letters or participated in the group. Eight members have been affiliated with the number-one defense contractor, Lockheed Martin, and seven have been associated with the number-three defense contractor, Northrop Grumman.[28] PNAC is one of several institutions that connect global dominance HCPE and large US military contractors.[29]

In September 2000, PNAC produced a 76-page report entitled *Rebuilding America's Defenses: Strategy, Forces, and Resources for a New Century.*[30] The report was similar to the Defense Policy Guidance document written by Lewis Libby and Paul Wolfowitz in 1992—not surprisingly, since both men participated in the production of the 2000 report. Steven Cambone, Dov Zakheim, Mark Lagan, and David Epstein were also heavily involved. Each of these individuals would go on to hold high-level positions in the George W. Bush administration.[31]

Rebuilding America's Defenses called for the protection of the American homeland, the control of space and cyberspace, and the ability to wage simultaneous theater wars and perform global constabulary roles. It claimed that the decade of the 1990s had been one of defense neglect and that the US had to increase military spending to preserve its geopolitical leadership as the world's superpower. The report claimed that in order to maintain a Pax Americana, potential rivals—such as China, Iran, Iraq, and North Korea—needed to be held in check. As many writers in this volume and elsewhere have pointed out, the report also, in calling for a transformation of the military, said that "the process of transformation... is likely to be a long one, absent some catastrophic and catalyzing event like a new Pearl Harbor."[32] September 11, 2001 was exactly the kind of catastrophe that the authors of *Rebuilding America's Defenses* thought was needed to accelerate a global dominance agenda.

Before 9/11, the development of strategic global dominance policies were likely to be challenged by members of Congress and liberal HCPE, who continued to hold a détente foreign policy that had been traditionally advocated by the Council of Foreign Relations and the State Department. Liberal and moderate HCPE in various think tanks, policy councils, and universities still hoped for a peace dividend, resulting in lower taxes and the stabilization of social programs, and the maintenance of a foreign policy based more on a balance of power than on unilateral US military global domination. Additionally, many HCPE were worried that the costs of rapidly expanding the military would lead to deficit spending.

These liberal/moderate HCPE were so shocked by 9/11 that they became immediately united in their fear of terrorism and in full support of the Patriot Act, Homeland Security, and legislation to support military action in Afghanistan and later Iraq. The resulting permanent war on terror led to massive government spending and the rapid acceleration of the neoconservative HCPE plans for military control of the world.[33]

Understanding Global Dominance Advocates within the HCPE

A group of Department of Defense (DoD) and Homeland Security contractors benefited significantly from expanded military spending after 9/11. For the purposes of this study, we included the top seven military contractors who derive at least one third of their income from DoD contracts. Additionally, we added in the Carlyle Group and Bechtel Group Inc. because of their high levels of political influence and revolving door personnel within the Reagan and both Bush administrations.[34] These corporations have benefited significantly from post-9/11 policies. Our goal is to identify the primary advocates for a global dominance policy within the HCPE and the principal beneficiaries of this policy (see Appendixes).

We believe that by identifying the most important policy advocates and those corporate heads who have the most to gain from a global dominance policy, we can begin to establish the parameters of the individuals involved in the Global Dominance Group (GDG) among the HCPE. Knowing the general parameters of the GDG will provide an understanding of who had the means, opportunity, and motive to have initiated a post-9/11 acceleration of neoconservative military expansion toward the goal of assuming full spectrum military dominance of the world. Understanding the parameters of the GDG will also allow researchers to explore the possibilities of insider pre-knowledge of the 9/11 attacks and the possibility that mercenaries working in conjunction with small elements of the GDG may have helped facilitate the events on September 11, 2001. These are classic sociological questions of who wins and who loses within class structures, policy processes, and state decision-making. In this study, we are not seeking to identify people involved in specific acts before or after 9/11. Rather we seek to understand the sociological phenomena of who, as collective actors the GDG within the HCPE, had the motive, means, and opportunity to gain from and perhaps facilitate such events.

To establish a GDG parameters list, we included the boards of directors of the nine DoD contractors identified earlier as those corporations earning over one third of their revenue from the government or having high levels of political involvement. We have also included members of sixteen leading conservative global-dominance-advocating foundations and policy councils.

Connections and associations listed in our GDG are not always simultaneous, but rather reflect links inside an increasingly important group within the HCPE extending over almost two decades. The list includes 236 names of people who have held high-level positions in the George W. Bush administration, sit on the boards of directors of major DoD contracting corporations, and/or are close associates of the above, serving as GDG advocates on policy councils or advocacy foundations. Deciding whom to include in such a list and how far to extend the links is difficult. We believe, however, that the people listed in Appendix C are many of the principal members of the core of the GDG. These people have been some of the strongest advocates for military global dominance and/or are the primary beneficiaries of such a policy. They tend to know each other through long periods of active involvement in policy circles, boards of directors, consulting positions, government agencies, and project-specific activities.

Although far more research on the GDG needs to be done, we can begin to have an understanding of the parameters and operational methods involved by showing major defense contractor links with the GDG and the policy benefits to such companies as Lockheed Martin, Halliburton, Carlyle, and Northrop Grumman.

Who Profits from GDG Policies?

Lockheed Martin has benefited significantly from the post-9/11 military expansion promoted by the GDG. The Pentagon's budget for buying new weapons rose from $61 billion in 2001 to over $80 billion in 2004. Lockheed Martin's sales rose by over 30 percent at the same time, with tens of billions of dollars on the books for future purchases. From 2000 to 2004, Lockheed Martin's stock value rose 300 percent.

New York Times reporter Tim Weiner wrote in 2004: "No contractor is in a better position than Lockheed Martin to do business in Washington. Nearly 80 percent of its revenue comes from the US Government. Most of the rest comes from foreign military sales, many financed with tax dollars."[35]

As of August 2005, Lockheed Martin stockholders had made 18 percent on their stock in the prior twelve months.[36] According to the Center for Public Integrity, Northrop Grumman has seen similar growth in the last three years, with DoD contracts rising from $3.2 billion in 2001 to $11.1 billion in 2004. Halliburton, with Vice President Dick Cheney as former CEO, has seen phenomenal growth since 2001. Halliburton had defense contracts totaling $427 million in 2001. By 2003, it had $4.3 billion in defense contracts, of which approximately a third were sole source agreements.[37] Cheney, not incidentally, continues to receive a deferred salary from Halliburton. According to financial disclosure forms, he was paid $205,298 in 2001; $162,392 in 2002; $178,437 in 2003; and $194,852 in 2004; and his 433,333 Halliburton stock options rose in value from $241,498 in 2004 to $8 million in 2005.[38]

The Carlyle Group, established in 1987, is a private global investment firm that manages some $30 billion in assets. Numerous high-level members of the GDG have been involved in the Carlyle Group, including Frank Carlucci, George H. W. Bush, James Baker III, William Kennard, and Richard Darman. The Carlyle Group purchased United Defense in 1997. It sold its shares in the company after 9/11, making a $1 billion dollar profit.[39] Carlyle continues to invest in defense contractors and is moving into the homeland security industry.[40]

GDG advocacy continues into the present. Thomas Donnelly—a PNAC participant, American Enterprise Institute resident scholar, and former director of communications for Lockheed Martin—published a book in May of 2005 advocating increasing the DoD budget by a third to $600 billion and adding 150,000 active duty military personnel. Donnelly calls for the continuation of today's "Pax Americana," a GDG euphemism for US global military domination of the world.[41]

Public-Private Partnerships

While it is important not to underestimate the profit motive within the top military defense contractors, the promotion of a global dominance agenda also involves neoconservative ideological beliefs and the formation of extremely powerful public-private partnerships at the highest levels of government, in order to create interlocking networks of global control. The continuing privatization of military services is but one example of this trend.[42] Another example is the recent appointment of Paul Wolfowitz, formerly deputy secretary of defense, to head the World Bank. His appointment gives the GDG strong control of another major institutional asset in the drive for full global dominance.

A global dominance agenda also includes penetration into the boardrooms of the corporate media. A research team at Sonoma State University recently finished conducting a network analysis of the boards of directors of America's ten big media organizations. The team determined that only 118 people comprise the membership on the boards of director of these giants. These 118 individuals in turn sit on the corporate boards of 288 national and international corporations. Four of the top ten media corporations have GDG–DoD contractors on their boards of directors, including William Kennard (*New York Times*, Carlyle Group), Douglas Warner III (GE [NBC], Bechtel), John Bryson (Disney [ABC], Boeing), Alwyn Lewis (Disney [ABC], Halliburton), Douglas McCorkindale (Gannett, Lockheed Martin).[43]

Given an interlocked corporate media network, it is safe to say that big media in the United States effectively represent the interests of corporate America. The media elite, a key component of the HCPE, are the watchdogs of acceptable ideological messages, the controllers of news and information content, and the decision-makers regarding media resources. Corporate media elites are subject to the same pressures as the higher-circle policy makers and, therefore, equally susceptible to reactionary response to our most recent Pearl Harbor.

An important case of Pentagon influence over the corporate media is CNN's retraction of the story about US military use of sarin (a nerve gas) in 1970 in Laos during the Vietnam War. CNN producers April Oliver and Jack Smith, after an eight-month investigation, reported on CNN in June of 1998 and later in *Time* magazine that sarin gas was used in Operation Tailwind in Laos and that American defectors were targeted. The story was based on eyewitness accounts and high military command collaboration. Under tremendous pressure from the Pentagon, Henry Kissinger, Colin Powell, and Richard Helms, both CNN and *Time* retracted the story, saying: "The allegations about the use of nerve gas and the killing of defectors are not supported by the evidence." Oliver and Smith were both fired by CNN later that summer. They have steadfastly stood by their original story as accurate and substantiated. Oliver feels that CNN and *Time* capitulated to the Pentagon's threat to lock them out of future military stories.[44]

Public Relations Companies and the GDG

A popular and arguably effective means of controlling public support for global dominance initiatives exists in the use of public relations (PR) firms. In recent years, PR corporations increased their profits through US and foreign contracts. While direct propaganda campaigns are generally illegal in the United States, governments and

PR firms creatively shape public opinion domestically by planting news in foreign papers that will instantly reach American readers.[45] While the government relies on these firms to generate a specific ideological response from the masses, the PR firms focus on profits. The concentration of power and capital at the top is not unique to the military defense contractors or to the government. It is also evident in the influence over public opinion exercised by public relations and crisis management agencies.

The images that have shaped support for a permanent war on terror include the toppling of the statue of Saddam, the dramatic rescue of Private Jessica Lynch, and dramatic tales of weapons of mass destruction.[46] During the 1991 Gulf War, the world witnessed testimony to Congress about babies taken from incubators and left on cold hospital floors and the heartfelt plea by the Kuwaitis to help liberate them from a ruthless Iraqi dictator. In truth, the CIA, using taxpayer money, funded these images, which were fabricated and disseminated by the Rendon Group, Hill and Knowlton, and other private public relations and crisis management companies.[47]

The agencies responsible for disseminating and shaping information are so interconnected that most public relations firms in the United States and Europe fall under the umbrella of three giant corporations. The big three—WPP, Omnicom Group, and Interpublic—have board members who also sit on the boards of the major media conglomerates, military contracting companies, and government commissions, including direct relationships in the executive and legislative branches of government.[48]

The Rendon Group is one of the firms hired for the PR management of America's pre-emptive wars. In the 1980s, the Rendon Group helped form American sentiment regarding the ousting of President Manuel Noriega in Panama.[49] It shaped international support for the 1991 Gulf War. And it created the Iraqi National Congress—from image, to marketing, to handpicking Ahmed Chalabi.[50] Rendon and similar firms follow the money, shaping public opinion to meet the needs of their clients. The conglomeration and corporatization of the PR industry, in service to the GDG, hinders public discourse and allows those with the most money to dominate news and information in the US and, increasingly, the world.

The ease with which the American population accepted the invasion of Iraq was the outcome of a concerted effort involving the government, DoD contractors, public relations firms, and the corporate media. These institutions are the instigators and main beneficiaries of a permanent war on terror. The importance of these connections lies in the fact that powerful segments of the GDG have the money and resources to articulate their propaganda repeatedly to the American people until those messages become self-evident truths and conventional wisdom.

Election Irregularities

In the fall of 2001, after an eight-month review of 175,000 Florida ballots never counted in the 2000 election, an analysis by the National Opinion Research Center confirmed that Al Gore actually won Florida and should have become president. However, coverage of this report was only a small blip in the corporate media, as a much bigger story dominated the news after September 11, 2001.[51]

The 2004 election was even more fraudulent. The official vote count in 2004 showed that George W. Bush won by three million votes. But exit polls projected a victory margin of five million votes for John Kerry. This eight-million-vote discrepancy is much greater than any possible margin of error. The overall margin of error should statistically have been under one percent. But the official result deviated from the poll projections by more than five percent—a statistical impossibility.[52] Edison Media Research and Mitofsky International were the two companies hired to do the polling for the Nation Election Pool (a consortium of the nation's five major broadcasters and the Associated Press). They refused to release their polling data until after the inauguration.

Election Systems & Software (ES&S), Diebold, and Sequoia are the companies primarily involved in implementing the new electronic voting stations throughout the country. All three have strong ties to the Bush administration. The largest investors in ES&S, Sequoia, and Diebold are government defense contractors Northrop Grumman, Lockheed Martin, Electronic Data Systems (EDS), and Accenture. Diebold hired Science Applications International Corporation (SAIC) of San Diego to develop the software security in its machines. Many of the officials on SAIC's board (identified in our GDG data) are former members of either the Pentagon or the CIA. They include Army General Wayne Downing, formerly on the National Security Council; Bobby Ray Inman, former CIA Director; Retired Admiral William Owens, former vice chairman of the Joint

Chiefs of Staff; and Robert Gates, another former director of the CIA.[53]

Black Box Voting has reported repeatedly that the voting machines used by over 30 million voters were easily hacked by relatively unsophisticated programs and that post-election audits of the computers would not show evidence of tampering. Irregularities in the vote counts indicate that something beyond chance happened in 2004.[54]

Conspiracy theories abound in America and are directly related to the lack of investigative reporting by the corporate media. Corporate media are principally in the entertainment business. The public, therefore, knows more about the 2004 murder case of California wife-killer Scott Peterson than about possibilities of national voter fraud. The corporate media are likewise ignoring many important questions related to 9/11.[55]

Unanswered Questions about 9/11 and the GDG

Philosophy of religion scholar David Ray Griffin has published his findings on the omissions and distortions of *The 9/11 Commission Report*. Griffin questions, among other things, why extensive advanced warnings from several countries were not acted upon by the administration. He asks how a major institutional investor chose to buy put-options (futures that hope a stock price will decline) on American Airlines, United Airlines, and various World Trade Center companies before 9/11. And he notes that the 9/11 Commission failed to address the reports that $100,000 was wired to Mohamed Atta from Saeed Sheikh, an agent for Pakistan's Inter-Service Intelligence (ISI), under the direction of the head of ISI, General Mahmud Ahmed.[56]

In Griffin's list of questions the 9/11 Commission failed to address, perhaps the most important was the reason for the collapse of building 7 of the World Trade Center (WTC) more than seven hours after the Twin Towers had collapsed. WTC 7 was a 47-story steel-frame building that, according to all photographic evidence, had only small fires on a few floors. WTC buildings 5 and 6 had much larger fires and did not collapse. These and other facts have led a number of critics to argue that WTC 7 was a planned demolition. The chapter in the present volume by physicist Steven E. Jones argues that the speed at which building 7 fell could only have been caused by controlled demolition.

Were members of the GDG involved in the events of 9/11 and voter fraud in 2004? We really do not know the answer to that question. We do know that a significant portion of the group has benefited financially from 9/11 and the 2000/2004 elections and that at least a portion of the GDG believed that a catastrophe on the order of 9/11 was necessary to facilitate their global dominance agenda. This establishes that there was clear motive within the GDG for wanting the 9/11 attacks to happen.

Additionally, a significant portion of the GDG had every opportunity to know in advance that the 9/11 attacks were imminent. Many countries — Afghanistan, Argentina, Britain, Cayman Islands, Egypt, France, Germany, Israel, Italy, Jordan, Morocco, and Russia — warned the US government of such attacks. Warnings from within the US intelligence community included intercepts of communications regarding al-Qaeda's specific plans. The Bush administration's claim that it had no idea that such an attack was coming or even possible is contradicted by the existence of a great number of warnings, which have been well documented.[57]

Foreknowledge of 9/11 would have enabled the GDG to act quickly to accelerate its global dominance agenda. People in the GDG had wanted an invasion of Afghanistan long before 9/11. The House International Relations Committee's Sub-Committee on Asia and the Pacific met in February of 1998 to discuss removing the government of Afghanistan from power. The US government told India in June of 2001 that a planned invasion of Afghanistan was set for October and *Jane's Defense News* reported in March of 2001 that the United States planned to invade Afghanistan later that year. The BBC reported that the US told the Pakistani foreign secretary prior to 9/11 of an invasion of Afghanistan planned for October.[58]

Did GDG Members Help Facilitate 9/11?

We have an abundance of evidence that some members of the GDG at least had foreknowledge that the attacks of 9/11 were scheduled. We now turn to our final question: Did some GDG members actually help facilitate the events of 9/11? Our attempt to answer this question is aided by the hearings of the Senate Judiciary Committee on September 21, 2005, which produced the following information.

In 2000, a team of US Army intelligence specialists working in cooperation with Orion Scientific Systems Inc. identified Mohamed Atta (who would later be considered the leader of the 9/11 terrorist group) and three other terror suspects as the center of a Brooklyn al-Qaeda cell. The Able Danger team under the command of US Special Operations Command (SOCOM) had been conducting "data mining" with Orion. (Data mining is the computer processing of vast amounts of communications, focusing in this case on known members of al-Qaeda.) During its operations, it was able to "map al-Qaeda as a world-wide threat with a surprisingly significant presence within the US."[59] On three occasions, the Able Danger team attempted to meet with FBI agents but was ordered by Pentagon officials to stand down and, ultimately, to destroy all its data. Former US Army Major Eric Kleinsmith, who was in charge of the operations, testified about the Pentagon orders. The Pentagon refused to allow all other members of the team who were still on active duty to testify at the hearings. The information destroyed was equal in amount to a quarter of the Library of Congress and included links of US citizens to al-Qaeda and the 9/11 terrorists.[60]

Although these hearings and the fact that the Able Danger team had pre-identified part of the 9/11 terror suspect group were widely covered in the corporate media, the information on possible involvement of American citizens has received little attention. The fact is that a high-level US military public-private partnership involving a major defense contractor and military intelligence uncovered US citizen links to the terror suspects. Officially, all this information was destroyed under direct orders from the Pentagon, although it is clear from the hearings that the data may still exist in private hands. Did members of the GDG cover up US citizen involvement in 9/11? Perhaps. We do not know the full story and much more investigation, based on government subpoena power, is needed.

In the meantime, Ken Cunningham from Penn State University writes:

> Current War-on-Terror levels [of expenditures] surpass the Cold War averages by 18 percent.... 9/11 and the War on Terror have enabled the assertion of an aggressive, preemptive, militarist bloc within the government and the National Security State.... The gravity of the current militarism is the nebulous, potentially limitless [permanent war].[61]

Resistance to the GDG within HCPE

By the end of 2005, the Global Dominance Group's agenda was well established within the HCPE and cunningly operationalized inside the US government. An important question remains. Can we see any evidence of moderates or liberals within the HCPE asserting resistance to the GDG agenda? Certainly the indictment of a key neocon within the Bush administration is a hopeful sign. But there is little evidence that the higher-circle policy elites have any interest in addressing questions regarding either 9/11 or national voter fraud.

Greg Palast reported on the split between the neocons in the Pentagon, on the one hand, and US oil companies and the State Department, on the other hand, over the privatization of the oil fields in Iraq. The GDG neocons were pushing for the US oil companies to purchase Iraq's oil fields outright and the oil companies balked, preferring simply to buy the oil from a stable pro-American Iraqi regime.[62]

Anther sign of resistance was a full-page ad in the *New York Times* on November 10, 2005, placed by a new policy advocacy group called the Partnership for a Secure America. The ad openly challenged the US policy of torture and was signed by numerous HCPE, including Lee Hamilton, Warren Christopher, Gary Hart, and Richard Holbrooke.

Still another sign of resistance is the fact that traditionally powerful long-term lobbying groups such as the US Chamber of Commerce, the National Association of Manufacturers, and the National Association of Realtors, have become concerned about the confidentiality of private files that "could too easily be reviewed" under the Patriot Act.[63]

These oppositional responses to GDG from higher-circle policy elites are hopeful but hardly significant in light of the extent of the global dominance agenda. Many in the HCPE are still fearful of terrorist attacks—a fear that the corporate media constantly reinforces.

Many in the HCPE believe in holding the course in Iraq out of fear of greater unrest in the region should we pull out. Without broad social movements and citizen protests that threaten the stability of HCPE's socioeconomic agendas and corporate profits, there will be little, if any, serious challenge to the GDG. Democratic control of the House and/or the Senate would probably only effect a slight slowing of the GDG agenda, not a reversal.

The events over the past couple of decades and especially the first five years of this century suggest that fascism has taken root in the United States, and there is little indication that a reversal is evident. Vice President Wallace wrote in the *New York Times* on April 9, 1944:

> The really dangerous American fascist… is the man who wants to do in the United States in an American way what Hitler did in Germany in a Prussian way. The American fascist would prefer not to use violence. His method is to poison the channels of public information. With a fascist the problem is never how best to present the truth to the public but how best to use the news to deceive the public into giving the fascist and his group more money or more power.

Wallace then added:

> They claim to be super-patriots, but they would destroy every liberty guaranteed by the Constitution. They demand free enterprise, but are the spokesmen for monopoly and vested interest. Their final objective toward which all their deceit is directed is to capture political power so that, using the power of the state and the power of the market simultaneously, they may keep the common man in eternal subjection.[64]

We are past the brink of totalitarian fascist-corporatism. Challenging the neocons and the GDG agenda is only the beginning of reversing the long-term conservative reactions to the gains of the 1960s. Re-addressing poverty, the UN Declaration of Human Rights, and our own weapons of mass destruction is a long-term agenda for progressive scholars and citizen democrats.

Appendixes to Chapter 11
Department of Defense Contracts

Company	Defense Contracts 2004	Total Revenue 2004	% from DoD
Lockheed Martin Corporation	$20,690,912,117	$35,526,000,000	58
General Dynamics Corporation	$9,563,280,236	$19,178,000,000	50
Raytheon Company	$8,472,818,938	$20,245,000,000	42
Northrop Grumman Corporation	$11,894,090,277	$29,853,000,000	40
Halliburton Company	$7,996,793,706	$20,464,000,000	39
Science Applications International	$2,450,781,108	$7,187,000,000	34
The Boeing Company	$17,066,412,718	$52,457,000,000	33
The Carlyle Group	$1,442,680,446	N/A	N/A
Bell Boeing Joint Program	$1,539,815,440	(Boeing)	N/A

Figures courtesy of Mergent Online Database

Global Dominance Group Organizations

Advocacy Organizations/Think Tanks

AEI	American Enterprise Institute
AIPAC	American Israel Public Affairs Committee
CLI	Committee for the Liberation of Iraq
CPD	Committee on the Present Danger
CSIS	Center for Strategic Studies and International Studies
CSP	Center for Security Policy
DPB	Defense Policy Board
HF	Heritage Foundation
HO	Hoover Institute
HU	Hudson Institute
JINSA	Jewish Institute of National Security Affairs
MI	Manhattan Institute
NIPP	National Institute for Public Policy
NSC	National Security Council
PNAC	Project for the New American Century
Team B	President's Foreign Advisory Board

Important Agencies and Other Organizations

CIA	Central Intelligence Agency
CFR	Council on Foreign Relations
DoC	Department of Commerce
DoD	Department of Defense
DoE	Department of Energy
DoJ	Department of Justice
DoS	Department of State
DoT	Department of Transportation
DPB	Defense Policy Board
NSA	National Security Agency
WHOMB	White House Office of Management and Budget

Note: In selecting the sixteen important neoconservative GPG advocacy organizations, we relied mostly on the International Relations Center website (rightweb.irc-online.org/), the Center for Public Integrity (www.publicintegrity.org), and other sources cited in Chapter Eleven.

Key Players

Individuals are listed with their known governmental and private sector affiliations. For abbreviations, see the previous two pages.

Abramowitz, Morton I.; PNAC, NSC, Asst. Sec. of State, Amb. to Turkey, Amb. to Thailand, CISS, Carlyle

Abrams, Elliott; PNAC, HF, DoS, HU, Special Asst. to President Bush, NSC

Adelman, Ken; PNAC, CPD, DoD, DPB, Fox News, CPD, Commander-in-Chief Strategic Air Command, Northrop Grumman, Arms Control Disarmament Agency

Aldrige, E. C. Jr.; CFR, PNAC, NSA, HU, HF, Sec. of the Air Force, Asst. Sec. of State, Douglas Aircraft, DoD, LTV Aerospace, WHOMB, Strategic Systems Group, Aerospace Corp.

Allen, Richard V.; PNAC, HF, HO, CFR, CPD, CNN, DPB, US Congress, CIA analyst, CSIS, NSC

Amitay, Morris J.; JINSA, AIPAC

Andrews, D. P.; SAIC

Andrews, Michael; L-3 Communications Holdings, Deputy Asst. Sec. of Research and Technology, Chief Scientist for the US Army

Archibald, Nolan D.; Lockheed Martin

Baker, James, III; Carlyle, Sec. of State (G. H. W. Bush), Sec. of Treas. (Reagan)

Barr, William P.; HF, HO, PNAC, CFR, NSA, US Congress, Asst. to President Reagan, Carlyle

Barram, David J.; Computer Sciences Corporation, DoC

Barrett, Barbara; Raytheon

Bauer, Gary; PNAC, Undersec. of Ed.

Bechtel, Riley; Bechtel

Bechtel, Steve; Bechtel

Bell, Jeffrey; PNAC, MI

Bennett, Marcus C.; Lockheed Martin

Bennett, William J.; PNAC, HU, NSA, Sec. of Ed.

Bergner, Jeffrey; PNAC, HU, Boeing

Berns, Walter; AEI, CPD

Biggs, John H.; Boeing, CFR

Blechman, Barry; CPD, DoD

Bolton, John; JINSA, PNAC, AEI, DoS, DoJ, Amb. to UN, WH Legis. Council, Agency Int'l Devel., Undersec. of State

Boot, Max; PNAC, CFR

Bremer, L. Paul; HF, CFR, administrator of Iraq

Brock, William; CPD, US Senate, Sec. of Labor

Brooks, Peter; DoD, HF, CPD

Bryen, Stephen; JINSA, AEI, L-3 Network Security, Edison Int'l, Disney, DoD

Bryson, John E.; Boeing
Bush, Jeb; PNAC, Governor of Florida
Bush, George H. W.; President, CIA dir., Carlyle
Bush, Wes; Northrop Grumman
Cambone, Stephen; PNAC, NSA, DoD, Los Alamos (specialized in theater nuclear weapons issues), Office of Sec. of Defense: Dir. Strategic Def., CSIS, CSP
Chabraja, Nicholas D.; General Dynamics
Chain, John T.; Northrop Grumman, Sec. of the Air Force, dir. of Politico Military Affairs at DoS, Chief of Staff for Supreme Headquarters Allied Powers Europe, Commander-in-Chief Strategic Air Command
Chao, Elaine; HF, Sec. of Labor, Gulf Oil, DoT, CFR
Chavez, Linda; PNAC, MI, CFR
Cheney, Lynne; AEI, Lockheed Martin
Cheney, Richard; JINSA, PNAC, AEI, HU, Halliburton, Sec. of Defense, Vice President
Cohen Eliot A.; PNAC, AEI, CLI, CPD, DPB, DoD
Coleman, Lewis W.; Northrop Grumman
Colloredo-Manfeld, Ferdinand; Raytheon
Cook, Linda Z.; Boeing
Cooper, Dr. Robert S.; BAE Systems, Asst. Sec. of Defense
Cooper, Henry; CPD, DoD, HF, Deputy Asst. Sec. of the Air Force, US Arms Control Disarm. Strategic Def. Initiative, Applied Research Assoc, NIPP
Cox, Christopher; CSP, Senior Associate Counsel to the President, Chairman: SEC.
Crandall, Robert L.; Halliburton, FAA Man. Advisor Bd.
Cropsey, Seth; PNAC, AEI, HF, HU, DoD, Undersec. of the Navy
Cross, Devon Gaffney; PNAC, HF, CPD, HO, DPB
Crouch, J. D.; CSP, Deputy National Security Advisor, DoD, Amb. to Romania
Crown, James S.; General Dynamics, Henry Crown and Co.
Crown, Lester; General Dynamics, Henry Crown and Co.
Dachs, Alan; Bechtel, CFR
Dahlburg, Ken; SAIC, DoC, Asst. to President Reagan, WHOMB
Darman, Richard G.; Carlyle, dir. of the WHOMB, Asst. to President Reagan, Deputy Sec. of Treas., Asst. Sec. of Commerce
Dawson, Peter; Bechtel
Decter, Midge; HF, HO, PNAC, CPD
Demmish, W. H.; SAIC
DeMuth, Christopher; AEI, WHOMB, Asst. to President Nixon
Derr, Kenneth T.; Halliburton
Deutch, John; CIA dir., Deputy Sec. of Defense, Raytheon
Dine, Thomas; CLI, US Senate, AIPAC, US Agency Int'l Development, Free Radio Europe/Radio Liberty, Prague, CFR
Dobriansky, Paula; PNAC, HU, AEI, CPB, DoS, Army, NSC European/ Soviet Affairs, USIA, ISS

Donnelly, Thomas; AEI, PNAC, Lockheed Martin

Downing, Wayne; General US Army, NSA, CLI, SAIC

Drummond, J. A.; SAIC

Duberstein, Kenneth M.; Boeing, WH Chief of Staff

Dudley, Bill; Bechtel

Eberstadt, Nicholas; AEI, CPD, PNAC, DoS (consultant)

Ebner, Stanley; Boeing, McDonnell Douglas, Northrop Grumman, CSP

Ellis, James O., Jr.; Lockheed Martin, Admiral US Navy, Commander US Strategic Command

Epstein, David; PNAC, Office of Sec. of Defense

Everhart, Thomas; Raytheon

Falcoff, Mark; AEI, CFR

Fautua, David; PNAC, Lt. Col. US Army

Fazio, Vic; Northrop Grumman, US House

Feith, Douglas; JINSA, DoD, L-3 Communications, Northrop Grumman, NSC, CFR, CPS

Feulner, Edwin J., Jr.; HF, HO, Sec. of HUD, Inst. European Def. & Strategy Studies, CSIS

Foley, D. H.; SAIC

Fradkin, Hillel; PNAC, AEI,

Frank, Stephen E.; Northrop Grumman

Fricks, William P.; General Dynamics

Friedberg, Aaron; PNAC, CFR, NSA, DoD, CIA consultant

Frost, Phillip; Northrop Grumman

Fukuyama, Francis; PNAC, HU, CFR

Gates, Robert; CIA dir., NSA, SAIC, Pres. Texas A&M Univ.

Gaffney, Frank; CPD, PNAC, *Washington Times*, DoD

Gaut, C. Christopher; Halliburton

Gedmin, Jeffrey; AEI, PNAC, CPD

Gerecht, Reuel Marc; PNAC, AEI, CIA, CBS

Gillis, S. Malcom; Halliburton, Electronic Data Systems Corp

Gingrich, Newt; AEI, CFR, HO, DPB, US House, CLI, CPD

Goodman, Charles H.; General Dynamics

Gorelick, Jamie S.; United Technologies Corporation, Deputy Attorney General, DoD, Asst. to the Sec. of Energy, National Com. Terrorist Threats Upon the US, DoJ, National Security Advisor, CIA, CFR

Gouré, Daniel; DoD, SAIC, DoE, DoS (consultant), CSP

Haas, Lawrence J.; WHOMB, CPD, Yale Univ. dir. of public affairs

Hadley, Stephen; NSA advisor to Bush, Lockheed Martin

Hamre, John J.; ITT Industries, SAIC, Deputy Sec. of Defense, Undersec. of Defense, Senate Armed Services Committee

Hash, Tom; Bechtel

Haynes, Bill; Bechtel

Hoeber, Amoretta; CSP, Defense Industry consultant, CPD, CFR, DoD

Horner, Charles; HU, CSP, DoS, staff member of Sen. Daniel Patrick Moynihan

Howell, W. R.; Halliburton, dir. Deutsche Bank

Hunt, Ray L.; Halliburton, Electronic Data Systems Corp, President's Foreign Intelligence Advisory Board

Inman, Bobby Ray; Admiral US Navy, CIA deputy dir., CFR, NSA, SAIC

Ikle, Fred; AEI, PNAC, CPD, HU, DPB, Undersec. of DoD, Def. Policy Board

Iorizzo, Robert P.; Northrop Grumman

Jackson, Bruce; PNAC, AEI, NSA, CFR, Office of Sec. of Defense, US Army Military Intelligence, Lockheed Martin, Martin Marietta, CLI, CPD

Jennings, Sir John; Bechtel

Johnson, Jay L.; General Dynamics, Admiral US Navy

Jones, A. K.; SAIC, DoD

Joseph, Robert; Undersec. of State for Arms Control and Int'l Security Affairs, DoD, CSP, NIPP

Joulwan, George A.; General Dynamics, General US Army

Kagan, Frederick; PNAC, West Point Military Academy

Kagan, Robert; PNAC, CFR, DoS (Deputy for Policy), *Washington Post*, CLI, contributing editor *Weekly Standard*

Kaminski, Paul G.; General Dynamics, Undersec. of DoD

Kaminsky, Phyllis; JINSA, CSP, NSC, Int'l Pub. Rel. Society

Kampelman, Max M.; PNAC, JINSA, CPD, Sec. of Housing and Urban Development, CPD

Keane, John M.; General Dynamics, General US Army, Vice Chief of Staff of the Army, DoD Policy Board

Kennard, William; Carlyle, *NY Times*, FCC

Kemble, Penn; PNAC, DoS, USIA

Kemp, Jack; JINSA, HF, Sec. of HUD, US House, CPD

Keyworth, George; CSP, HU, Los Alamos, General Atomics, NSC

Khalilzad, Zalmay; PNAC, Amb. to Iraq

King, Gwendolyn S.; Lockheed Martin

Kirkpatrick, Jeane; AEI, JINSA, CPD, CFR, NSA, Sec. of Defense Commission, US Rep. to UN, CLI, CPD, Carlyle

Kramer, H. M. J., Jr.; SAIC

Kristol, Irving; CFR, AEI, DoD, *Wall Street Journal* Board of Contributors

Kristol, William; PNAC, AEI, MI, CLI, Chief of Staff to VP Quayle, founding editor *Weekly Standard*

Kupperman, Charles; CPD, Boeing, NIPP

Lagon, Mark; PNAC, CFR, AEI, DoS

Lane, Andrew; Halliburton

Larson, Charles R.; Admiral US Navy, Northrop Grumman

Laspa, Jude; Bechtel

Ledeen, Michael; AEI, JINSA, DoS (consultant), DoD

Lehman, John; PNAC, NSA, DoD, Sec. of Navy

Lehrman, Lewis E.; AEI, MI, HF, G. W. Bush oil co. partner

Lesar, Dave; Halliburton

Libby, I. Lewis ("Scooter"); PNAC, Chief of Staff to VP Cheney, DoS,

Northrop Grumman, RAND, DoD, US House, Team B
Livingston, Robert; US House, CSP, DoJ
Loy, James M.; Lockheed Martin, Admiral US Navy
Malone, C. B.; SAIC, Martin Marietta, DynCorp, Titan Corp., CLI, CPD
Martin, J. Landis; Halliburton
McCorkindale, Douglas H.; Lockheed Martin
McDonnell, John F.; Boeing
McFarlane, Robert; National Security Advisor (Reagan), CPD
McNerney, James W.; Boeing, 3M, GE
Meese, Edwin; HF, HO, US Attorney General, Bechtel, CPD
Merrill, Philip; CSP, DoD, Import-Export Bank of US
Minihan, Kenneth A.; General US Air Force, BAE Systems, DoD, Defense
    Intelligence Agency
Moore, Frank W.; Northrop Grumman
Moore, Nick; Bechtel
Moorman, Thomas S.; CSP, Aerospace Corporation, Rumsfeld Space
    Commission, US Air Force, Vice Chief of Staff
Mundy, Carl E., Jr.; General Dynamics, General US Marine Corps
Muravchik, Joshua; AEI, JINSA, PNAC, CLI, CPD
Murphy, Eugene F.; Lockheed Martin, GE
Nanula, Richard; Boeing
Novak, Michael; AEI, CPD
Nunn, Sam; GE, US Senate, Chairman Senate Armed Services Committee
O'Brien, Rosanne; Northrop Grumman, Carlyle
Odeen, Philip A.; Defense and Arms Control Staff for Henry Kissinger, TRW,
    Northrop Grumman
Ogilvie, Scott; Bechtel
Owens, William; Admiral US Navy, DPB, Joint Chiefs of Staff, SAIC
Perle, Richard; AEI, PNAC, CPD, JINSA, HU, CLI, Carlyle, CFR, NSA,
    DoD, DPD
Peters, Aulana L.; Northrop Grumman, SEC
Pipes, Daniel; PNAC, CPD
Podhoretz, Norman; PNAC, CPD, HU, CFR
Poses, Frederic; Raytheon
Precourt, Jay A.; Halliburton
Quayle, Dan; PNAC, Vice President
Ralston, Joseph W.; Lockheed Martin, General US Air Force, Vice Chairman
    of Joint Chiefs of Staff
Reed, Deborah L.; Halliburton, Pres. Southern CA Gas & Elec
Ridgeway, Rozanne; Boeing, Asst. Sec. of State, Amb. to German Democratic
    Republic and Finland, DoD
Riscassi, Robert; L-3 Communications Holdings, UN Command/Korea,
    Army Vice Chief of Staff; Joint Chiefs of Staff
Roche, James; Sec. of the Air Force, CSP, Boeing, Northrop Grumman, DoS
Rodman, Peter W.; PNAC, NSA, Asst. Sec. of Defense for Int'l Security

Affairs, DoS

Rowen, Henry S.; PNAC, HO, CFR, DPB, DoD

Rubenstein, David M.; Carlyle, Deputy Asst. to the President for Domestic Policy (Carter)

Rubin, Michael; AEI, CFR, Office of Sec. of Defense

Rudman, Warren; US Senate, Raytheon

Ruettgers, Michael; Raytheon

Rumsfeld, Donald; PNAC, HO, Sec. of Defense, Bechtel, Tribune Co.

Sanderson, E. J.; SAIC

Savage, Frank; Lockheed Martin

Scaife, Richard Mellon; HO, HF, CPD, Tribune Review Publishing Co.

Scheunemann, Randy; PNAC, Office of Sec. of Defense (consultant), Lockheed Martin, CLI founder/dir., CPD

Schlesinger, James; DoE, Atomic Energy Commission, CIA dir., CSP

Schmitt, Gary; PNAC, CLI, DoD (consultant), CLI

Schneider, William, Jr.; BAE Systems, PNAC, DoS, House of Rep./Senate staffer, WHOMB, CSP, NIPP

Schultz, George; HO, AEI, CPD, CFR, PNAC, Bechtel, CLI, CPD, Sec. of State, Sec. of Treas.

Shalikashvili, John M.; Boeing, Chairman of Joint Chiefs of Staff, DoD, General US Army, CFR

Sharer, Kevin; Northrop Grumman, US Naval Academy, Lt. Com. US Navy

Sheehan, Jack; Bechtel, DPB

Shelman, Thomas W.; Northrop Grumman, DoD

Shulsky, Abram; PNAC, DoD

Skates, Ronald L.; Raytheon

Slaughter, John Brooks; Northrop Grumman

Sokolski, Henry; PNAC, HF, HO, CIA, DoD

Solarz, Stephen; PNAC, HU, CPD, Carlyle, DoS

Spivey, William; Raytheon

Statton, Tim; Bechtel

Stevens, Anne; Lockheed Martin

Stevens, Robert J.; Lockheed Martin

Stuntz, Linda; Raytheon, DoE

Sugar, Ronald D.; Northrop Grumman, Association of the US Army

Swanson, William; Raytheon, Lockheed Martin

Tkacik, John; PNAC, HF, US Senate

Turner, Michael J.; BAE Systems

Ukropina, James R.; Lockheed Martin

Van Cleave, William R.; Team B, HO, CSP, CPD, DoD, NIPP

Waldron, Arthur; CSP, AEI, PNAC, CFR

Walkush, J. P.; SAIC

Wallop, Malcolm; HF, HU, CSP, PNAC, US Senate

Walmsley, Robert; General Dynamics, Vice-Admiral Royal Navy, Chief of Defense Procurement for the UK Ministry of Defense

Warner, John Hillard; SAIC, US Army/Air Force Assn.

Watts, Barry; PNAC, Northrop Grumman

Weber, John Vincent (Vin); PNAC, George W. Bush Campaign Advisor, NPR

Wedgewood, Ruth; CLI, DoD, DoJ, DoS, CFR

Weldon, Curt; US House, CSP

Weyrich, Paul; HF, PNAC, US Senate

White, John P.; L-3 Communications, Chair of the Com. on Roles and Missions of the Armed Forces, DoD

Wieseltier, Leon; PNAC, CLI, literary editor *New Republic*

Williams, Christopher A.; PNAC, DPB, Undersec. for Defense, Boeing (lobbyist), Northrop Grumman (lobbyist), CLI

Winter, Donald C; Northrop Grumman

Wolfowitz, Paul; PNAC, HF, HU, Team B, Undersec. Defense, World Bank, Northrop Grumman, DoS

Wollen, Foster; Bechtel

Woolsey, R. James; PNAC, JINSA, CLI, DPB, CIA dir., Undersec. of Navy, NIPP

Wurmser, David; AEI, Office of VP Middle East Adviser, DoS

Yearly, Douglas C.; Lockheed Martin

Young, A. T.; SAIC

Zaccaria, Adrian; Bechtel

Zafirovski, Michael S.; Boeing

Zakheim, Dov S.; PNAC, HF, CFR, DoD, Northrop Grumman, McDonnell Douglas, CPD

Zinni, Anthony C.; General US Marines, BAE Systems, Commander-in-Chief US Central Command

Zoellick, Robert; PNAC, CSIS, US Trade Representative, DoS, CFR, DoJ

Contributors

Richard Falk is Milbank Professor of International Law, emeritus, Princeton University. Since 2002, he has been visiting professor of global studies at the University of California at Santa Barbara. He is chair of the Nuclear Age Peace Foundation and author of many books, three of the most recent being *The Great Terror War*, *The Declining World Order*, and (with Harold Friel) *The Record of the Paper: How the* New York Times *Misreports US Foreign Policy*.

Daniele Ganser is a Swiss historian who specializes in research on secret warfare and peace. He is a senior researcher at the Institute for Strategic Studies at Zurich University and teaches in the history department at the University of Basel. In 2005, he taught a seminar in the history department of Zurich University on the various 9/11 theories and the historical data used to back them up. His most recent book is *NATO's Secret Armies: Operation Gladio and Terrorism in Western Europe*.

David Ray Griffin is a professor of the philosophy of religion and theology, emeritus, at Claremont School of Theology and Claremont Graduate University in Claremont, California, where he remains a co-director of the Center for Process Studies. He is the author or editor of some 30 books, including *The New Pearl Harbor: Disturbing Questions about the Bush Administration and 9/11* and *The 9/11 Commission Report: Omissions and Distortions*.

Steven E. Jones is a professor of physics at Brigham Young University and a recipient in 2005 of its prestigious Alcuin Award. He is the author or co-author of over 40 peer-reviewed scholarly papers, published in such journals as *Nature, Physical Review Letters*, and *Scientific American*. His research interests include fusion energy, solar energy, and physics applied to archaeology.

Karen U. Kwiatkowski retired from the United States Air Force as a lieutenant colonel in 2003 after a twenty-year career, with assignments in the National Security Agency, in Headquarter Air Force, and in the Office of the Secretary of Defense. Her final military tour was as a staff policy officer within the undersecretary of defense for policy, Near East South Asia directorate. She has completed both Air Command and Staff College and the Naval War College seminar programs. She holds an M.A. in government from Harvard University, an M.S. in science management from the University of Alaska, and a Ph.D. in world politics from the Catholic University of America.

John McMurtry is a professor of philosophy and University Professor emeritus at the University of Guelph, Canada, and a fellow of the Royal Society of Canada. His latest book is *Value Wars: The Global Market versus the Life Economy*. He has been selected by the United Nations as the principal author and editor of the ongoing multi-volume set, *Philosophy and World Problems: Encyclopedia of Life Support Systems* (UNESCO/EOLSS).

Peter Phillips is a professor of sociology at Sonoma State University and director of Project Censored, a media research organization. Bridget Thornton and Celeste Vogler are senior research assistants at Sonoma State University with majors in history and political science, respectively.

Morgan Reynolds holds a Ph.D. in economics from the University of Wisconsin at Madison. Formerly the director of the Criminal Justice Center at the National Center for Policy Analysis in Dallas and the chief economist at the US Department of Labor in the first term of George W. Bush, he is now professor emeritus at Texas A&M University in College Station, Texas.

Kevin Ryan, who became a certified quality engineer after earning a B.S. in chemistry, was for many years the laboratory operations manager and then the site manager at Environmental Health Laboratories, a division of Underwriters Laboratories (UL). On the basis of knowledge about testing to national standards that he acquired in these positions, he was led to question the World Trade Center report issued by the National Institute of Standards and Technology (NIST). His employment at UL was terminated after he allowed his concerns to become public. He has since continued to work on behalf of 9/11 truth.

Peter Dale Scott is a former Canadian diplomat and professor of English at the University of California, Berkeley. His most recent book is *Drugs, Oil, and War: The United States in Afghanistan,*

Colombia, and Indochina. His next book is entitled *The Road to 9/11: Wealth, Empire, and the Future of America.* A poet, he was a winner in 2002 of the Lannan Poetry Award. His website is www.peterdalescott.net.

Ola Tunander is a research professor at the International Peace Research Institute in Oslo, Norway (PRIO). He received his Ph.D. in 1989 for a dissertation on US naval strategy. For several years, he headed PRIO's Foreign and Security Policy Program, where he contributed to projects and inquires for ministries of foreign affairs and defense. He has written or edited eleven books on geopolitics, political philosophy, security policy, military strategy and deception, including *Cold Water Politics: The Maritime Strategy and Geopolitics of the Northern Front* (1989), *Geopolitics in Post-Wall Europe: Security, Territory and Identity* (1997), and *The Secret War against Sweden: US and British Submarine Deception in the 1980s* (2004). Some of these books have been used as textbooks at universities and military colleges. He has also contributed to or acted as referee for journals such as *Review of International Studies, Geopolitics, International Security, Political Geography,* and *Millennium: Journal of International Studies.*

Notes

ONE: GRIFFIN

1 On the idea of moral principles common to all traditions, see Michael Walzer, *Thick and Thin: Moral Argument at Home and Abroad* (Notre Dame: University of Notre Dame Press, 1994), and Gene Outka and John P. Reeder Jr., eds., *Prospects for a Common Morality* (Princeton: Princeton University Press, 1993). This idea of a common morality presupposes moral realism, according to which some basic moral principles exist in the nature of things. I have defended moral realism in "Morality and Scientific Naturalism: Overcoming the Conflicts," in *Philosophy of Religion in the New Century: Essays in Honor of Eugene Thomas Long*, ed. by Jeremiah Hackett and Jerald Wallulis (Boston: Kluwer Academic Publications, 2004) 81–104, and in "Theism and the Crisis in Moral Theory: Rethinking Modern Autonomy," in *Nature, Truth, and Value: Exploring the Thought of Frederick Ferré*, ed. by George Allan and Merle Allshouse (Lanham, MD: Lexington Books, 2005) 199–220.

2 Hans Küng, *A Global Ethic for Global Politics and Economics* (New York: Oxford University Press, 1998) 97–98. This rule, in its negative form, is sometimes called the "silver rule."

3 Andrew J. Bacevich, *American Empire: The Realities and Consequences of US Diplomacy* (Cambridge: Harvard University Press, 2002) 30, 218–19.

4 Krauthammer's statement is quoted in Emily Eakin, "All Roads Lead To DC," *New York Times* 31 March 2002: Week in Review.

5 Charles Krauthammer, "The Bush Doctrine," *Time* 5 March 2001, quoted in Chalmers Johnson, *The Sorrows of Empire: Militarism, Secrecy, and the End of the Republic* (New York: Metropolitan Books, 2004) 68.

6 Robert Kagan, "The Benevolent Empire," *Foreign Policy* Summer 1998: 24–35.

7 Dinesh D'Souza, "In Praise of an American Empire," *Christian Science Monitor* 26 April 2002.

8 Charles Krauthammer, "The Unipolar Era," in Andrew J. Bacevich, ed., *The Imperial Tense: Prospects and Problems of American Empire* (Chicago: Ivan R. Dee, 2003) 47–65, at 59. This track record, he says, proves that "the United States is not an imperial power with a desire to rule other countries."

9 Noam Chomsky, *Hegemony or Survival: America's Quest for Global Dominance* (New York: Henry Holt [Metropolitan Books], 2003). As shown by this and many of Chomsky's previous books—one of which is entitled *Deterring Democracy* (New York: Hill and Wang, 1992)—his reading of America's "track record" is very different from Krauthammer's.

10 Richard Falk, "Will the Empire Be Fascist?" *Global Dialogues*, 2003; "Resisting the Global Domination Project: An Interview with Prof. Richard Falk," *Frontline* 20/8 (12–25 April 2003).

11 Johnson, *The Sorrows of Empire* 33, 4.

12 In light of the fact that the present chapter was, in an earlier form, delivered at the University of Wisconsin at Madison (18 April 2005), I should point out that Bacevich discusses two left-leaning historians from whose analysis of US foreign policy he has benefited, Charles Beard and William Appleton Williams, and that Williams studied at Madison (where Beard exerted great

influence) and then began teaching there in 1957, becoming the founding father of what historians have dubbed the "Wisconsin school" (see Bacevich, *American Empire* 3–31).

13 Bacevich, *American Empire* 7, 46, 52, 133.

14 See Chomsky's *Hegemony or Survival,* his *9-11* (New York: Seven Stories, 2001), and his foreword to Phyllis Bennis, *Before and After: US Foreign Policy and the September 11th Crisis* (Northampton: Olive Branch Press, 2003); for Rahul Mahajan, see *The New Crusade: America's War on Terrorism* (New York: Monthly Review Press, 2003) and *Full Spectrum Dominance: US Power in Iraq and Beyond* (New York: Seven Stories Press, 2003); for Johnson, see *The Sorrows of Empire.*

15 See www.zogby.com/news/ReadNews.dbm?ID=855. This information, however, was evidently not considered news fit to print by the *New York Times* and other mainstream sources. Also generally unknown is the fact that already in 2002, the *Atlanta Journal-Constitution,* believing that Congresswoman Cynthia McKinney had charged that the Bush administration had foreknowledge of the attacks, conducted a poll that asked its readers if they were "satisfied the Bush administration had no advance warning of the September 11 attacks." Surprisingly, 46 percent of the respondents said "No, I think officials knew it was coming." See "Poll Shocker: Nearly Half Support McKinney's 9/11 Conspiracy Theory," *Newsmax* 17 April 2002. I discussed the McKinney episode in *The New Pearl Harbor: Disturbing Questions about the Bush Administration and 9/11* (Northampton: Olive Branch Press, 2004) 161–64, 242–44nn. This book is henceforth cited as NPH.

16 See the *Toronto Star* 26 May 2004; Ian Johnson, "Conspiracy Theories about Sept. 11 Get Hearing in Germany," *Wall Street Journal* 29 September 2003; and "Zogby Poll Finds Over 70 Million Voting Age Americans Support New 9/11 Investigation" (www.911truth.org/article.php?story=20060522022041421).

17 Jean Bethke Elshtain, *Just War Against Terror: The Burden of American Power in a Violent World* (New York: Basic Books, 2003).

18 This interpretation is given in the most extreme, simplistic, and misleading terms in David Frum and Richard Perle, *An End of Evil: How to Win the War on Terror* (New York: Random House, 2003). To mention Frum and Perle as publicly endorsing the official view of the 9/11 attacks does not, of course, imply that they actually hold this view.

19 NPH 69.

20 See NPH Ch. 5 and David Ray Griffin, *The 9/11 Commission Report: Omissions and Distortions* (Northampton: Olive Branch Press, 2005) 49–58, 262–67. This book is henceforth cited as 9/11CROD.

21 This statement (which is quoted in NPH 69) is contained in the summary of the final report of the Joint Inquiry conducted by the House and Senate intelligence committees, posted at intelligence.senate.gov/press.htm under December 11, 2002.

22 *San Francisco Chronicle* 29 September 2001.

23 *The 9/11 Commission Report: Final Report of the National Commission on Terrorist Attacks upon the United States,* Authorized Edition (New York: W. W. Norton, 2004) 499n130.

24 UPI 13 February 2001; Michael Ruppert, "Suppressed Details of Criminal Insider Trading Lead Directly into the CIA's Highest Ranks," From the Wilderness (www.fromthewilderness.com) 9 October 2001.

25 William Norman Grigg, "Did We Know What Was Coming?" *The New American* 18/5 (www.thenewamerican.com) 11 March 2002.

26 Major Mike Snyder, a NORAD spokesman, was quoted right after 9/11 as saying that interceptions are carried out "routinely" (Glen Johnson, "Otis Fighter Jets Scrambled Too Late to Halt the Attacks," *Boston Globe* 15 September 2001. With regard to the figure of about 100 times a year, the FAA reported that NORAD had scrambled fighter jets 67 times between September 2000 and June 2001 (FAA News Release, 9 August 2002), and the *Calgary Herald* (13 October 2001) reported that NORAD had scrambled fighters 129 times in 2000. At an average of 100 a year, fighters would have been scrambled about 1,000 times in the decade prior to 9/11. One of the many falsehoods in a debunking essay entitled "9/11: Debunking Myths," which was published by *Popular Mechanics* (March 2005), is its claim that in the decade before 9/11, there had been only one interception, that of golfer Payne Stewart's Learjet. This essay's "senior researcher," 25-year old Benjamin Chertoff, has (on a radio show) tried to reconcile this claim with the statements by the FAA and the *Calgary Herald* by saying that these statements speak only of scrambles, not interceptions. But Chertoff's position would require the claim that only one of the 1,000 scrambles in that period resulted in interceptions—that the other 999 fighters were called back before they actually made the interception. Besides being highly improbable, this interpretation contradicts Major Snyder's statement that interceptions are carried out routinely.

Ben Chertoff is, not incidentally, the cousin of Michael Chertoff, the head of the Department of Homeland Security (see Christopher Bollyn, "Ben Chertoff of *Popular Mechanics*: Cousin of Homeland Security Director, Michael Chertoff" [www.911wasalie.com/phpwebsite/index.php?module=pagemaster&PAGE_user_o p=view_page&PAGE_id=33]). Young Chertoff's debunking article has itself been effectively debunked by many genuine 9/11 researchers. See Peter Meyer, "Reply to *Popular Mechanics* re 9/11" (www.serendipity.li/wot/pop_mech/ reply_to_popular_mechanics.htm) and Jim Hoffman, "*Popular Mechanics*' Assault on 9/11 Truth," *Global Outlook* 10 (Spring–Summer 2005): 21–42 (which was based on Hoffman, "*Popular Mechanics*' Deceptive Smear Against 9/11 Truth," 911Review.com, 15 February 2005 [911review.com/pm/markup/index.html]). Although these two critiques take different approaches in response to some of the issues, they both demonstrate that *Popular Mechanics* owes its readers an apology for publishing such a massively flawed article on such an important subject.

27 See 9/11CROD 143–51.

28 "Statement of Secretary of Transportation Norman Y. Mineta before the National Commission on Terrorist Attacks upon the United States, 23 May 2003" (available at www.cooperativeresearch.org/timeline/2003/ commissiontestimony052303.htm).

29 *The 9/11 Commission Report* 40.

30 Richard A. Clarke, *Against All Enemies: Inside America's War on Terror* (New York: Free Press, 2004) 7–8.

31 My accounts of the Report's lies aimed at defending the US military's behavior, which I cannot even begin to summarize here, fill Chapters 12–16 of 9/11CROD. A briefer version is provided in Griffin, "Flights of Fancy: The 9/11 Commission's Incredible Tales of Flights 11, 175, 77, and 93," published in *Global Outlook* 12 (Fall–Winter 2006), and in Griffin, *Christian Faith and the Truth behind 9/11* (Louisville: Westminster John Knox, 2006). It was previously

published as "Flights 11, 175, 77, and 93: The 9/11 Commission's Incredible Tales," 911Truth.org, 5 December 2005 (www.911truth.org/article.php?story=20051205150219651).

32 9/11CROD 159–64.

33 Thierry Meyssan, *Pentagate* (London: Carnot, 2002) 115, quoting "PAVE PAWS, Watching North America's Skies, 24 Hours a Day" (www.pavepaws.org).

34 Thierry Meyssan, *9/11: The Big Lie* (London: Carnot, 2002) 112, 116. With regard to his source of information, Meyssan has written (e-mail correspondence, 2005): "The presence of these anti-missile batteries was testified to me by French officers to whom they were shown during an official visit to the Pentagon. This was later confirmed to me by a Saudi officer." Testimony to the existence of anti-aircraft missiles has also been provided by John Judge, whose parents had worked at the Pentagon ("Pentagon and P-56 Preparations and Defenses and the Stand-Down on 9/11," *Ratville Times* 11 January 2006 [www.ratical.org/ratville/JFK/JohnJudge/P56A.html]). The Pentagon has, to be sure, denied that it had any anti-aircraft batteries at that time, saying that they were considered "too costly and too dangerous to surrounding residential areas" (Paul Sperry, "Why the Pentagon Was So Vulnerable," *WorldNetDaily* 11 September 2001 [www.wnd.com/news/article.asp?ARTICLE_ID=24426]). But can anyone believe that Pentagon officials would have let such considerations prevent them from protecting themselves?

35 Russ Wittenberg, who flew large commercial airliners for 35 years after serving in Vietnam as a fighter pilot, says that it would have been impossible for Flight 77 to have "descended 7,000 feet in two minutes, all the while performing a steep 270 degree banked turn before crashing into the Pentagon's first floor wall without touching the lawn." It would, he adds, have been "totally impossible for an amateur who couldn't even fly a Cessna to maneuver the jetliner in such a highly professional manner" (Greg Szymanski, "Former Vietnam Combat and Commercial Pilot Firm Believer 9/11 Was Inside Government Job," *Lewis News*, Sunday 8 January 2006 [www.lewisnews.com/article.asp?ID=106623]).

36 In "The Missing Wings" (www.physics911.net/missingwings.htm), A. K. Dewdney and G. W. Longspaugh argue that the absence of wing debris alone is sufficient to disprove the claim that the aircraft was a huge airliner. For more general discussions of the photographic evidence, see Eric Hufschmid, *Painful Questions*, Chapter 9; "September 11, 2001 Revisited: The Series: Act II, The Center for an Informed America" (www.davesweb.cnchost.com/nwsltr68.html); and "9-11 and the Impossible: Part One of an Online Journal of 9-11" (www.physics911.net/omholt.htm), by former pilot Ralph Omholt, who writes in a summary statement: "The expected 'crash' damage doesn't exist... . There was no tail, no wings; no damage consistent with a B-757 'crash.'" Discussing one photograph in particular, Omholt says: "there is no doubt that a plane did not hit the Pentagon. There is no hole big enough to swallow a 757. There is no distinctive impact damage to the façade of the building, from the supposed high-speed wings and tail."

37 Kwiatkowski speaks of the absence of the expected debris *outside* the building. For eyewitness accounts of the absence of the expected debris *inside* the building, see the statements by Ed Plaugher, the county fire chief, and Lee Evey, the head of the renovation project (DoD News Briefings, 12 and 15 September 2001; discussed in *NPH* 33). An eyewitness account to the lack of expected *damage* is provided by Isabelle Slifer, who has reported that her 4th-floor office,

which was immediately above the strike zone, was not damaged by the initial impact of the striking aircraft (Nikki Lowe, "Pentagon Survivor Donates $500 in Lieu of a Retirement Party: Isabelle Slifer Shares Her Story" [www.pentagonmemorial.net/site/News2?page=NewsArticle&id=5773]).

38 Won-Young Kim and Gerald R. Baum, "Seismic Observations during September 11, 2001, Terrorist Attack" (www.mgs.md.gov/esic/publications/ download/911pentagon.pdf).

39 For my discussion of these problems in the official story, see Chapter 2 and the Afterword of *NPH* (updated edition) or Chapter 3 of *9/11CROD*.

40 On the confiscation of the film from the Citgo gas station, see Bill McKelway "Three Months On, Tension Lingers Near the Pentagon," *Richmond Times-Dispatch* 11 December 2001 (news.nationalgeographic.com/news/2001/ 12/1211_wirepentagon.html). The confiscation from a nearby hotel was reported in Bill Gertz and Rowan Scarborough, "Inside the Ring," *Washington Times* 21 September 2001. On an attempt to get the Department of Justice to release the videos, see "Government Responds to Flight 77 FOAI Request," 911Truth.org, August 2005 (www.911truth.org/article.php?story=20050824131004151). On the videos released in 2006, see Pentagon Videos a Fiasco, Scholars Conclude" (www.scholars for 911truth.org/PressRelease22May2006.html).

41 See "High-Rise Office Building Fire One Meridian Plaza Philadelphia, Pennsylvania," by FEMA (www.interfire.org/articleres–file/pdf/Tr-049.pdf), and "Fire Practically Destroys Venezuela's Tallest Building" (www.whatreallyhappened.com/venezuela_fire.html).

42 See Griffin, "Explosive Testimony: Revelations about the Twin Towers in the 9/11 Oral Histories," 911Truth.org, 18 January 2006 (www.911truth.org/article.php?story=20060118104223192).

43 A Bronx firefighter named Joe O'Toole, who worked for many months on the cleanup efforts, said one day he saw a beam lifted from deep below the surface and "[I]t was dripping from the molten steel" (Jennifer Lin, "Recovery Worker Reflects on Months Spent at Ground Zero," Knight Ridder 29 May 2002. A company vice president who spent time at the site reported that "sometimes when a worker would pull a steel beam from the wreckage, the end of the beam would be dripping molten steel" (Trudy Walsh, "Handheld APP Eased Recovery Tasks," *Government Computer News* 21/27a, 11 September 2002 [www.gcn.com/21_27a/news/19930-1.html]). For more general testimonies about pools of molten steel, see the Jones essay, Chapter 3 of this book.

44 I have discussed eleven features of the collapses that cannot be explained by the official theory, but can easily be explained in terms of explosives, in "The Destruction of the World Trade Center: Why the Official Account Cannot Be True," in Paul Zarembka, ed., *The Hidden History of 9-11-2001* (Amsterdam: Elsevier, 2006); also available at 911Review.com (911review.com/articles/ griffin/nyc1.html), and in *Christian Faith and the Truth behind 9/11*.

45 The official investigators found that they had less authority than the clean-up crews, a fact that led the Science Committee of the House of Representatives to report that "the lack of authority of investigators to impound pieces of steel for examination before they were recycled led to the loss of important pieces of evidence" (www.house.gov/science/hot/wtc/wtc-report/WTC_ch5.pdf).

46 "Baosteel Will Recycle World Trade Center Debris," Eastday.com, 24 January 2002 (www.china.org.cn/english/2002/Jan/25776.htm).

47 This removal was, moreover, carried out with the utmost care, because

"the loads consisted of highly sensitive material." Each truck was equipped with a Vehicle Location Device, connected to GPS. "The software recorded every trip and location, sending out alerts if the vehicle traveled off course, arrived late at its destination, or deviated from expectations in any other way.... One driver... took an extended lunch break of an hour and a half.... [H]e was dismissed" (Jacqueline Emigh, "GPS on the Job in Massive World Trade Center Clean-Up," *Access Control & Security Systems* 1 July 2002; securitysolutions.com/ar/security_gps_job_massive).

48 For discussion of claims about significant structural damage, see the section on WTC 7 in Griffin, "The Destruction of the World Trade Center."

49 Chief Thomas McCarthy of the FDNY said that while the firefighters "were waiting for 7 World Trade to come down," there was "fire on three separate floors" (Oral History of Thomas McCarthy, 10–11). Emergency medical technician Decosta Wright said: "I think the fourth floor was on fire.... [W]e were like, are you guys going to put that fire out?" (Oral History of Decosta Wright, 11). These quotations are from the 9/11 oral histories recorded by the New York Fire Department at the end of 2001 but released to the public (after a court battle) only in August 2005, at which time they were made available on a *New York Times* website (graphics8.nytimes.com/packages/html/nyregion/20050812_WTC_GRAPHIC/met_WTC_histories_full_01.html).

50 A photograph taken by Terry Schmidt can be seen on page 63 of Eric Hufschmid's *Painful Questions: An Analysis of the September 11th Attack* (Goleta, CA: Endpoint Software, 2002). According to Schmidt, this photo was taken between 3:09 and 3:16 PM, hence only a little over 2 hours before Building 7 collapsed. It shows that on the north side of the building, fires were visible only on floors 7 and 12. Therefore, if there indeed were fired on the south side (which faced the Twin Towers), as some officials claimed, they were not big enough to be seen from the north side.

5 Maggie Burns, "Secrecy Surrounds a Bush Brother's Role in 9/11 Security," *American Reporter,* 9/2021, 20 January 2003.

52 "Secretary Rumsfeld Interview," *New York Times* 12 October 2001. Condoleezza Rice made a very similar comment, which is quoted in Chalmers Johnson, *The Sorrows of Empire* 229.

53 *The National Security Strategy of the United States of America,* September 2002 (www.whitehouse.gov/nsc/nss.html) 28.

54 David North, "America's Drive for World Domination," in Bacevich, ed., *The Imperial Tense* 66–77, at 66.

55 This document, which was signed in February 1997 by then USAF Commander in Chief Howell M. Estes III, was at one time available at www.spacecom.af.mil/usspace. This website is, however, no longer functional. Also, although the US military has a website devoted to "Joint Vision Historical Documents" (www.dtic.mil/jointvision/history.htm), the February 1997 document is not included. There *is* a document from *May* of that year entitled "Concept for Future Joint Operations," which is subtitled "Expanding *Joint Vision 2010.*" The website also has that previous document (*Joint Vision 2010*), which was published during the tenure of General John Shalikashvili as Chairman of the Joint Chiefs of Staff (1993 to 1997). But it is as if the document from February 1997 never existed; perhaps it was later deemed too candid. At this writing it could still be found on the website of Peace Action Maine (www.peaceactionme.org/v-

intro.html). And it was discussed in Jack Hitt, "The Next Battlefield May Be in Outer Space," *New York Times Magazine* 5 August 2001.

56 Air Force Space Command, "Strategic Master Plan FY06 and Beyond," 1 October 2003 (www.peterson.af.mil/hqafspc/library/AFSPCPADoffice/Final%2006%SMP--signed!vl.pdf).

57 Quoted in Hitt, "The Next Battlefield May Be in Outer Space." Although those who have warned that the United States plans to put weapons in space had long been dismissed as alarmists, the US military's plan to do just this was revealed in 2005 in a *New York Times* front page story (Tim Weiner, "Air Force Seeks Bush's Approval for Space Weapons Programs," *New York Times* 18 May 2005.

58 The Project for the New American Century, *Rebuilding America's Defenses: Strategy, Forces and Resources for a New Century*, September 2000 (www.newamericancentury.org).

59 *Rebuilding America's Defenses* 51.

60 This according to the *Washington Post* 27 January 2002.

61 *Report of the Commission to Assess US National Security Space Management and Organization* (www.defenselink.mil/pubs/spaceabout.html).

62 Department of Defense News Briefing on Pentagon Attack, 6:42 PM, 11 September 2001 (available at www.yale.edu/lawweb/avalon/sept_11/dod_brief02.htm). According to the transcript, the question was asked by Secretary Rumsfeld. But the flow of the discussion suggests that it came from a reporter. In either case, the 9/11 attacks were interpreted to mean that greater military spending was needed, "especially for missile defense."

63 Zbigniew Brzezinski, *The Grand Chessboard: American Primacy and Its Geostrategic Imperatives* (New York: Basic Books, 1997) 24–25.

64 Brzezinski, *The Grand Chessboard* 212; cf. 35–36.

65 See NPH 89–92 or 9/11CROD 122–28.

66 See NPH 92–95 or 9/11CROD 129–34.

67 *Rebuilding America's Defenses* 14.

68 Christine Spolar, "14 'Enduring Bases' Set in Iraq: Long-Term Military Presence Planned," *Chicago Tribune* 23 March 2004 (available at www.globalsecurity.org/org/news/2004/040323-enduring-bases.htm).

69 "Global Empire or Global Democracy: The Present Choice," Ch. 6 of *The American Empire and the Commonwealth of God: A Political, Economic, Religious Statement*, by David Ray Griffin, John B. Cobb, Jr., Richard Falk, and Catherine Keller (Louisville: Westminster John Knox Press, 2006).

70 This chapter is a slightly revised version of a lecture, "9/11 and the American Empire: How Should Religious People Respond," which was given at the University of Wisconsin at Madison, April 18, 2005. It was then broadcast on C-SPAN2 (BookTV) on April 30. This was the first time that this alternative understanding of 9/11 had been presented on a television program broadcast to a national audience. It was out of this lecture, along with the positive response it evoked, that the idea for the present book arose.

TWO: KWIATKOWSKI

1 George W. Bush, "Press Conference," Washington, DC, 13 March 2002 (www.whitehouse.gov/news/releases/2002/03/20020313-8.html).

2 See Silverstein's statement at Infowars.com.

3 See Alan Cabal, "Miracles and Wonders," *New York Press* 17–23 May 2006.

4 Bill McKelway "Three Months On, Tension Lingers Near the Pentagon," *Richmond Times-Dispatch*, 11 December 2001 (news.nationalgeographic.com/news/2001/12/1211_wirepentagon.html).

5 See White House, President's Remarks on Intelligence Reform, 2 August 2004.

6 David Harrison, "Revealed: The Men with Stolen Identities," *London News-Telegraph* 23 September 2001 "Hijack 'Suspects' Alive and Well," BBC News 23 September 2001.

7 Harrison, "Revealed."

8 Lyric Wallwork Winik, "Interview with Donald Rumsfeld," *Parade Magazine*, in Defenselink Transcripts, 12 October 2001 (www.defenselink.mil/transcripts/2001/t11182001_t1012pm.html).

THREE: JONES

1 Numbered photographs in this paper are displayed in color in the online version of this essay, which is at www.physics.byu.edu/research/energy.

2 See the video clip at www.plaguepuppy.net.

3 Click on the three photos at the top of 911research.wtc7.net/talks/wtc/videos.html. It helps to have sound. Then look at a video close-up of the southwest corner of WTC 7 as this corner begins its steady drop to the ground: st12.startlogic.com/~xenonpup/Flashes/squibs_along_southwest_corner.htm.

4 *The Structural Engineer* 3 September 2002: 6.

5 James Williams, "WTC a Structural Success," *SEAU NEWS: The Newsletter of the Structural Engineers Association of Utah*, October 2001: 3. (Although Leslie Robertson has often been credited with the design of the Twin Towers, he was, as Kevin Ryan points out in his chapter, at the time merely a junior member of the firm Worthington, Skilling, Helle, and Jackson. It was John Skilling who was really in charge of the design.)

6 *Penn Arts and Sciences,* Summer 2002 (www.sas.upenn.edu/sasalum/newsltr/summer2002/k911.html).

7 *Magazine of Johns Hopkins Public Health*, late fall, 2001.

8 FEMA, "World Trade Center Building Performance Study," May 2002 (www.fema.gov/library/wtcstudy.shtm); see also Jim Hoffman, "Metallurgical Examination of WTC Steel Suggests Explosives" (www.911research.wtc7.net/wtc/evidence/metallurgy/index.html).

9 Brent Blanchard, phone interview, 10 February 2006.

10 A. E. Cote, ed., *Fire Protection Handbook,* 17th ed. (Quincy, Maine: National Fire Protection Association, 1992).

11 *Fire Protection Handbook.*

12 T. W. Eagar and C. Musso, "Why Did the World Trade Center Collapse? Science, Engineering, and Speculation," *Journal of the Minerals, Metals and Materials Society*, 53/12 (2001): 8–11.

13 Andy Field, "A Look Inside a Radical New Theory of the WTC Collapse," *Fire/Rescue News* 7 February 2004 (available at cms.firehouse.com/content/article/article.jsp?sectionId=46&id=25807).

14 See "Metal Temperature by Color," Process Associates of America (www.processassociates.com/process/heat/metcolor.htm).

15 Gail Swanson, *Behind the Scenes: Ground Zero, World Trade Center, September 11, 2001* (New York: TRAC Team, Inc., 2003).

16 Available at www.cchem.berkeley.edu/demolab/images/ironred.jpg.

17 A manufacturer has written: "Nanoenergetics refers to a broad class of energetic materials and formulations that exploit mechanisms and properties that exist only at the nanoscale. For example, aluminum is a highly reactive metal when produced as nanopowder (size <100 nm). Metal powders are an important subset of nanoenergetics. Today it is well known that nanoenergetics can increase performance of explosives, propellants, and pyrotechnic devices. The interest and appeal of nanoenergetic formulations lies in their ability to release energy in a controllable fashion, coupled with their higher energy density, relative to conventional organic explosives" (www.nanoscale.com/markets_nanoenergetics.asp). Regarding bombs, see www.technologyreview.com/articles/ 05/01/wo/wo_gartner012105.asp?p=1.

18 See www.checktheevidence.com/911/Thermite2.htm, and media.putfile.com/thermitef.

19 J. R. Barnett, R. R. Biederman, and R. D. Sisson Jr., "An Initial Microstructural Analysis of A36 Steel from WTC Building 7," *Journal of the Minerals, Metals and Materials Society* 53/12 (2001): 18.

20 See www.dodtechmatch.com/DOD/Patent/ PatentDetail.aspx?type=description&id=6766744&HL=ON.

21 FEMA, "World Trade Center Building Performance Study," Appendix C.

22 A diagram of WTC 7's steel column arrangement is on my website. FEMA, Chap. 5; NIST (National Institute of Standards and Technology), "Final Report of the National Construction Safety Team on the Collapses of the World Trade Center Towers (Draft)," 2005.

23 For examples of complete, symmetrical collapses due to carefully pre-positioned explosives, see www.implosionworld.com/cinema.htm. The videos of the collapses of the Philips Building, Southwark Towers, and Schuylkill Falls Tower are particularly instructive.

24 FEMA, Ch. 5.

25 James Glanz, "Engineers are Baffled over the Collapse of 7 WTC; Steel Members Have Been Partly Evaporated," *New York Times* 29 November 2001.

26 Norman Glover, "Collapse Lessons," *Fire Engineering* October 2002 (fe.pennnet.com/Articles/Article_Display.cfm?Section=Archi&Subsection=Display &P=25&ARTICLE_ID=163411&KEYWORD=norman%20glover).

27 *Popular Mechanics*, "9/11: Debunking the Myths," March 2005 (www.popularmechanics.com/science/defense/1227842.html?page=1&c=y).

28 This equation is $y = \frac{1}{2} gt^2$.

29 An intriguing insight regarding this highly secure building is provided by *New York Times* writer James Risen, who says: "The CIA's undercover New York station was in the 47-story building at 7 World Trade Center.... The intelligence agency's employees were able to watch from their office windows while the twin towers burned just before they evacuated their own building" ("Secretive CIA Site in New York Was Destroyed on Sept. 11," *New York Times* 4 November 2001).

30 FEMA, Ch. 2.

31 See Jim Hoffman, "Video Evidence of the North Tower Collapse" (911research.wtc7.net/wtc/evidence/videos/wtc1_close_frames.html) and Ralph W. Omholt, "The Mystery of the WTC Collapse" (home.comcast.net/~skydrifter/collapse.htm).

32 James Glanz and Eric Lipton, "Towers Withstood Impact, but Fell to Fire, Report Says," *New York Times* 29 March 2002.

33 FEMA, Ch. 2.

34 James Dwyer, "City to Release Thousands of Oral Histories of 9/11 Today," *New York Times* 12 August 2005. These oral histories of eyewitnesses are available at the *New York Times* archives at graphics8.nytimes.com/packages/html/nyregion/20050812_WTC_GRAPHIC/met_ WTC_histories_full_01.html.

35 Donn de Grand Pre, "Many Questions Still Remain about Trade Center Attack," *American Free Press* 3 February 2002.

36 Dwyer, "City to Release Thousands."

37 Assistant Commissioner Stephen Gregory, FDNY, File No. 91 10008 (see note 34, above).

38 Rodriguez told me that even though he had given this testimony to the 9/11 commission, it was not included in the final report. He has observed that as the last person pulled from the rubble of the north tower, and a leader of the families who lost loved ones that day, his testimony (which is corroborated by other witnesses) is presented unedited all over the world—except in the US.

39 Field, "A Look Inside."

40 This point is clearly explained in Judy Woods, "The Case for Controlled Demolition" and Jim Hoffman, "The Twin Towers' Demolition: Exposing the Fraud of the Government's Story (911research.wtc7.net/talks/towers/index.html). See also, Griffin, "The Destruction of the World Trade Center: Why the Official Story Cannot Be True," Paul Zarembka, ed., *The Hidden History of 9-11-2001* (Amsterdam: Elsevier, 2006).

41 NIST, "Final Report" 80n1.

42 Tom Harris, "How Building Implosions Work" (science.howstuffworks.com/building-implosion.htm).

43 See Jim Hoffman, "Twin Towers' Rate of Fall Proves Demolition" (911research.wtc7.net/wtc/analysis/proofs/speed.html) and David Ray Griffin, NPH, Ch. 2.

44 This equation is $y = \frac{1}{2} gt^2$.

45 See Hoffman, "Twin Towers' Rate of Fall"; Griffin, NPH, Ch. 2; and Griffin, "The Destruction."

46 Harris, "How Building Implosions Work."

47 See photograph 16 of the online version of my paper (www.physics.byu.edu/research/energy/htm7.html), and www.911research.com/wtc/evidence/videos/docs/south_tower_collapse.mpeg.

48 See Chris Mooney, *The Republican War on Science* (New York: Basic Books, 2005).

49 Harris, "How Building Implosions Work."

50 FEMA, ch. 5.

51 Christopher Bollyn, "New Seismic Data Refutes Official Explanation" (www.americanfreepress.net/09_03_02/NEW_SEISMIC_/new_seismic_.html).

52 Harris, "How Building Implosions Work."

53 See Hoffman, "Videos Show Building 7's Vertical Collapse" (911research.wtc7.net/talks/wtc/videos.html). A great deal of further information is presented from a serious scientific point of view at Hoffman's other site, wtc7.net.

54 Zedenek P. Bazant and Yong Zhou, "Why Did the World Trade Center Collapse? Simple Analysis," *Journal of Engineering Mechanics* 128:2 (January 2002): 2.

55 Eagar and Musso, "Why."

56 NIST, "Final Report"; NIST, "WTC 7 Collapse (preliminary report), Part IIC."

57 B. Lane and S. Lamont, "ARUP Fire's Presentation Regarding Tall Buildings and the Events of 9/11," *ARUP Fire* April 2005 (www.arup.com/DOWNLOADBANK/download353.pdf).

58 Lane and Lamont.

59 Kevin Ryan, letter to Frank Gayle (2004), available at www.911truth.org/article.php?story=20041112144051451.

60 Dave Parker, "WTC investigators Resist Call for Collapse Visualisation," *New Civil Engineer* 6 October 2005.

61 William Manning, "Selling out the Investigation," Editorial, *Fire Engineering* January 2002.

62 Ryan, letter to Frank Gayle.

63 NIST, "Final Report,"81.

64 Quoted in Don Paul and Jim Hoffman, *Waking Up from Our Nightmare: The 9/11/01 Crimes in New York City* (San Francisco: Irresistible/Revolutionary, 2004) 25.

65 Field, "A Look Inside."

66 Paul and Hoffman, *Waking Up,* 26.

67 Eagar and Musso, "Why."

68 "Why the Towers Fell," *Nova,* PBS 30 April 2002 (see www.pbs.org/wgbh/nova/wtc/).

69 NIST, "Final Report" 142.

70 I gratefully acknowledge comments and contributions by Jim Hoffman, Alex Floum, Jeffrey Farrer, Carl Weis, Victoria Ashley, William Rodriguez, and Jeff Strahl, and Professors Jack Weyland, David Ray Griffin, James Fetzer, Bryan Peterson, Paul Zarembka, and Derrick Grimmer.

FOUR: RYAN

1 Richard Heinberg, "Götterdämmerung," Museletter 144, March 2004 (www.museletter.com/archive/144.html).

2 David Ray Griffin, *The 9/11 Commission Report: Omissions and Distortions* (Northampton: Olive Branch Press, 2005). Griffin summarizes the omissions and distortions in "The 9/11 Commission Report: A 571-Page Lie," 911 Visibility Project, 22 May 2005 (www.septembereleventh.org/newsarchive/2005-05-22-571pglie.php).

3 Angus K. Gillespie, *Twin Towers: The Life of New York City's World Trade Center* (New Brunswick: Rutgers University Press, 1999) 117.

4 "How Columns Will Be Designed for 110-Story Buildings," *Engineering News-Record* 2 April 1964: 48–49.

5 Jim Hoffman, "Building a Better Mirage: NIST's 3-Year $20,000,000 Cover Up of the Crime of the Century," 911Research.wtc7.net, 8 December 2005 (911research.wtc7.net/essays/nist/index.html).

6 Website for Teng & Associates (www.teng.com/teng2k3/mainframe.asp).

7 Website for National Directory of Expert Witnesses (national-experts.com/online.html).

8 Archived webcast video of NIST press briefing, NIST News Release website, 23 June 2005 (www.nist.gov/public_affairs/releases/wtc_briefing_june2305.htm) 01:15:10.

9 Sheila Barter, "How the World Trade Center Fell," BBC News, 13 September 2001 (news.bbc.co.uk/1/hi/world/americas/1540044.stm).

10 FEMA, "World Trade Center Building Performance Study," May 2005, Chapter 2.

1 James Glanz and Eric Lipton, *City in the Sky: The Rise and Fall of the World Trade Center* (New York: Times Books, 2003) 330.

2 Karl Koch III with Richard Firstman, *Men of Steel: The Story of the Family that Built the World Trade Center* (New York: Crown Publishers, 2002) 365.

3 Eric Hufschmid, *Painful Questions: An Analysis of the September 11th Attack* (Goleta, CA: Endpoint Software, 2002) 27.

14 Table of results from Underwriters Laboratories August 2004 floor model tests, as presented by NIST in October 2004 (wtc.nist.gov/media/P6StandardFireTestsforWeb.pdf) 25.

15 NIST, *Final Report of the National Construction Safety Team on the Collapses of the World Trade Center Towers* (Draft). (wtc.nist.gov/pubs/NISTNCSTAR1draft.pdf) 195.

16 Silverstein's statement is contained in "America Rebuilds," PBS documentary, 2002 (www.pbs.org/americarebuilds). It can be viewed (www.infowars.com/Video/911/wtc7_pbs.WMV) or heard on audio file (VestigialConscience.com/PullIt.mp3).

17 "Structures Can Be Beautiful, World's Tallest Buildings Pose Esthetic and Structural Challenge to John Skilling," *Engineering News-Record* 2 April 1964: 124.

18 Glanz and Lipton, *City in the Sky* 138.

19 Underwriters Laboratories e-mail correspondence, 1 December 2003.

20 Samuel H. Marcus, *Basics of Structural Steel* (Reston, VA: Reston Publishing, 1977) 20.

21 Underwriters Laboratories email correspondence, 1 December 2003.

22 Kevin Ryan, "The Collapse of the WTC," 911 Visibility Project, 11 November 2004 (www.septembereleventh.org/newsarchive/2004-11-11-ryan.php).

23 John Dobberstein, "Area Man Stirs Debate on WTC Collapse," *South Bend Tribune* 22 November 2004 (www.911truth.org/article.php?story=20041124095100856).

24 NIST, "Final Report" 196.

25 Comments from Underwriters Laboratories on NIST WTC report, NIST website (wtc.nist.gov/comments/ULI_Ganesh_Rao_8-5-05.pdf).

26 Archived webcast video of NIST press briefing, NIST News Release website, 23 June 2005 (www.nist.gov/public_affairs/releases/ wtc_briefing_june2305.htm) 01:18:50.

27 NIST presentation on WTC 7 collapse investigation, NIST website (wtc.nist.gov/pubs/June2004WTC7StructuralFire&CollapseAnalysisPrint.pdf).

FIVE: SCOTT

1 Western governments and media apply the term "al-Qaeda" to the whole "network of co-opted groups" who have at some point accepted leadership, training, and financing from bin Laden (Jason Burke, *Al-Qaeda: The True Story of Radical Islam* [London: I.B. Tauris, 2004] 7–8). From a Muslim perspective, the term "al-Qaeda" is clumsy and has led to the targeting of a number of Islamist groups opposed to bin Laden's tactics. See Montasser al-Zayyat, *The Road to Al-Qaeda: The Story of Bin Laden's Right-Hand Man* (London: Pluto Press, 2004) 100, etc.

2 Michael Griffin, *Reaping the Whirlwind: The Taliban Movement in Afghanistan* (London: Pluto Press, 2001) 115. Exploration in the 1990s has

considerably downgraded these estimates.

3 Peter Truell and Larry Gurwin, *False Profits: The Inside Story of BCCI, the World's Most Corrupt Financial Empire* (Boston: Houghton Mifflin, 1992) 132; Peter Dale Scott, *Drugs, Oil, and War* (Lanham, MD: Rowman & Littlefield, 2003) 42.

4 Robert Parry, *Secrecy & Privilege: Rise of the Bush Dynasty from Watergate to Iraq* (Arlington, VA: Media Consortium, 2004) 213–28, 235–39, 245–47.

5 For Hamilton's role on the conspiratorial whitewashing of contra drug activities, see Peter Dale Scott and Jonathan Marshall, *Cocaine Politics: The CIA, Drugs, and Armies in Central America* (Berkeley: University of California Press, 1998) 179–81. At least eight men in the current Bush administrations of George W. Bush were criticized for their roles in Iran-Contra, including two (Poindexter and Abrams) who were convicted.

6 Steve Coll, *Ghost Wars: The Secret History of the CIA, Afghanistan, and Bin Laden, from the Soviet Invasion to September 10, 2001* (New York: Penguin Press, 2004) 157; George Crile, *Charlie Wilson's War: The Extraordinary Story of the Largest Covert Operation in History* (New York: Atlantic Monthly Press, 2003) 521.

7 George Crile, *Charlie Wilson's War* (New York: Atlantic Monthly Press, 2003) 335 (car bombings); Steve Coll, *Washington Post*, 19 July 1992.

8 Rahman was issued two visas, one of them "by a CIA officer working undercover in the consular section of the American embassy in Sudan" (Peter L. Bergen, *Holy War, Inc.: Inside the Secret World of Osama bin Laden* [New York: Free Press, 2001] 67; cf. 218 (Khalifa). FBI consultant Paul Williams writes that Mohamed "settled in America on a visa program controlled by the CIA" (*Al Qaeda: Brotherhood of Terror* [Upper Saddle River, NJ: Alpha/Pearson Education, 2002] 117). Others allegedly admitted despite being on the State Department watch list include Mohamed Atta and possibly Ayman al-Zawahiri (Nafeez Mosaddeq Ahmed, *The War on Truth: 9/11, Disinformation, and the Anatomy of Terrorism* [Northampton, MA: Olive Branch Press, 2005] 205, 46).

9 Former State Department officer Michael Springmann, BBC, 6 November 2001; Ahmed, *The War on Truth*, 10.

10 *US v. Sheikh Omar Abdel Rahman et al*, Federal Court, SDNY, Testimony of Rodney Hampton-El, 3 August 1995.

11 Peter Lance, *Cover Up: What the Government Is Still Hiding about the War on Terror* (New York: Regan Books/HarperCollins, 2004) 25; Andrew Marshall, *Independent* 1 November 1998: "Mr. Mohamed, it is clear from his record, was working for the US government at the time he provided the training: he was a Green Beret, part of America's Special Forces.... A confidential CIA internal survey concluded that it was 'partly culpable' for the World Trade Center bomb, according to reports at the time." Williams writes that Mohamed's "primary task as a US soldier was to train Muslims to fight the Soviets in Afghanistan" (Williams, *Al Qaeda: Brotherhood of Terror* 117). Cf. *The 9/11 Commission Report* 68.

12 The most prominent example was the blocking by David Frasca at FBI headquarters of the investigation of Zacarias Moussaoui under the Foreign Intelligence Surveillance Act (FISA). Frasca also failed to act on the July 2001 request from the Phoenix FBI office urging a systematic review of Muslim students at US flight schools (Ahmed, *The War on Truth* 251–57).

13 *The 9/11 Commission Report* 171. This statement is one-sided and misleading. But so is the opposite claim of Yossef Bodansky: "The annual income of the Taliban from the drug trade is estimated at $8 billion. Bin Laden administers and manages these funds—laundering them through the Russian mafia..." (Bodansky, *Bin Laden: The Man Who Declared War on America* [New York: Random House/Prima, 2001] 315).

14 Thomas Goltz, *Azerbaijan Diary: A Rogue Reporter's Adventures in an Oil-Rich, War-Torn, Post-Soviet Republic* (Armonk, NY: M. E. Sharpe, 1999) 272–75. A fourth operative in MEGA Oil, Gary Best, was also a veteran of North's Contra support effort. For more on General Secord's and Major Aderholt's roles as part of Ted Shackley's team of off-loaded CIA assets and capabilities, see Marshall, Scott, and Hunter, *The Iran-Contra Connection* 26–30, 36–42, 197–98.

15 Goltz *Azerbaijan Diary* 272–75; Peter Dale Scott, *Drugs, Oil, and War* 7. As part of the airline operation, Azeri pilots were trained in Texas. Dearborn had previously helped Secord advise and train the fledgling Contra air force (Marshall, Scott, and Hunter, *The Iran-Contra Connection* 197). Richard Secord was allegedly attempting also to sell Israeli arms, with the assistance of Israeli agent David Kimche, another associate of Oliver North (see Scott, *Drugs, Oil, and War* 7, 8, 20). Whether the Americans were aware of it or not, the al-Qaeda presence in Baku soon expanded to include assistance for moving jihadis onward into Dagestan and Chechnya.

16 Cooley, *Unholy Wars* 180; Scott, *Drugs, Oil, and War* 7. These important developments were barely noticed in the US press, but a *Washington Post* article did belatedly note that a group of American men who wore "big cowboy hats and big cowboy boots" had arrived in Azerbaijan as military trainers for its army, followed in 1993 by "more than 1,000 guerrilla fighters from Afghanistan's radical prime minister, Gulbuddin Hekmatyar" (*Washington Post* 21 April 1994). The Azeri "Afghan Brigade" was formally dissolved in 1994, after which it focused more on sabotage and terrorism (Cooley 181).

17 Cooley, *Unholy Wars* 176.

18 As the *9/11 Commission Report* notes (58), the bin Laden organization established an NGO in Baku, which became a base for terrorism elsewhere. It also became a transshipment point for Afghan heroin to the Chechen mafia, whose branches "extended not only to the London arms market, but also throughout continental Europe and North America" (Cooley 176).

19 See Lewis Mackenzie (former UN commander in Bosnia), "We Bombed the Wrong Side?" *National Post* 6 April 2004: "Those of us who warned that the West was being sucked in on the side of an extremist, militant, Kosovo-Albanian independence movement were dismissed as appeasers. The fact that the lead organization spearheading the fight for independence, the Kosovo Liberation Army (KLA), was universally designated a terrorist organization and known to be receiving support from Osama bin Laden's al-Qaeda was conveniently ignored....The Kosovar Albanians played us like a Stradivarius violin. We have subsidized and indirectly supported their violent campaign for an ethnically pure Kosovo. We have never blamed them for being the perpetrators of the violence in the early 1990s, and we continue to portray them as the designated victim today, in spite of evidence to the contrary. When they achieve independence with the help of our tax dollars combined with those of bin Laden and al-Qaeda, just consider the message of encouragement this sends to other terrorist-supported independence movements around the world."

Cf. John Pilger, *New Statesman* 13 December 2004.

20 "'Many members of the Kosovo Liberation Army were sent for training in terrorist camps in Afghanistan,' said James Bissett, former Canadian ambassador to Yugoslavia and an expert on the Balkans. 'Milosevic is right. There is no question of their participation in conflicts in the Balkans. It is very well documented'" (*National Post* 15 March 2002). Cf. Frank Ciluffo of the Globalized Organized Crime Program, in testimony presented to the House of Representatives Judicial Committee (13 December 2000): "What was largely hidden from public view was the fact that the KLA raise part of their funds from the sale of narcotics." Contrast e.g. Michael Ignatieff, *Virtual War: Kosovo and Beyond* (New York: Metropolitan/Henry Holt, 2000) 13: "the KLA, at first a small band of poorly trained and amateurish gunmen...." For the al-Qaeda background to the UCK and its involvement in heroin-trafficking, see also Marcia Christoff Kurop, "Al Qaeda's Balkan Links," *Wall Street Journal Europe* 1 November 2001. "According to Michel Koutouzis, the DEA's website once contained a section detailing Kosovar trafficking, but a week before the US-led bombings began, the section disappeared" (Peter Klebnikov, "Heroin Heroes," *Mother Jones* January/February 2000).

21 George Monbiot, *Guardian* 15 February 2001.

22 BBC News 28 December 2004. Those who charged that such a pipeline was projected were initially mocked but gradually vindicated (*Guardian* 15 February 2001; Scott, *Drugs, Oil, and War* 34). See also Marjorie Cohn, "NATO Bombing of Kosovo: Humanitarian Intervention or Crime against Humanity?" *International Journal for the Semiotics of Law* March 2002: 79–106.

23 Klebnikov, "Heroin Heroes."

24 Patrick Fitzgerald, testimony before the 9/11 Commission, 16 June 2004, www.9-11commission.gov/hearings/hearing12.htm.

25 Fitzgerald must have known he was dissembling. Even the mainstream account by Daniel Benjamin and Steven Simon, *The Age of Sacred Terror* (New York: Random House, 2002) 236, records that "When Mohamed was summoned back from Africa in 1993 [sic: Mohamed in his confession says 1994] to be interviewed by the FBI in connection with the case against Sheikh Rahman and his coconspirators, he convinced the agents that he could be useful to them as an informant." Cf. Lawrence Wright, *New Yorker* 16 September 2002: "In 1989... Mohamed talked to an FBI agent in California and provided American intelligence with its first inside look at Al Qaeda." Larry C. Johnson, a former State Department and CIA official, faulted the FBI publicly for using Mohamed as an informant, when it should have recognized that the man was a high-ranking terrorist plotting against the United States. In Johnson's words: "It's possible that the FBI thought they had control of him and were trying to use him, but what's clear is that they did not have control" (*San Francisco Chronicle* 4 November 2001).

26 Lance, *1000 Years* 30; Williams, *Al-Qaeda: Brotherhood of Terror* 117; Bergen, *Holy War, Inc.* 128.

27 Bodansky, *Bin Laden* 106; cf. Richard H. Shultz Jr. and Ruth Margolies Beitler, *Middle East Review of International Affairs* June 2004 (meria.idc.ac.il/journal/2004/issue2/jv8n2a6.html). In 1995 Mohamed accompanied Ayman al-Zawahiri of Islamic Jihad, already effectively merged with al Qaeda, on a secret fund-raising trip through America (Bodansky 105; Peter L. Bergen, *Holy War, Inc.* [New York: Free Press, 2001] 201).

28 Cf. *The 9/11 Commission Report* 68. The *Globe and Mail* later concluded

that Mohamed "was working with US counter-terrorist agents, playing a double or triple game, when he was questioned in 1993" (*Globe and Mail* 22 November 2001).

29 Montasser al-Zayyat (see note 1) has written: "I am convinced that [Zawahiri] and not bin Laden is the main player in these events" (98). In contrast, *The 9/11 Commission Report* (151) assigns no role to Zawahiri in the 9/11 plot. Was Mohamed in touch with Zawahiri at this time? The *San Francisco Chronicle* has written that "until his arrest in 1998 [by which time the 9/11 plot was already under way], Mohamed shuttled between California, Afghanistan, Kenya, Somalia and at least a dozen other countries" (*San Francisco Chronicle* 21 October 2001).

30 Burke, *Al-Qaeda* 150 (see note 1).

SIX: GANSER

1 Thomas Kean (Chair), *The 9/11 Commission Report: Final Report of the National Commission on Terrorist Attacks upon the United States*, Authorized Edition (New York: W. W. Norton, 2004).

2 David Ray Griffin, *The 9/11 Commission Report: Omissions and Distortions* (Northampton: Olive Branch Press, 2005).

3 Griffin 14.

4 Books that have implicitly or explicitly argued that LIHOP or MIHOP theories describe 9/11 best include: David Ray Griffin's two books, *The New Pearl Harbor* (Northampton: Olive Branch Press, 2004) and the book mentioned above; Webster Griffin Tarpley, *9/11 Synthetic Terror: Made in USA* (Joshua Tree: Progressive Press, 2005); Michael Ruppert, *Crossing the Rubicon: The Decline of the American Empire at the End of the Age of Oil* (Gabriola Island: New Society Publishers, 2004); Jim Marrs, *Inside Job: Unmasking the 9/11 Conspiracies* (San Rafael: Origin Press, 2004); Andreas von Bülow, *Die CIA und der 11. September: Internationaler Terror und die Rolle der Geheimdienste* (Munich: Piper, 2004); Nafeez Ahmed, *The War on Truth* (Northampton: Olive Branch Press, 2005); Eric Hufschmid, *Painful Questions: An Analysis of the September 11th Attack* (Goleta, CA: Endpoint Software, 2002); Thierry Meyssan, *Pentagate* (London: Carnot, 2002).

5 Wikipedia, "Psychological Warfare" (en.wikipedia.org/wiki/Psychological_warfare).

6 During Italy's Cold War history, the military intelligence service had been involved in a number of shadow operations that, when discovered, led to public protests that repeatedly forced the intelligence service to change its label. Created on March 30, 1949, four years after the defeat of Italy in World War II but a few days before Italy became a founding member of NATO, the Italian military intelligence service was first called SIFAR (Servizio Informazioni delle Forze Armate), then SID (Servizio Informazione Difesa) from 1965 to 1977, and then its current designation, SISMI (Servizio per le Informazioni e la Sicurezza Militare).

7 Hugh O'Shaughnessy, "Gladio: Europe's Best Kept Secret," *Observer* 7 June 1992. Shaughnesssy writes: "They were the agents who were to 'stay behind' if the Red Army overran Western Europe. But the network that was set up with the best intentions degenerated in some countries into a front for terrorism and far-right political agitation."

8 *Newsnight*, BBC1 4 April 1991.

9 Quoted in *Senato della Repubblica: Commissione parlamentare d'inchiesta sul terrorismo in Italia e sulle cause della mancata individuazione dei responsabilii*

delle stragi: Il terrorismo, le stragi ed il contesto storico politico (Rome: Redatta dal presidente della Commissione, Senatore Giovanni Pellegrin, 1995) 261.

10 *Senato della Repubblica* 157.

11 *Senato della Repubblica* 220.

12 *Newsnight*, BBC1 4 April 1991.

13 *Observer* 18 November 1990.

14 Mario Coglitore, ed., *La Notte dei Gladiatori. Omissioni e silenzi della Repubblica* (Padua, 1992) 131.

15 Leo Müller, *Gladio: Das Erbe des Kalten Krieges: Der NATO-Geheimbund und sein deutscher Vorläufer* (Hamburg: Rowohlt, 1991) 27.

16 Reuters 12 November 1990.

17 Franco Ferraresi, "A Secret Structure Codenamed Gladio," *Italian Politics: A Review* 1992: 30. Ferraresi quotes directly from the document that Andreotti handed over to the parliamentary commission. The Italian daily *L'Unita* published the document in a special edition on 14 November 1990. It is also contained in Jean Francois Brozzu-Gentile, *L'affaire Gladio* (Paris: Editions Albin Michel, 1994).

18 Ferraresi 31, quoting directly from the Andreotti document.

19 Ed Vulliamy, "Secret Agents, Freemasons, Fascists... and a Top-level Campaign of Political 'Destabilisation': 'Strategy of Tension' That Brought Carnage and Cover-up," *Guardian* 5 December 1990.

20 Italian political magazine *Europeo* 16 November 1990. Miceli had indeed been sentenced to go to prison in the 1970s and spent six months in a military hospital. In 1974 the Italian investigating judge, Giovanni Tamburino, in the course of his investigation into right-wing terrorism in Italy, had taken the unprecedented step of arresting General Miceli on the charge of "promoting, setting up, and organizing, together with others, a secret association of military and civilians aimed at provoking an armed insurrection to bring about an illegal change in the constitution of the state and the form of government." (See also the British political magazine *Statewatch* January 1991.) During his trial in November of 1974, Miceli, previously responsible for the NATO Security Office, angrily confirmed that a special unit did indeed exist within the military secret service, SID, but that he was not to blame: "A Super SID on my orders? Of course! But I have not organized it myself to make a coup d'état. This was the United States and NATO who asked me to do it!" (See also Brozzu-Gentile 105.) It was the end of his career in the Italian military secret service. After his time in prison, he became a parliamentarian in 1976 and for the rest of his life enjoyed parliamentary immunity from prosecution as deputy of the neofascist Movimento Sociale Italiano (MSI). Reelected twice, he resigned in 1987 on grounds of ill health and died three years later.

21 As quoted in Ferraresi 31.

22 Norberto Bobbio, as quoted in Ferraresi 32.

23 *Washington Post* 14 November 1990. The only other article by the *Post* that features the keyword "Gladio" appeared on 8 August 1993. A comparison with a leading British newspaper, the *Guardian*, which had 39 articles on Gladio during the same period, indicates how poorly the Gladio phenomenon was covered in the US press.

24 Philip P. Willan, *Puppetmasters: The Political Use of Terrorism in Italy* (London: Constable, 1991) 28.

25 *Independent* 1 December 1990.

26 Jonathan Kwitny, "The CIA's Secret Armies in Europe," *Nation* 6 April 1992: 445.

27 *Senato della Repubblica: Commissione parlamentare d'inchiesta sul terrorismo in Italia e sulle cause della mancata individuazione dei responsabiliy delle stragi: Stragi e terrorismo in Italia dal dopoguerra al 1974. Relazione del Gruppo Democratici di Sinistra l'Ulivo* (Rome, June 2000). Quoted as "Italian Senate 2000 report on Gladio and the massacres."

28 Quoted in Philip Willan: "US 'Supported Anti-left Terror in Italy.' Report Claims Washington Used a Strategy of Tension in the Cold War to Stabilize the Centre-Right," *Guardian* 24 June 2000.

29 Philip Willan, "Terrorists 'Helped by CIA' to Stop Rise of Left in Italy," *Guardian* 26 March 2001. Willan, an expert on US covert action in Italy, published the very valuable book *Puppetmasters* (see note 24).

30 Jeffrey McKenzie Bale, "The 'Black' Terrorist International: Neo-Fascist Paramilitary Networks and the 'Strategy of Tension' in Italy, 1968–1974" (Ann Arbor, Mich.: UMI Dissertation Services, 1996).

31 Arthur Rowse, "Gladio: The Secret US War to Subvert Italian Democracy," *Covert Action Quarterly* 49 (Summer 1994).

32 *Times* (London) 19 November 1990.

33 *Observer* 18 November 1990.

34 See Daniele Ganser, *NATO's Secret Armies: Operation Gladio and Terrorism in Western Europe* (London: Frank Cass, 2005).

35 *European* 9 November 1990.

36 *European* 9 November 1990. It seems that the NATO official who issued the correction was Robert Stratford. Cf. Regine Igel, *Andreotti: Politik zwischen Geheimdienst und Mafia* (Munich: Herbig Verlag, 1997) 343.

37 *Observer* 18 November 1990.

38 Letter of Lee McClenny, NATO head of press and media, to the author, dated 2 May 2001

39 "Gladio. Un misterio de la guerra fria. La trama secreta coordinada por mandos de la Alianza Atlantica comienza a salir a la luz tras cuatro decadas de actividad," *El País* 26 November 1990.

40 *El País* article.

41 Reuters News Service 15 November 1990.

42 Debates of the European Parliament (official transcripts) 22 November 1990.

43 See note 34.

44 Quoted in Brozzu-Gentile 141. Also quoted by the Associated Press 13 November 1990.

45 Kwitny, "The CIA's Secret Armies in Europe" 446, 447.

46 Kwitny.

47 Roger Faligot and Pascal Krop, *La Piscine: Les Services Secrets Francais 1944–1984* (Paris: Editions du Seuil, 1985) 165.

48 Quoted in Stuart Christie, *Stefano Delle Chiaie* (London: Anarchy Publications, 1984) 32. Also in *Lobster* (October 1989) 18. This document was allegedly found in the former office of Guerain-Serac after the Portuguese revolution of 1974.

49 *Commissione parlamentare d'inchiesta sul terrorismo in Italia e sulle cause della mancata individuazione dei responsabili delle stragi.* 9th session, 12 February 1997 (www.senato.it/parlam/bicam/terror/stenografici/steno9.htm).

50 Besides not implementing Lemnitzer's plan, Kennedy transferred him to Europe, where he served as NATO's Supreme Allied Commander from January 1963 to July 1969. He was replaced by General Andrew Goodpaster, who served

as SACEUR from 1969 through 1974, during the years when the terrorist operations took place in Italy.

51 On the homepage of the National Security Archive at www.gwu.edu/~nsarchiv/news/20010430.

52 James Bamford, *Body of Secrets: Anatomy of the Ultra-Secret National Security Agency* (New York: Anchor Books, 2002) 91.

SEVEN: REYNOLDS

1 See www.lewrockwell.com/reynolds/reynolds12.html.

2 Texas A&M has since taken this web page down, but it can be found 911blimp.net/cached/DrGates-stmtTAMU.htm.

3 Hans-Hermann Hoppe, "Interview with Chronicle of Higher Education," Ludwig von Mises Institute, 27 February 2005 (www.mises.org/fullstory.aspx?Id=1756); Hans-Hermann Hoppe, "My Battle with the Thought Police," Ludwig von Mises Institute, 12 April 2005 (www.mises.org/story/1792).

4 Defense Secretary Rumsfeld claims: "This is not a criminal action. This is war" (Paul Thompson, *The Terror Timeline* [New York: Reganbooks, 2004] 463). But war does not excuse destruction of evidence.

5 For proof—plenty of it—that there was a cover-up, see David Ray Griffin, *The 9/11 Commission Report: Omissions and Distortions* (Northampton, MA: Olive Branch Press, 2005).

6 See www.teamliberty.net/id267.html.

7 For a superb history of false-flag operations, see Webster Griffin Tarpley, *9/11 Synthetic Terror: Made in USA* (Joshua Tree, CA: Progressive Press, 2005). //

8 *The Wordsworth Dictionary of Idioms* (Hertfordshire, UK: Wordsworth Editions, 1995) 258.

9 www.tamu.edu/00/data/about.html.

10 www.clearchannel.com.

11 www.salon.com/ent/clear_channel.

12 www.buzzflash.com/farrell/04/03/far04009.html.

13 Tarpley 443.

14 student-rules.tamu.edu/aggiecode.htm.

15 student-rules.tamu.edu/foreword.htm.

16 www.tamu.edu/vision2020.

17 The document, signed in February 1997 by then USAF Commander in Chief Howell M. Estes III, was at one time available at www.spacecom.af.mil/usspace but the website is now gone. As David Ray Griffin says, perhaps it was too candid. It can, in any case, still be found at Peace Action Maine (www.peaceactionme.org/v-intro.html). It was discussed by Jack Hitt, "The Next Battlefield May Be in Outer Space," *New York Times Magazine* 5 August 2001.

18 Quoted in Hitt.

19 David Ray Griffin, *The New Pearl Harbor* (Northampton, MA: Olive Branch, 2004) 100.

20 www.af.mil/bios/bio.asp?bioID=5317.

21 www.mcc.org/ask-a-vet/military_oath.html. It appears that for them, obeying presidential orders is more important than defending the Constitution, which says, among other things, that the military should not go overseas to fight wars unless declared by Congress (www.lewrockwell.com/hornberger/hornberger61.html).

22 en.wikipedia.org/wiki/Space-grant_university.

23 "Resisting the Global Domination Project: An Interview with Prof. Richard Falk," *Frontline* 20/8 (12–25 April 2003).

24 See Chapter 11 and Appendix C, for insight on Gates's place within the elite ruling group of this country.

25 Robert M. Gates, *From the Shadows: The Ultimate Insider's Story of Five Presidents and How They Won the Cold War* (New York: Touchstone, 1996). While Gates credits Western political pressure symbolized by SDI in winning the Cold War, the opposite interpretation, provided by Chalmers Johnson, is that Gates's CIA had "an almost unbroken record of mistaken assessments" of the USSR during its final decade and that "US intelligence agencies did not see the crisis of the Soviet Union coming.... [T]he USSR succumbed to a domestic coup d'etat thanks to an internal process of delegitimization that Gorbachev himself had initiated. The United States had little or nothing to do with it" (Chalmers Johnson, *The Sorrows of Empire* [New York: Henry Holt, 2004] 17–18).

26 For the neoconservative argument that a "galvanizing event" like a new Pearl Harbor would promote the global domination project, see Project for the New American Century, *Rebuilding America's Defenses* (September 2000) 63. This argument, in somewhat different words, had been made earlier in Zbigniew Brzezinski, *The Grand Chessboard: American Primacy and Its Geostrategic Imperatives* (New York: Basic Books, 1997) 24–25.

27 Lou Cannon and Bob Woodward, "Gates to Withdraw as CIA Nominee; Reagan's Choice Facing Senate Rejection," *Washington Post* 2 March 1987.

28 Tom Polgar, "Gates: The Wrong Choice to Head the CIA," *Washington Post National Weekly Edition* 1–7 July 1991: 24.

29 See www.fas.org/irp/offdocs/walsh/chap_16.htm.

30 See, for example, James McConnachie and Robin Tudge, *The Rough Guide to Conspiracy Theories* (London and New York: Rough Guides, 2005), which says: "[C]ampaign chief, Bill Casey, devised the so-called Iran-Contra scheme, originally known only to a few top officials under the code name 'the Enterprise.' The money from the missile sales would be diverted directly to the Contras" (186).

31 Relevant here is the wisdom of libertarian economist and historian Murray Rothbard who said, "only a few key people need be in on the original crime, while lots of government officials can be in on the subsequent cover-up, which can always be justified as 'patriotic,' on 'national security' grounds, or simply because the president ordered it. The fact that the highest levels of the US government are all-too capable of lying to the public, should have been clear since Watergate and Iran-Contra" ("The J.F.K. Flap," in Lew Rockwell, ed., *The Irrepressible Rothbard* [Burlingame, CA: Center for Libertarian Studies, 2000] 307).

32 Kitty Kelley, *The Family: The Real Story of the Bush Dynasty* (New York: Doubleday, 2004) 533.

33 Kelley 533.

34 See www.answers.com/topic/george-bush. There is powerful evidence that Bush, the effective chief of all covert action and *de facto head* of US intelligence, was at the center of Iran-Contra; see www.tarpley.net/bush18.htm.

35 The 9/11 Commission Executive Summary (www.9-11commission.gov/report/911Report_Exec.htm) 2.

36 Tarpley 7–8. He continues: "It requires expert terrorist controllers. Because of this, the starting point for realistic appraisal of 9/11 is not primarily

the sociology of the Middle East, but rather the historical record of NATO and CIA state-sponsored terrorism in western Europe and elsewhere in the post-World War II period. For it is here, and not in some distant cave of the Hindu Kush, that we can find the methods and personnel which produced 9/11."

37 Nafeez Mosaddeq Ahmed, *The War on Truth: 9/11, Disinformation, and the Anatomy of Terrorism* (Northampton, MA: Olive Branch, 2005) 130–33; Craig Unger, *House of Bush, House of Saud* (New York: Scribner, 2004); J. H. Hatfield, *Fortunate Son* (Brooklyn: Soft Skull, 2002); Alex Jones, *9-11 Descent into Tyranny* (Austin, TX: AEJ, 2002) 66.

38 Ahmed chs. 4–6.

39 Besides the evidence I cite in this section, see the books by Ahmed, Griffin, and Tarpley, as well as several of the other essays in the present volume.

40 www.state.gov/secretary/rm/2005/54176.htm.

41 *Arkansas Democrat-Gazette*, October 3, 2005: 4B.

42 911research.wtc7.net/disinfo/retractions/romero.html.

43 "Tech Receives $15 M for Anti-Terrorism Program" (infohost.nmt.edu/mainpage/news/2002/25sept03.html), citing *Influence Magazine* December 2002. Strangely, when the Pentagon was attacked, Romero was in Washington, DC, en route to an office building near the Pentagon to seek new funding for his institute.

44 www.911truth.org/article.php?story=20041112144051451.

45 E-mail to Frank Gayle, deputy chief of the metallurgy division, Material Science and Engineering Laboratory, at the National Institute for Standards and Technology (www.septembereleventh.org/newsarchive/2004-11-11-ryan.php).

46 911research.wtc7.net/talks/towers/text.

47 911research.wtc7.net/wtc/analysis/fires/steel.html.

48 Murray N. Rothbard, "The Case for Revisionism (and against A Priori History)," Mises Institute 22 June 2004 (www.mises.org/fullstory.aspx?control=1541).

49 A little-known outrage for our so-called democracy, once a constitutional republic, happened on November 1, 2001, when President George W. Bush signed Executive Order 13233, which ordered that a former president's private papers can be released only with the approval of both that former president (or his heirs) and the current one. Since the Reagan administration had a "stop the clock" granted, new Iran-Contra evidence can be withheld indefinitely, protecting Bush's father from further revelations. Prior to this new secrecy order, "the National Archives had controlled the release of documents under the Presidential Records Act of 1978, which stipulated that all papers, except those pertaining to national security, had to be made available 12 years after a president left office." Since when can executive fiat overrule national law? Congress must contest this usurpation.

50 www.st911.org.

EIGHT: FALK

1 There has been a great deal of writing recently on this theme of American exceptionalism and its implications for international law and world order. See two recently published edited volumes for the range of viewpoints: Amy Bartholomew, ed., *Empire's Law: The American Imperial Project and 'War to Remake the World'* (London: Pluto Press, 2006), and Michael Ignatieff, ed., *American Exceptionalism and Human Rights* (Princeton: Princeton University Press, 2005), especially John Ruggie's contribution, "American Exceptionalism,

Exemptionalism, and Global Governance," 304–338.

2 On continuities and discontinuities, see perceptive discussion, emphasizing economic dimensions of global dimension, in Neil Smith, *The Endgame of Globalization* (New York: Routledge, 2005) 27. From a more conservative and political perspective, see Walter Russell Mead, *Power, Terror, Peace, and War: America's Grand Strategy in a World at Risk* (New York: Knopf, 2004).

3 See Michel Chossudovsky, "Nuclear War Against Iran," *Global Research* 3 January 2006; James Petras, "Israel's War Deadline: Iran in the Crosshairs," *Counterpunch* 24–25 December 2005 (www.counterpunch.org/ petras12242005.html); and Bill and Kathleen Christison, "Let's Stop a US/Israeli War on Iran," *Counterpunch* 29 December 2005 (www.counterpunch/ christison12292005.html).

4 The descriptive term "pancapitalism" to denote the current phase has been coined by Majid Tehranian, *From Silk to Silicon: Civilization, Communication, and Terror in the Global Village* (unpubl. ms., 2005).

5 "Rebuilding America's Defenses," Project for the New American Century, September 2000. Note the disingenuousness of the title, considering that American military forces were world dominant, with annual expenditures exceeding those of the next fifteen countries, and were not "defenses" but globally deployed imperial forces ready to strike from bases on every continent and from navies in every ocean.

6 The most persuasive rationale for a posture of extreme suspicion is provided in two books by David Ray Griffin: *The New Pearl Harbor: Disturbing Questions about the Bush Administration and 9/11* and *The 9/11 Commission Report: Omissions and Distortions* (both Northampton: Olive Branch Press, 2004, 2005).

7 See the Griffin books in the previous note for detailed consideration.

8 See also Paul Rea, *Still Seeking the Truth About 9/11: Exposing Fallacies in the "Official Story"* (Newark, CA: Bayside Press, 2005).

9 See Anne Norton, *Leo Strauss and the Politics of American Empire* (New Haven: Yale University Press, 2004), on the importance of distinguishing between Strauss and Straussians on this matter; but also see Strauss on persecution and deception.

10 I am now embarrassed by the fact that I subscribed to such a view in the early aftermath of the 9/11, which despite some qualifications represented a faulty assessment from the perspective of both security and the real priorities of the Bush presidency. See Falk, *The Great Terror War* (Northampton: Olive Branch Press, 2003) esp. 1–73. My more recent views are better reflected in the final chapter of *The Declining World Order: America's Imperial Geopolitics* (New York: Routledge, 2004), entitled "Will the Empire be Fascist?" (241–52).

11 This conclusion is convincingly argued by the veteran journalist Kathy Gannon, who has covered Afghanistan for many years, in her book *I is for Infidel: From Holy War to Holy Terror* (New York: Public Affairs, 2005).

12 In this spirit, note the call of John Yoo— Berkeley Law School professor and former Justice Department official who wrote the main "torture memos"—for assassination of suspected terrorists as a natural outcome of wartime. Yoo has been quoted as saying: "A nation at war may use force against members of the enemy at any time, regardless of their proximity to hostilities of their activity at the time of the attack" (Paul M. Barrett, "Young Lawyer Proposes Assassinating More Suspected Terrorists," *Wall Street Journal* 12 October 2005). For a comprehensive argument as to the essentially unlimited powers of the president in

his role as commander-in-chief to initiate and wage war as he determines, see Yoo's book, *The Powers of War and Peace: The Constitution and Foreign Affairs After 9/11* (Chicago: University of Chicago Press, 2005).

13 See Christopher Scheer, Robert Scheer, and Lakshmi Chaudhry, *The Five Biggest Lies Bush Told Us about Iraq* (Brooklyn: Akashic Books and New York: Seven Stories Press, 2003). The text of the first "Downing Street Memo" also confirms the view that the Bush presidency was determined to invade Iraq even in the absence of evidence of an Iraqi threat (www.downingstreetmemo.com/docs/memotext.pdf).

14 See the revealing front-page story by David Streitfeld, "US Labor in Retreat as Global Forces Squeeze Pay and Benefits," *Los Angeles Times* 18 October 2005. For a broader analysis of these effects of neoliberal globalization, see my *Predatory Globalization: A Critique* (Cambridge, UK: Polity Press, 1999). For a devastating critique of the impact of economic globalization on the poor and with respect to widening income and wealth disparities throughout the world, both among and within countries, see Judith Blau & Alberto Moncada, *Human Rights: Beyond the Liberal Vision* (Lanham, MD: Rowman & Littlefield, 2005) esp. 85–114.

15 For elaboration, see Falk, *The Declining World Order* 3–44 and note 10.

16 "Resisting the Global Domination Project: An Interview with Prof. Richard Falk," *Frontline* 20/8 (12–25 April 2003).

17 For an the insider account of how the Iraq disaster came to pass written from a neoconservative outlook, see Adam Garfinkle, "The Wrong Stuff," *The American Interest* 1/1 (Autumn 2005): 119–124.

NINE: MCMURTRY

1 Evidence that the 2000 election was stolen has been provided by many writers. For example, Gregory Palast, in *The Best Democracy That Money Can Buy* (New York: Penguin, 2003), showed that Database Technologies Corporation (now ChoicePoint Corporation), acting under the direction of Jeb Bush's party-loyalist Secretary of State, Katherine Harris, illegally removed at least 7,000 lawful Afro-American voters (estimated as 93 percent Democratic) from voter lists. More generally, see Daniel Lazare, *The Velvet Coup: The Constitution, the Supreme Court, and the Decline of Democracy* (London: Verso Books, 2001).

2 See www.crimesofwar.org/thebook/crimes-against-peace.html.

3 The torture began as routine as soon as the invasion of Afghanistan occurred, with all of the methods exposed in Iraq three years later used primarily on ordinary people picked up at random. "The tortures were in many ways worse," observed the Human Rights Watch in the area, "not operated even nominally in accordance with the Geneva Conventions—the whole system operates outside the rule of law." The Independent Human Rights Commission set up in June 2002 by the European Union "Bonn Agreement" concurred: "From those who are talking about human rights and democracy, it is a great shock" (Duncan Campbell, "America's Afghan Gulag," *Guardian Weekly* 2–8 July 2004: 15–16). Over two years before, a press report had revealed that prisoners had been held in inhuman conditions at the US Bagram airbase in Afghanistan with fatalities from the criminal abuse (Dana Priest and Barton Gellman, "US Decries Abuse, but Defends Interrogations," *Washington Post* 26 December 2002).

4 Ignacio Ramone, "'Torture in a Good Cause,'" *Le Monde Diplomatique*

June 2004: 1.

5 Cited by Nicola Short, "The Challenges of Bush's Foreign Policy," *Science for Peace Bulletin* May 2004: 2.

6 US Ambassador to Iraq, John Negroponte, was described by UN Secretary-General Kofi Annan as "an outstanding professional, a great diplomat, and a wonderful ambassador here" a year after the US invasion (Robin Wright and Colum Lynch, "Tough Road ahead for Negroponte," *Washington Post/Guardian Weekly* 29 April–5 May 2004: 29). Negroponte first presided over the funneling of weapons, money, and political support to war-criminal attacks on Nicaragua as ambassador to Honduras from 1981 to 1985. He was then the US representative to the UN Security Council when the US perpetrated "the supreme crime under international law" by directly invading Iraq in 2003 while UN arms inspections were proceeding. (Annan was UN Secretary-General at the time.)

7 In 1933, President Roosevelt's US Ambassador to Germany, William Dodd, warned: "A clique of US industrialists is hell-bent to bring a fascist state to supplant our democratic government and is working closely with the fascist regime in Germany" (see the impeccably documented summary by Richard Sanders, *Facing the Corporate Roots of American Fascism* [Ottawa: Coalition to Oppose the Arms Trade, 2004] 3). President George W. Bush may be understood from a biographical standpoint as carrying on a family tradition originating with his maternal and paternal grandfathers, George Herbert Walker and Prescott Bush, who were investigated by the Roosevelt government for collaboration with the Nazis—Prescott Bush as a primary financial operative in the banking structure of the Nazi war machine (see Webster Tarpley, "Legacy of Prescott Herbert Bush," *Global Outlook* Summer/Fall 2003: 54). Transnational corporations that armed, equipped, and financed the Nazis also included major subsidiary operations of General Motors, Ford, I.B.M., Dupont, IT&T, and Standard Oil (now Exxon).

8 See www.newamericancentury.org. The full statement is: "Further, the process of transformation, even if it *brings revolutionary change, is likely to be a long one, absent some catastrophic and catalyzing event*—like a new Pearl Harbor" (emphasis added).

9 "The new flexibility of the US on working with international partners" was featured in the world press across continents. That the social infrastructure of Iraq was destroyed, that over a million of its people were dead from US-led invasions and embargoes, and that its possibility of a secular socialist future was eradicated were not problems that registered for the UN Security Council, which voted unanimously to approve the continuing US occupation.

10 As Jonathan Schell points out on the basis of the administration's own statements, "the new 'sovereign' Iraq will not: possess authority over either American forces or its own; be able to pass legislation; control its own news media; make decisions about the economy of the country" (Jonathan Schell, "Politicizing the War," *TomDispatch* 28 May 2004).

11 Julian Borger, "The CIA Finally Gets Its Man," *Guardian Weekly* 4–10 2004: 9.

12 Exhaustive documentation of Canadian government complicity with the United States in its war crimes and illegal militarization of space, while publicly asserting the opposite so as not to be elected out of office, is provided by Richard Sanders, *Canada's Role in the 'Missile Defense' Weapons Program, Parts I and II* (Ottawa: Coalition Against the Arms Trade, 2005).

13 The "Comprehensive Privatization Plan for Iraq" was issued as a 101-

page US State Department document prescribing the total revolution of privatization and deregulation (Liam Lacey interview with Gregory Palast, *CCPA Monitor* December–January 2004: 18–19).

14 US decrees in Iraq explicitly connected its control over Iraq's resources to the right to self-defense of the United States in such forms as Executive Order 130303: "Threat of attachment or judicial process against the [US-controlled] Development Fund for Iraq, Iraqi petroleum and petroleum products, and interests therein constitutes an unusual threat to the national security and foreign policy of the United States" (Ibrahim Warde, "Iraq: A Licence to Loot the Land," *Le Monde Diplomatique* May 2004: 2). Observe how the US here not only institutes its right to war-criminal expropriation of control over and right to Iraq's oil as the law of Iraq (itself a war crime under law), but defines any "judicial process" against this criminal expropriation of possessions as "an unusual threat to the national security of the US." Here we see an assumption of lawless power that first puts itself above the law, then treats as a cause of war any lawful recourse against its criminal actions. Our account of the "religion of America" below explains the logic of the group-mind that produces such policy decisions as benevolent necessity.

15 Denis Halliday, "The UN Failed the Iraqi People," *Global Outlook* Winter 2004: 48.

16 See, for example, Michel Chossudovsky, *America's War on Terrorism* (Pincourt, Quebec: Global Research, 2005), and Nafeez Mossadeq Ahmed, *Behind the War on Terror: Western Strategy and the Struggle for Iraq* (Gabriola: New Society Publishers, 2002).

17 Needless to say, the facts of Kuwait's slant-drilling into Iraq's oilfields from its artificially created oil-state were not observed, although the US green-light to Saddam to invade and the concocted atrocity story of "babies in incubators cut off from electricity by Saddam's armed forces" (a story arranged by a US advertising firm working with the daughter of the Kuwait ambassador to Washington) were ephemerally reported before disappearing to restore the normality of group-mind perception.

18 See, for example, Ahmed, *Behind the War on Terror.*

19 One might ask to whom the "I" of this sentence refers: Bush or Blair? The answer is that "one mind," a single "I," emerges from this "*cojones* meeting of Bush and Blair"—the "I" of the ruling group-mind. In Bush and Blair's oneness of conviction of the goodness and necessity of their war-criminal invasion of Iraq—a shared conviction that eventually disgraced Blair's political legacy in Britain—we may see the deepest grip of the ruling group-mind, the first-person identification with it across persons and societies at the top. The grip goes wide as well as deep. Blair's ambassador in Washington before and during the US–British invasion of Iraq observed in late 2005 that although the British prime minister was personally "seduced, by the glamour of US power," in this invasion, there was no one in official society speaking up anywhere. "I do not know anyone with any stature," he stated, "who was going around saying that Iraq did not have this stuff [the weapons of mass destruction threatening the world]." Observe the implication of the British ambassador's public comment (cited by Julian Glover and Ewen MacAskill, "Blair's Repeated Failures in Iraq—Envoy's Verdict," *Guardian Weekly* 11–17 November: 1). Everyone "of any stature" in the official world believed a story for which there was no evidence whatever—although their completely unfounded certitude of the official myth caused a major international war crime

that has only grown in murder and crimes against humanity as the facts have become clear. Such is the hold of the ruling group-mind thrall. Such is the nature of the 9/11 Wars and the 9/11 story that has allowed their perpetation.

20 "The sites targeted for looting and burning—the Ministries of Planning, Information, and Health—support the speculation that a concerted attempt has been made to destroy crucial data—[while] there was heavy guarding of Oil and Interior Ministries by US tanks and soldiers.... The data from pre-Gulf War health records is critical to establish a baseline showing increases in post-Gulf War levels of cancers and birth defects in Iraq... [from] the direct bombing of cities with 'depleted' uranium weapons" (press release, Association of Humanitarian Lawyers, UN NGO, 25 April 2003). "Major funds to restore food and relief supplies to the Iraqi people" amounted to 21 cents (US) per capita per day for the "emergency period."

21 Thus Pierre Bordieu's concept of "habitus" cannot explain the phenomenon of the regulating group-mind because "habitus" is always rooted in practice or locale. Nor can Antonio Gramsci's concept of "hegemony," because that is grounded in productive class membership. I first identified the phenomenon of the "regulating group-mind" or, in its sociopolitical form, the "ruling group-mind," in *Value Wars: The Global Market versus the Life Economy* (London and Sterling, VA: Pluto Press, 2001). That book provides detailed study of the phenomenon but little theoretical development of the concept as a formal category of explanation. More systematic attention to the ruling group-mind as a regulating and ruling structure of consciousness across individuals and cultures is provided in my earlier essay, "The Shadow Subject of History: Understanding 9/11 and the 9/11 Wars" (scienceforpeace@sa.utoronto.ca).

22 Thus legendary socialist and worker leader of Brazil, President Lula da Silva, heading up a delegation of 450 people, met with Communist Party officials in China in the first week of June to further "Brazil's success in locking into Chinese markets" by mass supply of soya grown from a 50 percent increase in burnt-out and clearcut Amazon rainforests ("from 30 to 60 million hectares under agriculture"), while China simultaneously planned to remove 300 million people from their ancestral rural lands to the mega-cities of China (Associated Press 4 June 2004). The global market formula is in such ways universalized as "progress and development" by the leading heirs of socialism and communism.

23 Zbigniew Brzezinski, *The Grand Chessboard: American Primacy and Its Geostrategic Imperatives* (New York: Basic Books, 1997) 124, 211.

24 At the behest of American friends who were disquieted by the belittling dismissal by editor Michael Albert and Z-Net regulars of allegations of administration foreknowledge of 9/11, I wrote a reply as a Z-Net Commentary (22 May 2002), whose introductory overview read: "The most telling documented evidence has been altogether ignored, and not a jot of counter-evidence has been thought necessary to disconfirm the foreknowledge hypothesis. Instead we are once more treated to name-calling with no refutive substance." Albert kindly published and replied to my article, but did not engage any fact or argument of my reply. Albert's general argument (and Noam Chomsky's, with whom he has elsewhere shared authorship of the position) is that "institutional analysis" must eschew particularist "conspiracy theory." While I sympathize with this method, I note that 9/11 denial is itself an institution, one based on a deeper and comprehensive institution, the market group-mind.

25 Documentation for this and subsequent facts I report ahead about the

construction of the 9/11 attack can be found in Nafeez Ahmed, *The War On Freedom: How and Why America Was Attacked* (Joshua Tree, CA. Tree of Life Publications, 2002); Michel Chossudovsky, *War and Globalisation: The Truth Behind 9/11* (Canada: Global Outlook, 2002); Thierry Meyssan, *9/11: The Big Lie* (London: Carnot, 2002), which is the translation of *L'Effroyable Imposture* (Paris: Les editions Carnot, 2002); and—in definitive summary—David Ray Griffin, *The New Pearl Harbor* (Northampton: Olive Branch Press, 2004). Paul Thompson, "September 11: Minute By Minute," Center for Cooperative Research (www.cooperativeresearch.org) provides exact time coordinates of the events. Much of Thompson's timeline has now been published as *The Terror Timeline: Year by Year, Day by Day, Minute by Minute: A Comprehensive Chronicle of the Road to 9/11—and America's Response*, by Paul Thompson and the Center for Cooperative Research (New York: HarperCollins [ReganBooks], 2004.

26 I am indebted to Professor John Valleau, Chemistry-Physics Research Group, University of Toronto, for drawing my attention to this scientific anomaly of the plane-impact causal sequence. (See also Griffin, *The New Pearl Harbor*.) The hypothesis of demolition wiring of the WTC has been since confirmed by the systematic findings of Brigham Young University physicist Steven E. Jones, in his chapter in this volume. Jones concludes that the evidence of the symmetry and speed of the buildings' fall into their footprints is consistent with "explosive demolition" and "satisfies tests of repeatability and parsimony." On the other hand, the official explanation of fire damage by jet diesel fuel combining with inflammatory building contents has no scientific basis or precedent in the history of fires in steel-support-column buildings. Most significantly, "the delay that must be expected due to conservation of momentum [is] one of the foundational laws of physics," he observes. "As upper falling floors strike lower floors—and intact steel support columns—the fall must be significantly impeded by the impacted mass." Yet no such impediment of fall registered in the fall of the World Trade Center buildings, which plunged at the speed of gravity into their footprints. The mysterious free-fall speed of the buildings is thus altogether inexplicable by the received story, but is "easily resolved by the explosive demolition hypothesis." Since, moreover, a non-demolition collapse would leave piled up concrete toppled onto the site, while the towers were in fact mostly converted to flour-like powder, the official explanation is again in contradiction with the known physical effects. The only conclusion in accord with the undisputed hard evidence and the laws of physics is that the buildings fell as they did from explosive demolitions. Since there is no physical science or factual support for the official story, and since US government-funded reports nowhere explained or analyzed this phenomenon, the story is demonstrably false. When the known facts and the laws of physics are thus systematically repressed in concealing the truth of 9/11, we appear to have the scientific counterpart of a smoking gun.

27 Even Michael Moore's famous documentary, *Fahrenheit 9/11*, was refused contracted US distribution by the Disney Corporation and otherwise blocked and attacked, although its attention was centered on the long-term Bush–bin Laden business affiliations and mutual profits from the 9/11 Wars by their families as well as by Vice President Cheney's Halliburton Corporation and the Wall Street Carlyle Group, in which the senior Bush and James Baker are invested. These interests in war-profiteering are understood here as collateral re-enforcers of the regulating market group-mind, whose rule, as Moore's documentary confirms, is internalized by the poor and the enlisted as their own set-points of emotional identification and aggression.

28 Irving L. Janis, *Groupthink: Psychological Studies of Policy Decisions* (Boston: Houghton Mifflin, 1972).

29 Greg Palast's *The Best Democracy that Money Can Buy* systematically exposes the facts of the corrupt election and policy behavior of the Bush administration before and since 9/11. The nature of the police-state legislation outside of the US since 9/11 is most economically explained by the Canadian Association of University Teachers in "Civil Liberties, Human Rights and Canada's Security Legislation" (Ottawa: CAUT/ACPPU, 2004).

30 An examination of "real-time war as pop culture" is provided by Paul Rutherford, *Weapons of Mass Persuasion* (Toronto: University of Toronto Press, 2004).

31 The choice-path structure towards the 9/11 Wars is explained by the ruling market group-mind, but only as one set of dramatic expressions of it. An exact account of its phenomena, if not of its inner logic, is provided by Mark Blyth in *Great Transformations* (New York: Cambridge University Press, 2002). He explains how "business repertoires" of thought and action "which resonate with the core identities" of businessmen preceded revolutionary policy attacks on public sectors to dismantle them across the world in the 1980s and 1990s, with no compelling economic evidence to justify them. "Absent the transformative effect of such ideas on agents' perceptions of their self-interest and the policy choices of the heirs of embedded liberalism make no sense," Blyth concludes (269). While Blyth provides masterful evidence for the phenomena and expressions of what I define as "the regulating group-mind," his concept of it as the expressed "ideas" of the business misses the deeper and wider syntax of social perception and judgment at work.

32 These were the highlights of the "opposing" program proclaimed by the Democratic National Convention in July 2004. I am indebted for its contents to an active Convention attendant, Eileen Dannemann, Director of the National Coalition of Organized Women. A committee proposal at the Democratic Party Convention for a new Department of Peace was rejected, in predictable accordance with the "religion of America" explained in the next section.

33 Gilbert Achcar, "Greater Middle East: The US Plan," *Le Monde Diplomatique* April 2004: 6. Bilateral trade treaties with the US, "free trade zones," and membership in the WTO were other market remedies proposed by the UNDP in collaboration with the US and the Arab Fund for Social and Economic Development (AFSED). That none of the latter "market transformations" had worked in achieving greater life security, or more basic needs fulfillment, or better education and cultural opportunity, for any society in market-reformed "Central and East Europe" did not compute to the group-mind that now regulated official thought across the former Eastern bloc and the Islamic world as magically "transformative" to the better, whatever the contrary evidence.

34 The Project for the New American Century (PNAC) thus headlines the US geostrategic plan to be followed by its armed force deployments as "Control the New International Commons of Space and Cyberspace," explaining that its text shows how to "pave the way... to control" and "determine the future shape of international politics here on earth."

35 Joseph Stiglitz, *Globalization and Its Discontents* (New York: Norton, 2002), penetrates the structure of delusion at work in the IMF, but seldom confronts the defining principles of the regulating market program as such. His comment regarding the failures of IMF Structural Adjustment Programs across the world—"the IMF simply assumed that markets arise quickly to meet every need"

(55)—applies in general.

36 The definitive study of the military-market-machine interlock of contemporary economic theory is provided in detail by Joseph Mirowski, *Machine Dreams: Economics Becomes a Cyborg Science* (Cambridge: Cambridge University Press, 2002).

37 Glenn Kessler, "Kerry: Democracy Can Wait," *Guardian Weekly* 4–10 June 2004: 7.

38 One should distinguish between the Religion of the Market and the Religion of America, but they are as complementary as the Invisible Hand and its Incarnation. In each case, the monotheist properties of supreme power, infallibility, and benevolence of will are assumed as given.

39 Consider George Kennan's oft-cited post-war declaration of US right, the logic of which is not deviated from today: "We have about 50 percent of the world's wealth, but only 6 percent of its population.... Our real task in the coming period is to devise a pattern of relationships which will permit us to maintain this position of disparity without positive detriment to our national security." What has changed other than the numbers since Kennan's policy statement is that the religion of America has become otherworldly.

40 Susan Jacoby, *A History of American Secularism* (New York: Metropolitan/Holt, 2004).

TEN: TUNANDER

1 George W. Bush, "Address to a Joint Session of Congress and the American People," 20 September 2001 (www.whitehouse.gov/news/releases/2001/09/print/20010920-8.html).

2 Donald H. Rumsfeld, "Transforming the Military," *Foreign Affairs* 81/3 (May/June 2002): 31.

3 Charles Krauthammer, "The Unipolar Moment," *Foreign Affairs* 70/1 (Winter 1990–1991): 23–33.

4 See, for example, ESDP Presidency Report 2003 and 2004 (www.agoria.be/gen-en/presente/secteurs/bsdi/esdp.htm; requires ID & PW www.eu2004.ie/templates/standard.asp?sNavlocator=4,18,299; www.eu2004.ie/templates/news.asp?sNavlocator=66&list_id=517).

5 Quoted in "Secretary Rumsfeld Interview with *Parade Magazine*," United States Department of Defense, 12 October 2001 (www.defenselink.mil/transcripts/2001/t11182001_t1012pm.html).

6 Quoted in Nicholas Lehman, "The Next World Order," *New Yorker* 1 April 2002.

7 Prepared Testimony by US Secretary of Defense Donald H. Rumsfeld, Senate Armed Services Committee, 9 July 2003: 5–6.

8 Alyson Bailes, "US, NATO and Europe: Is there Still a Common Agenda?" (talk at the Cicero Foundation, Paris, 12 December 2002).

9 Daniele Ganser, *NATO's Secret Armies: Operation Gladio and Terrorism in Western Europe* (London & New York: Frank Cass, 2005).

10 Ole Wæver, "Securitization and Desecuritization," Ronnie D Lipschutz, ed., *On Security* (New York: Colombia University Press, 1995).

11 Confidential interview with PFLP associate.

12 Quoted in Craig Unger, *House of Bush, House of Saud: The Secret Relationship between the World's Two Most Powerful Dynasties* (New York &

London: Scribners, 2004) 105.

13 Quoted in Robert Sam Anson, "The Journalist and the Terrorist," *Vanity Fair* August 2002 (www.cooperativeresearch.org/timeline/2002/vanityfair0802.html).

14 "The British Jackel," *Sunday Times* (London) 21 April 2002 (available at meaindia.nic.in/bestoftheweb/2002/04/21bow02.htm).

15 Confidential interview with PFLP associate.

16 Colin Smith, *Carlos—Portrait of a Terrorist: The Murderous Career of the World's Most Wanted Man* (London: Mandarin Paperback, 1995).

17 Claire Hoy and Victor Ostrovsky, *By Way of Deception: An Insider's Devastating Exposé of the Mossad* (London: Arrow Books, 1991) 202–214.

18 "Overt Assistance from Pakistan May Bring Dire Consequences," *Jane's Intelligence Digest*, September 20, 2001 (www.janes.com/security/international_security/news/jid/jid010920_1_n.shtml).

19 Joseph Neff and John Sullivan, "Al-Qaeda Terrorist Duped FBI, Army," *Raleigh News & Observer* 24 October 2001 (www.knoxstudio.com/shns/story.cfm?pk=ALIMOHAMED-10-24-01&cat=AN); see also Tom Hays and Sharon Theimer (AP), "Egyptian Led a Life of Double-Crosses," *Tulsa World* 30 December 2001; Reed Irvine, "Bin Laden's Military Mole," 8 November 2001 (www.aim.org/aim_column/A1449_0_3_0_C/) Lawrence Wright, "The Man Behind bin Laden," *New Yorker* 16 September 2002 (www.newyorker.com/fact/content/ articles/020916fa_fact2g).

20 James Taranto, "Our Friends the Pakistanis," *Wall Street Journal* 9 October 2001 (referring to the Pakistani Newspaper *Dawn*); Taranto, "Our Friends the Pakistanis," *Wall Street Journal* 10 October 2001. See also "India Accuses Ex-Pakistan Spy-Chief of Links to US Attackers: Report," AFP, 10 October; Manoj Joshi, "India Helped FBI to Trace ISI-Terrorist Links," *Times of India* 10 October 2001; Nick Fielding, "The British Jackal: From British Public School to the Shadow of the Noose," *Sunday Times* (London) 21 April 2001.

21 Daniel Klaidman, "Federal Grand Jury Set to Indict Sheikh," *Newsweek* website 13 March 2002 (www.msnbc.com/news/723527.asp; also available at www.cooperativeresearch.org/timeline/2002/newsweek031302.html).

22 Fielding, "The British Jackal."

23 Daniel Klaidman, "Federal Grand Jury Set to Indict Sheikh."

24 *Pittsburgh Tribune-Review* 3 March 2002 (www.pittsburghlive.com/x/tribune-review/opinion/datelinedc/s_20141.html).

25 Alexander B. Calahan, "Countering Terrorism: The Israeli Response to the 1972 Munich Olympic Massacre and the Development of Independent Covert Action Teams" (thesis submitted to the Faculty of the Marine Corps Command and Staff College) April 1995 (www.fas.org/irp/eprint/ca/ahqn.htm).

26 David Ignatius, "The Secret History of US–PLO Terror Talks," *Washington Post* 4 December 1988. See also www.washingtonpost.com/ac2/wp-dyn/A34478-2001Sep14.

27 Patrick Seale, *Abu Nidal: A Gun for Hire* (London: Hutchinson, 1992).

28 Carl Schmitt, *The Theory of the Partisan: A Commentary/Remark on the Concept of the Political* (East Lansing: Michigan State University Press, 2004) 8–9; see also Andreas Behnke, "Terrorising the Political: 9/11 Within the Context of the Globalisation of Violence," *Millennium* 33/2 (2004): 289.

29 Schmitt, *Theory of the Partisan* 43–45.

30 Walter Laquer, *The Age of Terrorism* (London: Weidenfeld & Nicholson, 1987) 16, 134–35; Tore Bjørgo and Danial Heradstveit, *Politisk Terrorism* (Oslo:

Tano, 1993).

31 See Livia Rokach, *Israel's Sacred Terrorism* (Belmont, MA: AAUG Press, 1980). Rokach's study drew on the diaries of former Israeli prime minister Moshe Sharett (in whose government Rokach's father had served as minister of the interior); see also David Hirst, *The Gun and the Olive Branch: The Roots of Violence in the Middle East* (New York: Thunder's Mouth Press/Nation Books, 2003) 290–96.

32 Seale, Abu Nidal.

33 Franco Ferraresi, *Threats to Democracy: The Radical Right in Italy after the War* (Princeton: Princeton University Press, 1996); see also David J. Whittaker, ed., *The Terrorism Reader* (London: Routledge, 2001) 218.

34 *Sentenza – ordinanza del Guidice Istruttore presse il Tribunale Civile e Penale di Milano, dr Guido Salvini, nel procedimento penale nei confronti di ROGNONI Giancarlo ed altri*, 1995–2001 (www.strano.net/stragi/tstragi/salvini/index.html); "Gladio, Part II, The Puppeteers," BBC, June 1992; Jeffrey McKenzie Bale, "The 'Black' International: Neo-Fascist Paramilitary Networks and the 'Strategy of Tension,'" (Ann Arbor, Mich.: UMI Dissertation Service, 1994); Ferraresi, *Threats to Democracy*; Ganser, *NATO's Secret Armies*, 2005.

35 Quoted in Ferraresi, *Threats to Democracy*, 93.

36 Philip Willan, *Puppetmasters: The Political Use of Terrorism in Italy* (London: Constable, 1991), 198-199; see also interview with Federico Umberto D'Amato in "Gladio Part III, The Foot Soldiers," BBC, 10 June 1992.

37 Willan, *Puppetmasters* 205.

38 "Gladio Part III, The Foot Soldiers"; see also Ganser, *NATO's Secret Armies* 2005.

39 Interview with former US Secretary of Defense Caspar Weinberger, "Striptease," Swedish TV2, 7 March 2000; printed in Ola Tunander, *The Secret War Against Sweden: US and British Submarine Deception in the 1980s* (London & New York: Frank Cass, 2004).

40 Tribunali Civile e Penale di Milano, 1995–2001.

41 "Red Cell: Secret SEAL 'Terrorist' Operations" (Video Interview with Captain Richard Marcinko and Admiral James Lyons), Boulder: Paladin Press, 1993; see also Tunander, *The Secret War Against Sweden*, and Thomas Hunter, "Red Cell" www.specialoperations.com/Navy/Red_Cell/Default.htm.

42 "Secretary Rumsfeld Interview with *Parade Magazine*."

43 Rumsfeld interview; see also "Vastly More Deadly Attacks Possible, Rumsfeld Says," Associated Press 31 January 2002.

44 Commissioner Jamie Gorelick reported that Wolfowitz made this comment in a statement to the Commission. See "Day One Transcript: 9/11 Commission Hearing," *Washington Post* 23 March 2004 (www.washingtonpost.com/wp-dyn/articles/A17798-2004Mar23.html).

45 Rumsfeld's testimony as quoted in "Day One Transcript: 9/11 Commission Hearing," *Washington Post* 23 March 2004 (www.washingtonpost.com/wp-dyn/articles/A17798-2004Mar23.html).

46 Project for the New American Century (PNAC), *Rebuilding America's Defenses: Strategy, Forces and Resources for a New Century* (September 2000) 50–51.

47 Report of the Commission to Assess United States National Security Space Management and Organization, 11 January 2001 (www.defenselink.mil/pubs/spaceintro.pdf)15.

48 David Armstrong, "Dick Cheney's Song of America: Drafting a Plan for

Global Dominance," *Harper's* October 2002: 76–83.

49 Armstrong, "Dick Cheney's Song." See also Nicholas Lehman, "The Next World Order," and Elliot Abrams et al., "The Honorable William J. Clinton, President of the United States," Project for the New American Century, 26 January 1998 (www.newamericancentury.org/iraqclintonletter.htm).

50 This document, according to David Armstrong ("Dick Cheney's Song of America"), was crafted by Lewis Libby and Eric Edelman under the supervision of Paul Wolfowitz, who has later argued that he never saw the original draft before it was leaked to the *New York Times* (Deputy Secretary Wolfowitz Interview with Sam Tannehaus, *Vanity Fair* 9 May 2003).

51 Nick Cohen, "With a Friend Like This. . . . America Divides to Control," *Observer* 7 April 2002.

52 Quoted in Armstrong, "Dick Cheney's Song of America."

53 Memorandum for Secretary of Defense by Joint Chiefs of Staff, 13 March 1962, signed by the Chairman of the JCS, General Lyman Lemnitzer (declassified in 2001, National Security Archive: www.gwu.edu/~nsarchiv/news/20010430/). This memorandum is also printed in Thierry Meyssan, *9/11: The Big Lie* (London: Carnot) 198–205.

54 Jon Elliston, "Bomb School," *Independent Weekly* 5 June 2002.

55 Robert Baer, *See No Evil: The True Story of a Ground Soldier in the CIA* (New York: Random House, 2002) 31.

56 On August 25, 1998, German TV Channel ZDF exposed CIA and Mossad links to the 1986 Berlin disco bombing. Amairi's lawyer confirmed that his client worked for Mossad. See "German TV Exposes CIA, Moassad Links to 1986 Berlin Disco Bombing," 27 August 1988 (100777.com/node/101; see also usa.mediamonitors.net/content/view/full/22038 and www.nadir.org/nadir/periodika/jungle_world/_98/36/09a.htm).

57 Victor Ostrovsky, *The Other Side of Deception: A Rogue Agent Exposes the Mossad's Secret Agenda* (New York: Harper, 1994).

58 Bale, "The 'Black' International: Neo-Fascist Paramilitary Networks and the 'Strategy of Tension,'" 155, 180–82.

59 Quoted in Bale 139, 179, 186.

60 Giovanni Maria Bellu, "Strage di Piazza Fontana spunta un agenta Usa," *La Republica* 11 February 1998, Tribunali Civile e Penale di Milano, 1995–2001 (www.strano.net/stragi/tstragi/salvini/index.html; www.almanaccodeimisteri.info/sentenzaordinanzapiazzaFontana5.htm).

61 Philip Willan, "Terrorists 'Helped by the CIA' to Stop Rise of Left in Italy," *Guardian* 26 March 2001; see also "Ex-Spy Alleges CIA Endorsed Italy Bombings in 1970s," Reuters 4 August 2000 (marx.econ.utah.edu/archives/autopsy/2000m08/msg00024.htm).

62 Agents linked to the CIA—including Italians Giovanni Bandoli, Carlo Digilio, and Sergio Minetto, as well as US Navy Captain David Carret and his replacement in 1974, Captain Theodore Richard—were involved in this NDS terrorist activity. See Bellu, "Strage di Piazza Fontana spunta un agenta Usa," and Tribunali Civile e Penale di Milano (1995–2001); see also Ganser, *NATO's Secret Armies*; Bale, "The 'Black' International"; and the Italian Parliamentary Investigation on Terrorism (1998), available at www.parlamento.it/parlam/bicam/terror/stenografici/steno38a.htm; see also Ferraresi, *Threats to Democracy*; and a number of interviews in "Gladio—Parts I–III."

63 Ralph Boulton, "Turkey's New Govt. Faces Challenge," *Dawn* 30 January

2003. In Turkey but also elsewhere the concept of "deep state" is used frequently for a kind of security structure able to operate outside the law. See, for example, Shahram Chubin and Jerrold D. Green, "Turkish Society and Foreign Policy in Troubled Times," RAND Conference Proceedings (Geneva: Center for Middle East Public Policy & Geneva Center for Security Policy, 2001).

64 Carl Schmitt, *Political Theology* (Cambridge, MA: MIT Press 1985 [originally 1922]).

65 Krauthammer, "The Unipolar Moment," 24–25.

66 See, for example, Zbigniew Brzezinski, *The Choice: Global Domination or Global Leadership* (New York: Basic Books, 2004).

67 There is also an increasing amount of technical evidence related to 9/11 and other attacks, which is discussed in other chapters of this volume, that is impossible to explain in terms of so-called "regular terrorist operations."

68 EUOBSERVER, "Poll Controversy as Israel and US Labelled Biggest Threats to World Peace" (MIFTAH's Dialogue & Instant Polls, 30 October 2003).

69 Thanks to John Carville at PRIO for his comments on an earlier version of this chapter.

ELEVEN: PHILLIPS, THORNTON, VOGLER

1 See G. William Domhoff, *Who Rules America?* 5th ed. (New York: McGraw Hill, 2006), and Peter Phillips, "A Relative Advantage: Sociology of the San Francisco Bohemian Club," 1994 (libweb.sonoma.edu/).

2 Early studies by Charles Beard, published as *An Economic Interpretation of the Constitution of the United States* (1929), established that the economic elites formulated the US Constitution to serve their own special interests. Henry Klein, in a 1921 book entitled *Dynastic America and Those Who Own It*, argued that wealth in America had power never before known in the world and was centered in the top 2 percent of the population, which owned some 60 percent of the country. In 1937, Ferdinand Lundberg published *America's Sixty Families*, which documented inter-marrying, self-perpetuating families, for whom wealth was the "indispensable handmaiden of government." C. Wright Mills determined in 1945 ("American Business Elites," *Journal of Economic History*, December) that nine out of ten business elites from 1750 to 1879 came from well-to-do families.

3 See R. Brady, *Business as a System of Power* (New York: Columbia University Press, 1943), and Val Burris, "Elite Policy Planning Networks in the United States," 1991 paper for the American Sociological Association.

4 C. Wright Mills, *The Power Elite* (New York: Oxford University Press, 1956).

5 See Michael Soref, "Social Class and Division of Labor within the Corporate Elite," *Sociological Quarterly* 17 (1976), and two works by Michael Useem: "The Social Organization of the American Business Elite and Participation of Corporation Directors in the Governance of American Institutions," *American Sociological Review* 44 (1979), and *The Inner Circle* (New York: Oxford University Press, 1984).

6 T. Koenig and R. Gobel, "Interlocking Corporate Directorships as a Social Network," *American Journal of Economics and Sociology* 40 (1981); Peter Phillips, "The 1934–35 Red Threat and the Passage of the National Labor Relations Act," *Critical Sociology* 20/2 (1994).

7 Dwight D. Eisenhower, Military-Industrial Complex Speech, Public Papers of the Presidents, 1961: 1035–1040.

8 For an understanding of the anti-military sentiment of the 1930s, see Smedley D. Butler (major general, US Marines), *War is a Racket* (New York: Round Table Press, 1935) and "The Washington Arms Inquiry," *Current History* November 1934.

9 *Economic Concentration and World War II: A Report of the Smaller War Plants Corporation to the Special Committee to Study Problems of American Small Business*, US Senate (Washington, DC: Government Printing Office, 1946).

10 US Office of Management and Budget, *Budget of the United States Government, Historical Tables, Fiscal Year 1995* (Washington Printing office, 1994) 36–43, 82–87.

11 Michael Putzel, "Battle Joined in Peace Dividend," *Boston Globe* 12 January 1992: 1.

12 Eric Pianin, "Peace Dividend Efforts Dealt Blow," *Washington Post* 27 March 1992: A4.

13 Sam Meddis, "Peace Dividend Is No Guarantee, Aspin Says," *USA Today* 6 December 1994.

14 Margaret Tauxe, "About That Peace Dividend: The Berlin Wall Fell, But a Wall of Denial Stands," *Pittsburgh Post Gazette* 12 November 1999: A–27.

15 Guy Caron, "Anatomy of a Neo-Conservative White House," *Canadian Dimension* 1 May 2005.

16 Alain Frachon and Daniel Vernet, "The Strategist and the Philosopher: Leo Strauss and Albert Wohlstetter," *Counterpunch* 2 June 2003 (originally in French in *Le Monde* 16 April 2003).

17 Anne Hessing Cahn, "Team B: The Trillion-Dollar Experiment," *Bulletin of the Atomic Scientists* 49/3 (April 1993).

18 John Pilger, "A New Pearl Harbor," *New Statesman* (London) 16 December 2002 (www.ifamericansknew.org/us_ints/nc-pilger.html).

19 Peter Phillips, "The Neoconservative Plan for Global Dominance," in Peter Phillips, *Censored 2006: The Top 25 Stories* (Censored) (New York: Seven Stories Press, 2005), also at www.projectcensored.org. Excerpts from the 1992 "Defense Planning Guidance" draft are at www.pbs.org/wgbh/pages/frontline/shows/iraq/etc/wolf.html.

20 Patrick E. Tyler, "Senior US Officials Assail Lone-Superpower Policy," *New York Times* 11 March 1992: A6.

21 Anna Rich and Tamar Gabelnick, "Arms Company of the Future: BoeingBAELockheedEADS, Inc," *Arms Sales Monitor* January 2000.

22 Guy Caron, "Anatomy of a Neo-Conservative White House."

23 Martha Honey, "Guns 'R' Us," *In These Times* August 1997.

24 See Carl Grossman, "US Violates World Law to Militarize Space," *Earth Island Journal* Winter 1999, and Bruce Gagnon, "Pyramids to the Heavens," *Towards Freedom* September 1999. "Vision for 2020" can be read at www.fas.org/spp/military/docops/usspac/lrp/ch02.htm.

25 Quoted in Peter Phillips, "A Relative Advantage: Sociology of the San Francisco Bohemian Club," 1994 (libweb.sonoma.edu/regional/faculty/phillips/bohemianindex.html) 104. Note: Although I heard this speech myself, a pre-agreement with my host required that the name of the speakers and other participants be kept confidential.

26 Project for the New American Century, "Statement of Principles," 3 June 1997 (www.newamericancentury.org).

27 Positions held by PNAC founders in the George W. Bush administration:

Elliot Abrams, National Security Council; Dick Cheney, vice president; Paula Dobriansky, undersecretary of global affairs, Dept. of State; Aaron Friedberg, vice president's deputy national security advisor; Francis Fukuyama, President's Council on Bioethics; Zalmay Khalilzad, US ambassador to Afghanistan; Lewis Libby, chief of staff for the vice president; Peter Rodman, assist. secretary of defense for international security; Henry S. Rowen, Committee on Intelligence Capabilities, Defense Policy Board; Donald Rumsfeld, secretary of defense; Vin Weber, National Commission on the Public Service; Paul Wolfowitz, deputy secretary of defense, president of the World Bank.

28 Ted Nace, *Gangs of America* (San Francisco: Berrett-Koehler, 2003), 186.

29 For a full review of the Global Dominance Group, listing key advocates for military expansion and affiliates of the major defense contractors, see the Appendixes.

30 The Project for the New American Century, *Rebuilding America's Defenses: Strategy, Forces, and Resources for a New Century*, September 2000 (www.newamericancentury.org).

31 David Epstein, Office of Secretary of Defense; Steve Cambone, NSA; Dov Zakheim, Dept. of Defense CFO; Mark Lagan, Deputy Assist. Secretary of State.

32 *Rebuilding America's Defenses* 51.

33 William Rivers Pitt, "The Root of the Bush National Security Agenda: Global Domination and the Pre-emptive Attack on Iraq First," www.Truthout.org, 27 February 2003.

34 See Appendix A for listing of the top DoD Contractors from 2004.

35 Tim Weiner, "Lockheed and the Future of Warfare," *New York Times* 28 November 2004: Sunday Business, 1.

36 Jerry Knight, "Lockheed Rules Roost on Electronic Surveillance," *Washington Post* 29 August 2005: D-1.

37 See the Center for Public Integrity, "Pentagon Contractors: Top Contractors by Dollar" (www.publicintegrity.org).

38 Raw Story, "Cheney's Halliburton Stock Options Rose 3,281% Last Year, Senator Finds," 11 October 2005 (www.rawstory.com).

39 M. Asif Ismail, "Investing in War: The Carlyle Group Profits from Government and Conflict," 18 November 2004 (www.publicintegrity.org).

40 M. Asif Ismail, "The Sincerest Form of Flattery: Private Equity Firms Follow in Carlyle's Footsteps," 18 November 2004 (www.publicintegrity.org).

41 Martin Walker, "Walker's World: Neo-Con Wants More Troops," UPI 31 May 2005.

42 Greg Guma, "Privatizing War," UPI 8 July 2004; John Sisco, "Pentagon Increases Private Military Contracts," in Peter Phillips, *Censored 2004* (New York: Seven Stories Press, 2003) 98.

43 Phillips, *Censored 2006* 248.

44 April Oliver, "The Censored Side of the CNN Firings over Tailwing," in Peter Phillips, ed., *Censored 1999* (New York: Seven Stories Press, 1999) 158.

45 Treasury, Postal Service, Executive Office of the President, and General Government Appropriations Act of 2000, Pub. L. No. 106–58 § 632, 113 Stat. 430, 473 (1999) ("General Government Appropriations Act of 2000"), which prohibits the use of appropriated funds for "publicity or propaganda purposes."

46 Jack Shafer, "The *Times* Scoops That Melted: Cataloging the Wretched Reporting of Judith Miller," *Slate* 25 July 2003.

47 Ian Urbina, "Broadcast Ruse: A Grad Student Mimicked Saddam Over the

Airwaves," *Village Voice* 13–19 November 2002.

48 Bill Berkowitz, "Tapping Karen Hughes," *Working for Change* 18 April 2005.

49 James Bamford, "The Man Who Sold the War: Meet John Rendon, Bush's General in the Propaganda War," *Rolling Stone* December 2005.

50 "India/Iraq: Worldspace Bids for Contract to Rebuild Iraqi Media Network," Global News Wire–Asia Africa Intelligence Wire BBC Monitoring International Reports, 17 December 2003.

51 The National Opinion Research Center (NORC), University of Chicago, "The Florida Ballot Project: Frequently Asked Questions" (www.norc.uchicago.edu).

52 See Peter Phillips, "Another Year of Distorted Election Coverage," and Dennis Loo, "No Paper Trail Left Behind," both in Peter Phillips, ed., *Censored 2006: The Top 25 Censored Stories* (New York: Seven Stories Press, 2005) 48, 185.

53 Peter Phillips, "The Sale of Electoral Politics," in *Censored 2005* (New York: Seven Stories Press, 2004) 57.

54 See www.blackboxvoting.org. For recent updates on voting machine hacking, see "12–13–05: Devastating Hack Proven" (www.bbvforums.org/cgi-bin/forums/board-auth.cgi?file=/1954/15595.html).

55 For more on 9/11, see "Unanswered Questions of 9/11" (www.projectcensored.org).

56 David Ray Griffin, *The 9/11 Commission Report: Omissions and Distortions* (Northampton, MA: Olive Branch Press, 2005). Note: General Ahmed resigned his position less than one month later. The *Times of India* reported that Indian intelligence had given US officials evidence of the money transfer ordered by Ahmed and he was dismissed after the US authorities sought his removal.

57 See Jessica Froiland, "9/11 Pre-warnings," in *Censored 2006*. Also see David Ray Griffin, *The New Pearl Harbor: Disturbing Questions about the Bush Administration and 9/11* Ch. 6, "Did US Officials Have Advance Information about 9/11," and *The 9/11 Commission Report: Omissions and Distortions* (Northampton, MA: Olive Branch Press, 2004) Ch. 5, "Advance Information about the Attacks."

58 "India in Anti-Taliban Military Plan, Indiareacts.com," 26 June 2001; George Arney, BBC News, 18 September 2001; Rahul Bedi, "India Joins Anti-Taliban Coalition," *Jane's Defense News* 15 March 2001.

59 "Able Danger and Intelligence Information Sharing: Hearings Senate Judiciary Committee," Federal News Service 21 September 2005: 15.

60 Bart Jansen, "Sept. 11 Military Cover-Up Alleged," *Portland Press Herald* (Maine) 22 September 2005: A1. Kleinsmith has more recently worked for Lockheed Martin doing private data mining in Iraq under contract with the US military.

61 Ken Cunningham, "Permanent War? The Domestic Hegemony of the New American Militarism," *New Political Science* 26/2 (December 2004).

62 Greg Palast, "OPEC and the Economic Conquest of Iraq," *Harpers* October 2005.

63 "Business Groups Want to Limit Patriot Act," San Francisco Indy Media 17 October 2005 (www.sf.indymedia.org).

64 Cited from Davidson Loehr's sermon, "Living Under Fascism," Unitarian Universalist Church of Austin, 7 November 2004 (www.uua.org/news/2004/voting/sermon_loehr.html).

Index

Belgium, 92, 94
Ben-Veniste, Richard, 25
bin Faisal, Prince Turki, 153
bin Laden, Abdullah, 153
bin Laden, Osama, 5, 21, 22, 153
    and Bush family, 110, 227 n.27
    drug trafficking by, 214 n.13,
        214 n.18
    false connection to Saddam
        Hussein, 16
    and Kosovo Liberation Army
        (KLA), 219 n.19
    as orchestrator of 9/11, vii,
        80–81, 103
    as al-Qaeda leader, 122, 212 n.1
    US covert backing of, 74–75,
        77, 123, 146, 154–155
biological weapons, 150, 151
black box, 69, 70
Black September, 152–153, 154, 155
Blair, Tony, 134, 225 n.19
Blanchard, Brent, 36
Bloom, Allan, 172
Blyth, Mark, 228 n.31
Boeing Company, 178, 189, 191–197
Bohemian Club, 175
Boland Amendments, 73, 109
Bologna, Italy, 86
Bordieu, Pierre, 226 n.21
Bosnia, 153
Bowen, Ray, 106
Brazil, 226 n.22
Brescia, Italy, 86
Brussels, 93, 95
Bryson, John, 181
Brzezinski, Zbigniew, 16
Bulgaria, 76
Bush family, 108, 132
Bush, George H.W., 107–108, 109,
    173, 178, 180, 192, 220 n.34,
    227 n.27
Bush, George W., 12–13, 15, 22, 24,
    105, 114, 134, 140, 149, 160,
    221 n.49, 224 n.7, 225 n.19
Bush (George W.) administration
    aggressive global agenda of, 2,
        14, 16, 117–118, 123–124,

130–131, 138, 149, 160, 166
    appointment of neoconservatives
        and loyalists to, 12, 176–179,
        235 n.27
    dissent by former officials of, x,
        101
    and election irregularities, 183,
        228 n.29
    foreknowledge of 9/11, 3–4, 13,
        31, 121–122, 137, 185
    indictments of officials, 187
    and official account of 9/11, 25,
        79–80
Bush, Marvin, 12
Bush, Prescott, 224 n.7
Business Council, 170
Business Roundtable, 170
Byrd, Robert C., 174

C

Cachia, Edward, 45
Caesar, Julius, 80
Canada, 77, 224 n.12
Canadian Public Broadcasting
    Corporation (CBC), 135
capitalism, 144–148
    capitalist dream, 132
    free market, 134, 136
    inner logic of, 145
Carlyle Group, 178–181, 191–197,
    227 n.27
Carret, David, 158, 164, 237 n.62
Casey, William, 73, 109
Caspian Basin, 73
Casson, Felice, 84–85, 86–88
Castro, Fidel, 97
casus belli, 142
Center for Security Policy, 175
Central Intelligence Agency (CIA), x,
    5, 81, 103, 107–110, 132, 138,
    161, 165
    and Bay of Pigs, 98
    and Diebold, 184
    and drugs, 73, 75, 76
    and France, 94, 95
    and Italy, 87, 88, 89–91
    and public relations funding, 182

and al-Qaeda, 74, 75, 76–77
and terrorism, 74, 75–76, 155,
    157, 162, 163–164, 232 n.62
Chalabi, Ahmed, 182
Chapin, Tom, 68, 69, 70
Chechnya, 75, 214 n.15, 214 n.18
Cheney, Richard, 8, 15, 160,
    173–174, 176, 179–180, 192,
    227 n.27, 235 n.27
Chertoff, Benjamin, 203 n.25
Chertoff, Michael, 203 n.25
Chicago Tribune, 63
China, 161, 165, 166, 226 n.22
Chomsky, Noam, 2–3, 13, 201 n.9,
    226 n.24
Citgo gas station, 24, 205 n.40
civil liberties, vii
Clancy, Tom, *Executive Orders*, 27
Clandestine Planning Committee
    (CPC), 88
    See also NATO.
Clarke, Richard A., 8
Clarridge, Duane R., 110
Clear Channel Communications, 105
Clinton (Bill) administration, 117,
    118, 125, 126, 172, 174, 175
CNN, 102, 181
Cold War, x, 79, 87, 88, 89, 90–91,
    164, 166, 171, 172
    post, 92, 94, 146, 150, 165
    and secret warfare, 80, 82
    and terrorism, 151–152, 166
Committee on the Present Danger, 173
Comprehensive Privatization Plan,
    132, 225 n.13
Conservation of Momentum, 47,
    227 n.26
conspiracy theory, vii–viii, 26, 32,
    80, 101, 102–103, 115, 120,
    136–137, 139, 184, 226 n.24
Contras, 73–74, 109–110, 214 n.14,
    214 n.15
controlled demolition
    See World Trade Center.
Corley, Gene, 65, 66
Corus Construction Corporation, 113
Cossiga, Francesco, 87–88

Council on Foreign Relations, 170,
    177, 191–197
covert operations (US), ix–x, 158
    See also Central Intelligence
        Agency.
Craxi, Bettino, 87–88
C-Span, 63
Cuba, 97–98, 161–162

D

Dannemann, Eileen, 228 n.32
da Silva, Lula, 226 n.22
Dayan, Moshe, 157
Dearborn, Ed, 75, 214 n.15
deep state, 158, 164, 166, 233 n.63
Defense Planning Guidance report,
    174, 177
Defense Science Board, 174
de Gaulle, Charles, 95–96
delle Chiaie, Stefano, 157
Democratic Party, 143, 228 n.32
Department of Defense, 31, 83,
    106–107, 160, 175, 178–180,
    183, 191–197
Department of Peace, 228 n.32
Diebold, 183
Dien Bien Phu, 96
Digilio, Carlo, 163, 232 n.62
Dixie Chicks, 105
Dobriansky, Paula, 235 n.27
Dodd, William, 224 n.7
Donnelly, Thomas, 180
drugs (illegal), x, 205 n.20
    See also heroin.
D'Souza, Dinesh, 2
Dupont, 224 n.7

E

Eagar, Thomas, 36, 40, 50, 58
Eaton, Keith, 34
Eberhart, Ralph E., 107
Edleman, Eric, 232 n.50
Edison Media Research, 183
Egypt, 76, 157
Eisenhower, Dwight, xi, 171
Election Systems & Software (ES&S),
    183–184

stay-behind armies, 88, 92, 93, 96
Stern, Howard, 105
Stewart, Payne, 23, 203 n.25
Stiglitz, Joseph, 228–229 n.35
strategy of tension, xi, 79, 82–86,
    87, 90, 92, 94–98
Strauss, Leo, 121, 172
Sudan, 123
Sunder, Shyam, 46
Supreme Headquarters Allied
    Powers Europe (SHAPE), 88,
    92, 93–94
    See also NATO.
surprise theory, 80
Switzerland, 79, 92

T

Tajikistan, 75
Taliban, 21, 75, 110, 122, 123, 160,
    214 n.13
Team B, 173
Teng & Associates, 65
terrorism, 85, 131, 133, 143, 152,
    153–154, 156–157, 158–159,
    163, 164, 167
    as asymmetric warfare, 151,
        152–154
    definition of, 150–152
    and drug-trafficking, 73, 75, 76
    to establish new world order,
        149–150, 167
    as false-flag operation, 110,
        156, 159, 161, 162
    and intelligence organizations,
        154–156
    as pretext for war, 160–164
    as psychological operation
        (PSYOP), 151, 158
    as a strategy of tension, 83, 164
    as a vehicle for Pax Americana,
        163, 165–167
Texas, 101
Texas A&M University, x, 101–102,
    104–108
thermate, 35, 41, 47
thermite, 35, 38, 40, 41, 43, 59
Thompson, James, 25

Thornton and Tomasetti, 66
Thornton, Charles, 66, 70
Times (London), 92
Tomasetti, Richard, 66
torture, 129, 228 n.3
Tunander, Ola, xi
    See also Chapter 10.
Turkey, 92, 94, 233 n.63
Turner, Stansfield, 90
Twin Towers. See World Trade Center.

U

Underwriters Laboratories (UL), viii,
    ix, 52, 53, 56, 59, 63, 66–70, 112
UNICOL, 123
UPI, 101
United Airlines Flight 93 (UA 93), 8, 23
United Airlines Flight 175 (UA 175), 23
United Nations, 118, 124, 125, 149,
    166
    Development Program (UNDP),
        143, 228 n.33
    Security Council, 131–132,
        224 n.6
    weapons inspectors, 134, 135
United States
    Chamber of Commerce, 187
    Congress, x, 21, 125, 141, 160
    Constitution, 107, 238 n.2
    and empire, viii, 144
    foreign perception of, 125
    and God, 146–148
    Joint Vision 2010, 206 n.55
    lawlessness of, 129–130
    multinational corporations, 133,
        135, 137
    national security, 138, 139
    visa programs, 74, 76, 213 n.8
    See also covert operations;
        Central Intelligence Agency.
United States military
    aircraft transponder, 9–10
    interceptions by, 8–9
    radar systems of, 9
    Space Command, 14–15,
        106–107, 175
    Special Operations Command